Celebrating Divine Presence:
Journeys into God

☀ ❖ ◉

This book is dedicated
to those committed to the journey into God,
who acknowledge and live the truth
of our Oneness, like "beads on one string."
May we travel together as brothers and sisters
— in peace.

Beads on One String gathering in Flagstaff, November 4, 2007.
(L–R) Ameeta Vora, Thom Knoles, Laurent
Weichberger, Kelly McCabe, Haring Singh Khalsa, Esther
Stewart, (not present: Yaakov Weintraub, Karl Moeller, and
Lopon Tsultim Wangmo).

CELEBRATING DIVINE PRESENCE:
JOURNEYS INTO GOD

Lopon Tsultim Wangmo

Yaakov Weintraub

Laurent Weichberger

Ameeta Vora

Haring Singh Khalsa

Thomas M. Knoles

Kelly William McCabe

Karl Moeller

Mary Esther Stewart

COMPANION BOOKS PUBLISHER

Celebrating Divine Presence:
Journeys into God

Published by
Companion Books
228 Hammersmith Grove
London, W6 7HG UK

3RD printing: July, 2009
ISBN: 0 9525097 9 2

Printed by Lightning Source, USA.

Cover art by Haidee O. Cooke, "Luminous Return."
This book was designed and set into type by Ed Legum and Alison Govi.
Photos of Avatar Meher Baba courtesy of the MSI collection India,
used by permission.

Contents

Prologue
Wayne Smith

W HEN I MENTIONED TO LAURENT that maybe not all who opened this book would be familiar with the name "Meher Baba" (referred to here by Don Stevens), he asked me to try rectify this by adding some words to the Foreword. I immediately expressed my concern, for where do you start trying to describe the indescribable, capturing the ineffable in words – it's a bit like trying to pour the ocean into a cup, or drawing down an infinite blue sky and folding it away inside your pocket.

The term "Avatar" is another word you might also encounter for the first time in this book and one which does capture for me the very essence of who Meher Baba really is. It's an ancient Hindu term, literally an "incarnation," a concept which refers specifically to the incarnation of transcendent God into a visible, tangible form. This form is usually experienced by humanity as being that of another human being, what has been referred to in other traditions as the "Christ," or the "Messiah." But, as Meher Baba has explained, this most magical and exalted of all spiritual transformations isn't just restricted to the human form, for whenever God is brought down into Creation, like crystal veined through rock or sunlight that cuts through dust, " ... God mingles with mankind as man and with the world of ants as an ant, etc. But the man of the world cannot perceive this and hence simply says that God has become man and remains satisfied with this understanding in his own world of mankind." *

---

*From *God Speaks*, by Meher Baba, p.252 (New York: Dodd, Mead & Co., 1973).

7

Personally this concept of the avatar is my favorite in all the spirituality that I have so far encountered, especially also because this incarnating of God doesn't just happen the once, but periodically according to Meher Baba, about every thousand years or so, " ... whenever there is too much evil in the world", as Krishna explained to Arjuna all those years ago. A truth, I feel, that still holds true today.

Foreword
Don E. Stevens

Meher baba's london address to the press: Shortly after arriving for his second visit to England in 1932, Meher Baba addressed the British press by telling them in London that he had not come to found a new religion, but to gather together the world's great existing faiths like beads on one string,* and that he would revivify them and thus make their doctrines available to the seekers of the truth. After that stunning statement he did not refer at any later date to what he might have done during his lifetime in this regard. He did, however, speak many times of a New Humanity and also of a New Life and even of a New Age, all of which might have had something to do with each other and also with what he had said he would do related to the existing great religions.

There the matter rested largely for decades after the departure of Meher Baba from Creation. That is, apparently these momentous statements of intent had had no follow-up on his part. Then all that began to stir in the late 70s when some films that Meher Baba had asked me to take for him in the early 60s started a very quiet but important stirring into life. This came about due to the curiosity of several devotees who had heard about their existence and insisted that if these filmed locations had been important enough to Meher Baba to ask that they be filmed, then they were also automatically important to his devotees as well.

---

* "I intend to bring together all religions and cults like beads on one string and revitalize them for individual and collective needs" –Meher Baba. See also, *Lord Meher*, Vol. 5, p. 1554.

9

The nagging on this topic continued until 2004, when I got fed up, oddly enough not with the decades of nagging, but with my own continued postponement of what I knew would be an exhausting journey which undoubtedly would finally come to rest on my shoulders. As by that time I was well into my 80s, it was not a very pleasant holiday to look forward to at that time of life. But, to my amazement, I heard the words, "Then let's do it now!"

Now it just so happened that Meher Baba, as was his rather frequent habit, had involved me in several other obviously important but totally unexplained events dealing with spots of historical importance or religious veneration. The chief of these latter was Kailash Temple among the Ellora Caves near Aurangabad. Meher Baba had asked me to visit it in the early evening in company with his chief male devotee, Eruch Jessawala, who would stand guard at the entry to the temple while I made my way to the chief temple room and sat, at Baba's instructions. Those instructions from Baba were no more than to sit until I felt I had finished. Finished what, was not examined, before or ever after, until I put a few dots together and made up my own story.

Shortly after sitting down that evening in the pitch black temple room I began to feel a pressure develop in my chest region, and this increased at an alarming rate. I feared at first I had caught a galloping bronchial infection, but then discarded this line of reasoning. I simply got up and left the temple room, whereupon the chest pain disappeared. I told my story to Eruch, who was waiting at the gate to the temple. He made not comment. Nor did Baba when he got the brief story out of me the following morning on my return to Meherazad. Nor did either Baba or Eruch ever again refer to that Kailash Temple episode.

Pilgrimage

It was only in 2004 when I returned with the first pilgrimage group to visit this and the other sites Baba had me film, that the next chapter rolled out quickly and simply. As I leaned up against my favorite pillar in the temple I began to feel the identical chest pressure, but before it had reached the acute stage I abruptly and positively identified it. It was the force of Meher Baba's spiritual presence which in some manner he had impregnated into the locale of Kailash, and which I now knew from having experienced it on various important occasions when I had accompanied Meher Baba on several of his important public visits. But it was not "instead of" the natural spiritual force of Kailash, but harmoniously "in addition to."

Here I must insert another chapter of which Eruch is also the principal figure. Very near the end of Eruch's life he told me on a visit to India that he had finally had the opportunity to see the films that Baba had asked me to take for him, about which Eruch knew the planning part, but had never seen the filmed results. Now he told me very simply that all of the spots Baba had had me film were also places that Baba had asked Eruch on repeated occasions to take Baba to visit, completely anonymously, without this being known even to the very close Mandali of Baba. When they would arrive there, Eruch said, Baba would rest in deep meditation, and then they would leave without Baba explaining anything about the purpose of this operation.

Such was the story of Eruch, and he emphasized that Baba had done this repeatedly at each locale, and never explained to Eruch and always completely unknown to the Mandali. Baba was often like that, and we had grown used to the fact that such events often became clear through later events, but some are still in the file of unexplained happenings that occurred in Baba's presence.

When I left the Hammersmith Hospital after returning from that 2004 Pilgrimage, suddenly the thought came to me, This is all about the beads on one string, and now it all makes sense. Baba was busy all those years putting in the basic investment, and now it is clearly up to us to build the next steps onto what he has put in place.

End of story? Not quite. Beloved Eruch supplied to me one more essential, many years ago when he was telling me details of events that happened with Baba during the three year period of the new Life which several of the close ones spent in Baba's company. Eruch's words were, "Don, you cannot imagine the glory of the companionship with the Avatar that we experienced in those times in his close presence."

Don E. Stevens · Paris, France
September 20, 2007

Introduction
Jane Chin, Ph.D.

T HIS BOOK CAME TO ME at a time when I was going through a life transition: I had just become a parent.

Ten years ago, when I was a biochemistry graduate student, I did "timed" experiments in the laboratory. I was supposed to add chemicals to cells in petri dishes every two hours and observe how the chemicals affected cell growth over time. I would often miss one or two time-points because I couldn't wake up in time, even when I slept overnight at the lab. In the early months as a new mother, I woke up every two hours to feed my baby, a feat that I am relieved that I was able to accomplish. I have "adaptation scars," however: a gash on my ankle when I tripped over myself in the pitch black of night and cut my right ankle with my left toenail; a cut on my finger in a moment of fatigue when I pushed my fingers against the inside metal edge of the formula container; a welt on my scalp where I pushed the hairpins too hard too quickly in my hurry to tie back my hair to see what I was doing at 2 A.M.

Those of you who have parented a newborn will understand why I saw "getting through each day" as a meditation in itself. Every day was different, unpredictable, full of highs and lows, with the promise to do it all again the next day.

Yet what caught me off-guard was not the sleep deprivation or blurred boundaries between night and day. What blind-sided me was the revelation of how much I had equated myself with external qualifiers and the roles I had played. I defined myself by the goals I achieved, money I made, and how well I performed as a career professional and entrepreneur. In making a conscious decision to become a stay-at-home mom for at least my son's first year of life, I was ill prepared for the ego pathologies that would emerge.

This switch of gears from "performance to participation" led me to ask the question, "Who Am I?"

I had asked this question before, but now more was at stake. My son may ask me this question one day.

When I first received this book, I thought I was going to learn about different religions and faith traditions. What I did not expect was an invitation to the intensely personal journey of the struggle and desire for truth.

As I read each personal account of a faith tradition, I saw a reflection of my thoughts and feelings in the thoughts and feelings of my fellow travelers. You learn about the basic tenets of each faith.

You may form an idea of the similarities and differences between faiths, and, like me, you may gain insight into the origin of faith-based conflict. But I am most grateful for the companionship each contributing author offers for what is a solitary journey to the Self. Each explores in his or her own unique way the question – Who Am I? – through a personal journey to the Divine, and ultimately a return to the Self.

There is no shortage of commercially available packages for enlightenment and spiritual prescription. Workshops and seminars abound, each claiming to be a solution that I may be seeking. In the past, I had been quick to discard and discount what I considered "a spiritual fad." Given today's ease of connecting through technology, viral marketing has left its mark on spiritual programs. Gurus partner with talk show hosts. Celebrities lend leverage to spiritual products and services. In

Karl Moeller's account of the Sufi tradition, where our spiritual
journey is not only about rules or guidelines, I considered the
possibility that all solutions may be potentially valid solutions
for someone, somewhere, at some time in the course of their
life. The idea that there is "no single recipe for enlightenment"
made sense to me. What does not work for me may help another
as our journeys converge. I embraced the idea that popularizing
spiritual exploration engages those who may otherwise not give
this subject a second glance.

Having spent decades in school, I came to see knowledge
as critical; after all, "knowledge is power." If I acquired more
knowledge, wouldn't this get me closer to the truth I sought? As
I read Thomas M. Knoles' explanation of Vedanta, I understood
that information is not the end, but a means. Knowledge in itself
is not power without the Knower, because knowledge is a scaffold
that we build from or a ledge we can spring forth to increased
understanding. The journey is about merging into something
bigger. The aim is not to expand the "known", but instead, to
expand the "Knower". Only then can I shift from desiring to
experience inspiration to becoming inspiration.

This book also came to me at a time when I began questioning the role of spiritual teachers, philosophers, and gurus. I
was puzzled by popular philosophers who espoused evolution
of consciousness yet exhibited behaviors that appeared to fly in
the face of what they preached. Therefore, reading Kelly William
McCabe's vivacious description of Hinduism gave me relief and
excitement. I was relieved as I read the words that confirmed my
suspicion that the true spiritual teachers in this world are not
those who have the gift of spiritual gab, but people whose manifestation of light and love are visible without clever marketing.
Many of these people are not charismatic spiritual celebrities

and don't have sophisticated websites, yet the way they conduct themselves through their lives and in relationship with other human beings are exemplary of goodness and truth.

When I came to this line by McCabe: "I remember reading about some young famous western philosopher ... and finding out what a mess he had made of his life and thinking 'why in the world would anybody pay attention to the ideas – however intellectually brilliant they may be – of someone who was so obviously screwed up?' I wrote in the margins, Yes. I want to shake [McCabe's] hand for saying this. Common sense has become a rarity in books dealing with spiritual topics. What I had found in these words is an affirmation that a spiritual "system" is relevant to me if it helps me get closer to my journey home.

Philosophical eloquence may satiate my intellectual mind temporarily, but words do not get me closer to my authentic self. Words that come from those who work by double standards are like a person with bad credit trying to tell me I have poor financial sense.

If you are considering a spiritual path and reading this book to decide "which one," what I have learned from these authors is simply "start." Any beginning is a worthwhile beginning to your journey.

Through your intention of searching, you may discover as I have discovered, that in the process of aiming for your destination, the beauty of your path unfolds in magical ways. Sacredness is not in the show of miracles, but in the subtle beauty of ordinary lives, including your own. You only have to connect with the gifts that come your way every day, pay attention when a gift shows up, and say "yes" to invitations that resonate with you. I said yes to the commitment of spending one year to doing only what I love to do. This led me to say yes to an online *Friend Request* from Laurent Weichberger, which led me to say yes to many profound conversations with him, to this point of saying yes to sharing my thoughts with you here. Lopon Tsultim Wangmo said yes to an invitation on a postcard that was mistakenly delivered to her. This led her to say yes to hours of chanting in a foreign language she did not understand, which led her to the Buddhist path. Will you say yes to an invitation to your personal journey's magical unfolding?

"That I Am" is at once the path and the destination in this personal journey into the Divine, but until I read this book, I had forgotten that the key word here is "personal." The single most critical variable we get to work with – that we *can* work with – in this lifetime, is ourselves.

In closing, if I may suggest an approach to reading this book, I would recommend that you allow Laurent's chapter, Listening, be your guide. Many of us listen for the sake of grabbing the baton and speaking our views. I know I am often guilty of letting my mind chatter ceaselessly instead of purely listening to the speaker. Laurent takes the art of listening one step further and reminds us to beware of listening only for our own experiences for the purpose of turning the conversation to ourselves. Laurent's chapter asks that we focus on the speaker even as we are unsure where the speaker is taking us. Isn't this embrace in the unknown, to follow without constantly wanting to lead, the very act of faith?

In Gratitude,
Jane Chin, Ph.D.

Mehera J. Irani* with Avatar Meher Baba at Meherabad, India, in 1936.

*Meher Baba said, "She is my very breath without which I cannot live," from *Mehera*, by Mehera J. Irani with Janet Judson and Shelley Marrich (New Jersey: Beloved Books, 1989). He said Mehera loved him more than any other being, and he gave her the highest status in his circle of disciples.

CHAPTER ONE

Listening
Laurent Weichberger

WHEN I HAD JUST FINISHED A DRAFT OF MY CHAPTER, Ancient Mysticism, I had a dream in which there was a saintly man, and he had just read the chapter. Naturally, I asked him his feelings about it. He was pensive, and said he liked it very much but there was something missing, that I should add to it. I eagerly asked him, "What should I add?" Instead of responding in words, he turned to the front page of the chapter and wrote in ink the word "Listening." I woke up, and knew exactly what he meant. This chapter is what I am adding to that original writing.

There are many levels of listening. For some reason, in this present age where there is so-incredibly-much information, we as a global culture have lost touch with what it means to simply listen to another person, or for one group of souls to listen to another group, or for one faith to listen to another faith. I see an image of most communication as being pushed outward from an individual, or from a group, or from a faith toward another and then a sense of wait for the next opportunity to push more. However, I feel what is indicated as the next stage of listening development reveals a circular (and reciprocal) flow of energy, where the listening encourages more sharing, and one grows through the receiving of what is being shared, and flourishes within the experience of sensitive, honest, and nurturing communication.

I am reminded of visits I made to the Monastery of the Holy Spirit in Georgia, where Father Anthony used to tell us about the lives of the monks who live by the Rule of Benedict. What I remember is that the monks there have their time divided each day into preset-parts, such as reading scripture, devotions and praying, meditation and contemplation, as well as other spiritual practices. Lastly, and quite importantly, another aspect, vital to the monk, was not doing anything but simply – to be – and listen for the Lord. This final aspect struck me as extraordinary. Shortly after my writing the above a dear spiritual sister, Alison (who was completely unaware that I wrote about this Benedictine practice), reminded me of this type of "listening" within the Benedictine Order, and so I feel now it is confirmed that I should share it here.

How much time do we set aside to just be with & listen to the Divine, our loved ones, children, spouse, sisters and brothers, parents, and friends? If we belong to a certain faith, or spiritual path, do we "tune people out" when we have decided they are "other" and therefore not worthy of being listened to? Do we pre-judge people as unworthy of being listened to?

One of the jokes that Anthony told us, which has become a favorite of mine is this: One day a man who had been engrossed in his worldly life finally got fed up, and disgusted with the ways of the world. He decided he wanted to be a monk and live a holy life, and so he found a monastery in the countryside and requested one of the monks there for a meeting with the Abbot, and waited. Finally the Abbot came, and standing before the man says, "Yes my son?" The man hangs his head, and starts to explain, "I have had enough of the world, I want to come live here with you, to become a monk, and ..." but the Abbot interrupts him and says, "Oh no my son, let me tell you about our life here, and then you can decide." The man looks up at him and listens. "First of all, we live a very simple life, there is no excitement here. You get one small room, and it is quite Spartan. The food is not the rich food

you are used to eating. Also, we live a celibate life, and we remain
completely silent." The man thinks all of this over and says to the
Abbot, "I understand all that you have said, and I still want to join
you and live your holy life." That day the man becomes a monk,
with the Abbot's blessing, but the Abbot tells him, "I will allow
you only two words every five years." So the new monk moves
into his small room, and the years roll by. After five years there
is a knock at his door, and answering it he sees the Abbot there,
who asks, "Well?" And the new monk says, "Hard bed," but he
remains a monk. The years continue to unfold, with prayers, and
readings, and meals and dishes, and after another five years, there
is a knock at the monk's door. Again it is the Abbot who says,
"Well?" And the monk replies, "Cold food," But he remains a
monk. Now getting a little grey, the monk continues another five
years, and after 15 years on this path there is a knock at the door.
Opening it he sees his Abbot standing there with the customary,
"Well?" But this time the monk replies, "I quit!" And the Abbot
says, "Well, it's no wonder, all you've done since you came here
is bitch and moan!"

Speaking of which, one of the criticisms I have had of my
own spiritual community over two decades is that they tend to
put up on a stage, with a microphone, only those who have met
the Spiritual Master in his human form. Those who have met
him purely spiritually (within) tend not to be invited to speak.[1]
Even if the same truths be told, the messenger is often deemed
unworthy if they lack the stamp of a physical meeting with the
Master. This is misguided. My feeling is that it should probably
be the opposite, as those whose faith and experience is so strong
that they follow the Master year after year, without having met
him physically, are most worthy of being listened to carefully
and having our full attention. The difficulty which arises then
is that we must use our inner sense, our intuition, to determine

the truth as it is shared. This is no doubt a vital process that many are now being called upon to engage in fully.

Another way of saying the same thing is that if a child were to speak the same truth into a microphone as, let us say, St. Francis or a disciple of Buddha, would the audience be able to hear and receive this truth as told by the child? If not, there is something terribly wrong with the picture. I like to keep a diary, and looking back over past entries can help me become more aware of my own process, and spiritual unfoldment in general. I also make it a point not to tell (or teach) my children about God, but to allow them to receive through their own experience, to find their own way. Just yesterday, I read this entry from August, 2000, where I quoted my daughter saying, "We are always God. God does everything we do." So when Aspen (at age five) shared that with me, you bet I was listening.

Listening, at least in part, means embracing the Truth of the situation and hearing the truth as it manifests, sometimes in places and ways unexpected. The truth should be perceived and not simply accepted based on the package, or wrapping on the container of the message. This is our individual responsibility as the listener, to discern and distinguish based on experience and intuition. If a drug addict speaks the truth, it is Truth and should be honored as such. This means listening for Truth in and through all forms. How well do we listen as individuals to others? Do we need to remember how to listen, or work at learning how to listen? What are the tools of listening? How well do we listen as a group, or a nation, or a faith, to other groups?

Exemplars of Listening
My wife, Lilly, reminded me, "There have been examples throughout history of leaders and prophets listening to the Divine within them, and within the people surrounding them,

LISTENING 23

which have led to great changes in the world. Martin Luther King, Jr. listened to the state of his people and their suffering when he put his neck on the line to lead the Civil Rights Movement in a non-violent manner. This led to the adoption of equal rights for minorities in this country."[2]

The Prophet Zarathustra listened to the state of those around him when he gave humanity extremely straightforward precepts, "Think truly. Speak truly. Act truly." He also gave them an image of living fire to represent the purity and reality of Beloved God. These seemingly simple commands are even today found to be so difficult to live up to by most people, showing that the path to Truth is often made unnecessarily complicated. Meher Baba has shown me that the Truth can be expressed in the most simple terms.

Abraham listened to his Lord YHWH (the Hebrew name of God) when the Lord asked him to sacrifice his son as a burnt offering, and Abraham again listened when an angel of the Lord commanded him to stop before slaying this precious son. Who can have such obedience, so total and complete?[3] This story continues to inspire Jews, Christians, and Muslims alike.

Prince Rama listened to his stepmother, Kaikeyi, when she exercised her "wish" and exiled Rama for 14 years solely so that her own son, Bharata, could be made King instead of Rama.[4] Afterwards, when Rama did become King after all, the Hindu people were given the example of His divine life of perfect humility, and called him Lord Rama. Over 5000 years later, Rama's story proves to be a constant example to millions of Hindus the world over, of how best to behave in a variety of challenging circumstances.

Krishna listened to his disciples. When Arjuna and his brothers, especially Yudhisthira, decided it was time for war, Krishna became Arjuna's chariot driver. Krishna demonstrated that the divine life can be perfectly at peace in any role. That Krishna could be an integral part of a violent war between ruling royal families gave many a new view about what it means to be detached from the ways of the world.

Prince Buddha listened to his inner voice when it told him he must renounce his royal surroundings, including his wife and child, and live penniless as a wandering mystic until he reached enlightenment. Not that anyone should take this as an example and leave their family, but that a Prince would renounce not only his family, but all the princely trappings, for a life of come-what-may and spiritual austerities, was a dramatic example of living from one's gut.

Jesus listened to God, His Father, in the Garden of Gethsemane when they made the Divine decision to go forward with the crucifixion to benefit all humanity. The result, as we know, is the perfect story about the man of love despised by those to whom He reached out with perfect tenderness, and humility.

Saint Catherine[5] listened to Jesus when He came to her in her bedroom, and gently, but firmly, ordered to her to leave her room, to re-enter the world, and work for Him and promised to guide her. She did, going first into the kitchen to help her mother, then becoming a nurse. Finally, she corresponded with the Pope in France, boldly begging him to return the papacy to Italy. She was made a "Doctor of the Church," although she was barely able to read and write.

Mohammed (peace be upon him) listened to his own human nature when he decided to flee from Mecca to Medina, as the Arabian tribes sent representatives to his house to assassinate him in his sleep. He was saved by his own chief disciple, Ali who waited for them instead so that Mohammed could get away safely. Such is love. Mohammed's humanness was exalted by God, and he became the perfect man to hundreds of millions.

And Meher Baba listened to the state of the 20TH century world, when he decided that since God's principles and precepts had been ignored by humanity at large, in this present Avataric form he would observe total silence. What happens when the one who should be speaking keeps silent so that those who are saying nothing can have the floor? My uncle Dieter shared with me recently that, "What is demanded of us is that we learn a new way of listening to what Baba says without speaking."[6] To me this begs the questions, Can a spiritual being speak without words, and what is the spiritual value of silence? The life of Baba speaks volumes.

Effective Listening
I am reminded of a conversation I had with Lilly, after we watched a popular movie called *Juno* the other night with our daughter Aspen (now age 13). The plot has a girl, named Juno, a teenager (age 16) give birth to a healthy baby boy which she gives away in a closed adoption. Lilly asked me if Meher Baba had said anything about "abortion" and I told her a story I had heard, wherein Baba was approached by a young Hindu couple. My understanding was that they were not married, but she was pregnant. Baba heard their request for help in this extremely delicate situation, as Hinduism is famously conservative on this particular issue, and arranged that she come stay with him for six months provided her parents agreed. She did not tell her parents of the pregnancy. Baba himself found a married couple and arranged for the baby, once born, to be placed with them. The girl gave birth, the new-born was given a home, and the young woman returned home after the six months period. I can hear much in this story if I listen carefully. Also, I didn't like the film *Juno* much, because I was disappointed in her lack of emotional involvement with her baby, and the mixed messages I heard the film sending.

I have been asked to give examples of how we can listen more effectively. What I know is that most people seem to listen only for what the sharing means to them, meaning, they hear only that which resonates with their own experience, and then turn the conversation in a direction to which they can continue to relate. Usually, this turns the conversation away from the speaker, so that now they have something to say. I am sure we have all been in this situation. To me, truly effective listening means keeping the focus on the speaker, even if unsure of where the conversation is going, and when drawn to comment (or give feedback) to go deeper into what the speaker is trying to get across. This means really going toward unity of understanding, not continually shifting the conversation around. In this way, the focus remains on the issue at hand, and does not go back and forth from one person's self-interest to the other. When practicing this, I have found, the listener's intuition may elucidate something fundamental and important in what the speaker is conveying, and sharing that intuition helps both the listener and the speaker go deeper into the heart of the matter. In other words, the ego must let go of its desire to be the center of attention and to focus fully on the other for effective listening to take place, and somehow this gives an opportunity for intuition to speak up as well.

In a group setting, I believe, one group may listen effectively to another when, instead of making demands to be heard, the group sincerely tries to put itself into the mind-set of the other group, and listen for the meaning or issues that are being wrestled with. For example, a group of Christians may desire to listen to a group of Muslims, and in order to accomplish this effectively, the Christians must try to put themselves into the Islamic view, and not push a Christian view into that process. By Islamic view, I mean, imagine that you met a prophet who shared with you what the Archangel Gabriel said to him last night, and what you experienced from this man was divinity in action. Try to forget the senseless acts of violence committed in anyone's name, whether Mohammed or Jesus, or for any cause, and just imagine what the early Muslims experienced. It is difficult but certainly not impossible, and the fruits of this type of listening are astounding.

To give another example, I will tell you what Father Anthony said about the visit from the Dalai Lama to the Monastery in Georgia. Anthony told us that when the Dalai Lama came to Georgia, he asked his American assistant, are there monks living here? And someone said, yes, but in Conyers at the Monastery of the Holy Spirit. So he said, "Let's go there." And he went with his own monks who accompanied him on his tour, and his translator. When he arrived, according to Father Anthony, he wanted to meet the Abbot and some of the Roman Catholic monks, and introduce his Tibetan Buddhist monks, so that together they could start to share their "experiences." The gist of it was not sharing dramatic Hollywood-experiences of powers and visions, but simply their experiences of living as monks on a spiritual path, and the beauty of that walk.

What astounded Father Anthony was that as the sharing went on over some hours, something became crystal clear to all the monks, regardless of their faith: they all shared the same experience, but the terminology and culture surrounding that experience was different. In other words, at an essential level, each monk had progressed according to common experiential truths, regardless of the ideology or religious background. As a Meher Baba follower who had been given numerous examples by Baba of the unity of all religious ideals, this made perfect sense to me. Anthony's story was a dramatic confirmation that there is essentially one Divine Truth, and according to Baba, one Infinite God for all humanity, no matter how many ways humans have come to regard this Beloved Divine Being, or which names they use to address that One in their tender moments.

As a result, there are so many faiths all over the world, each striving to move closer to the Truth of Oneness, to please God in one form or another. The question that must be asked is how can we learn to listen to one another? What can each faith learn from the other faiths to help bring a state of Oneness amongst all mankind? I believe if we beseech the Divine for the answers to such questions, that One will surely guide us. I am now certain that listening is an aspect of love, and love is an aspect of forgiveness, and to me both love and forgiveness are Divine attributes. Let us move closer to the truth of Oneness through practicing that love which God has exemplified throughout the ages, by sending into the world matchless prophets, avatars, masters, saints and sincere lovers of God, who continue to inspire humanity to embrace and celebrate the Divine Presence in any and all forms.

☼   ❖   ▣

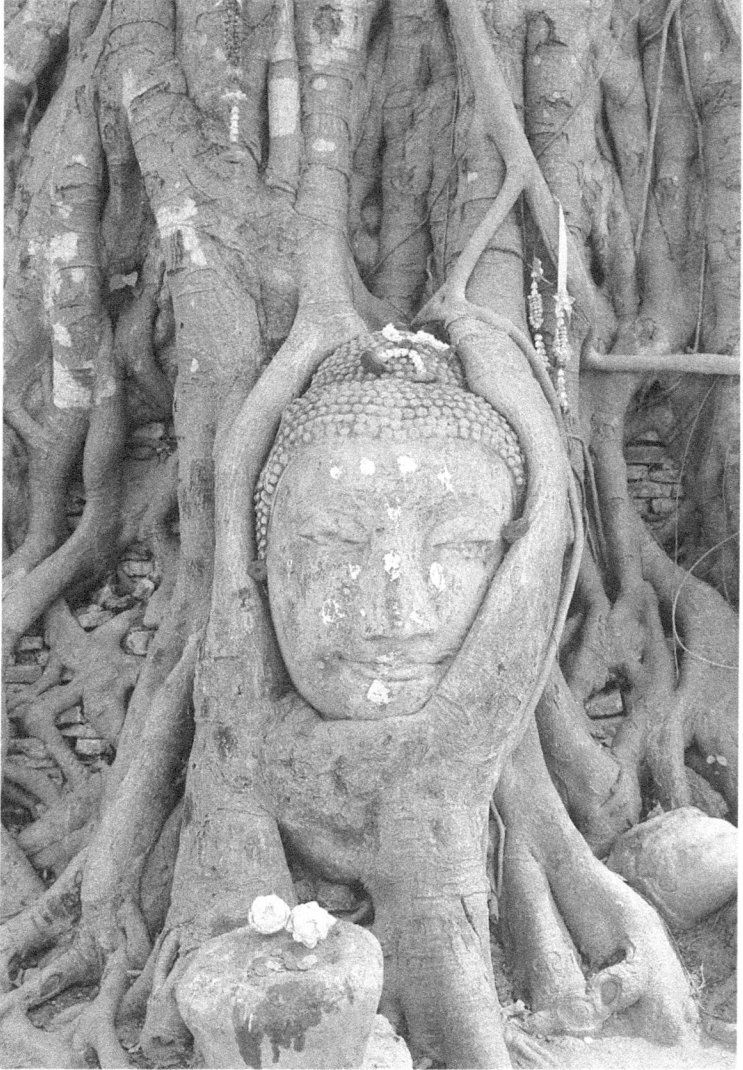

A Buddha from Ayutthaya, Thailand. *

---

* ... it is indeed stone. It seems that a bird, which had just eaten a fig from a Pipal tree, landed on the statue, perhaps as long as a thousand years ago. After digesting the fruit it left behind one seed, which grew into a monumental specimen that engulfed the statue with its trunk & air roots. It is in a small courtyard surrounded by broken walls and filled with the ruins of an old monastery. –JO (NYC: September 4, 2008).

CHAPTER TWO

Ancient Mysticism
Laurent Weichberger

I WAS BORN AND RAISED IN MANHATTAN. We lived in Westbeth, an experimental artist housing community, about a mile from where the World Trade Center used to be. The national tragedy on September 11 struck very close to home for me and my family. My dear mother still lives in our apartment there, and we had to work with her in her process around living there and staying there after such horrific events.

Shortly after that, there are two things that happened in my life which inspired me to bring together such beautiful souls of different faiths in a symposium, Beads on One String, to share directly with the world. First, I got a package in the mail from Jon, a friend of mine in Berkeley and inside was a Meher Baba T-shirt. He knew I'd been following Meher Baba for quite some time, and he thought it would be a nice surprise. I put this new shirt on and went outside. It was a beautiful day, and I was walking down the sidewalk when a young man stopped me, literally he stepped in front of me, and said, "Tell me about your shirt." He was intense. So, I sort of gauged him quickly and said, "It's Meher Baba, my spiritual master."

He looked at the image, and read the quote underneath, "When the Word of my love breaks out of its silence and speaks in your hearts, telling you who I really am, you will know that that is the Real Word you have been always longing to hear."[1] And then the young man said to me, "You'd better watch out, even Sikhs are being shot right now!"

Something really touched my heart – to be careful about revealing my association with an Eastern Spiritual Master in my love for God. I didn't feel threatened by him. I felt that he was giving me a warning, and he could be threatening, but he didn't seem to be an immediate threat to me. I am a big guy, and felt confident and clear. I responded, "Ignorance prevails, but not forever." It just spontaneously came out of me. Then I thought, What does that mean? But he liked those words, and he reached out and shook my hand and then stepped aside. That experience had a profound effect on me; it created a lasting impression.

Just a few days later I got an email from Robby, a close friend. He had heard the story of a Muslim family living in Minnesota who had a six-year-old son. That boy had gone to school – a kindergarten – on September 12, and his own classmates ganged up on him, started beating him, and then crashed his head into the pavement repeatedly, cracking his skull and putting him into a coma. Why? Because his name is Yussuf. His olive complexion is darker than most Americans and the other boys knew that he is a Muslim. They punished him for being a Muslim, and so he wound up in a coma. He did eventually recover from the beating, but he has permanent facial scarring, and psychologically, obviously he's in a long term process around healing.

These two events combined really upset me deeply. Then, I went camping down in Fossil Canyon, Arizona, with my buddy Jim Courson. We sat under the stars and I shared about my struggle and process around these issues. While we were trading thoughts in this majestic scene of bright stars – no air pollution, no light pollution, a beautiful campfire, just sitting and enjoying spiritual companionship – I got this tremendous inspiration: The way to heal these issues is not by waving a flag. It's not by creating a unified America. Unified against what? What are we unified for? Why? That is not what this is all about. Right then, this became an intensely personal issue around ignorance, and knowledge. Ignorance of what's important, what's really going on in the world. How could this six-year-old boy, Yussuf, have anything to do with the problem? He simply cannot. How can I convey any of the knowledge I have received from my Master, Avatar Meher Baba, about how to be tolerant, accepting, loving towards one and all, not because we are created equally, but because we are all essentially one? How do I share the knowledge of the One God present in all that lives?

I concluded that we need to find out what the problem really is, and to provide a healing and a lasting solution. For me, the problem is colossal ignorance around faiths and cultures of the East fueled by hatred and anger which devolves into the worst kinds of thoughtless violence. Unless we start to educate ourselves about the real meaning of these faiths and cultures, such fatal prejudice and idiotic behavior will no doubt continue. When I say the meaning of the faith, it is a reference to the fact that all of the Masters who are looked upon as "founders" of world faiths tried to live in peace, and share divine love. None of them wanted fighting and warring and violence.

So, what is the difference between a Muslim and a Sikh? What do real Muslims believe? And by "real" I mean not the extremists who have hijacked their faith and perverted it for fundamentalist aims. And, what is a Jain? Some of us have never even heard of Jainism. What does it mean to be Jain, or to be a Sufi? What about Hindus? Does a Buddhist believe in God? I have heard people ask hundreds of questions like these over many years of research into the roots of spiritual wisdom, in both the East and West. How did so many of these ancient traditions bring us to where we are today? Then, what about modern mysticism? Are there mystics alive today, full of divine knowledge, full of wisdom, giving, and constantly serving humanity? What would they be giving? Where are they helping and how? Can we meet them? Have we passed them in the street? Can we go somewhere to find them? Can we find a deeper knowledge and wisdom within ourselves? So many mystical questions. I have heard that sometimes the questions are more important than the answers. If you have a superficial question, then the answer to that question is not so important. Formulating the right questions can be extremely difficult.

This chapter is intended to serve as an overview of ancient mystical traditions and is based on my understanding* after spending 20 years following my Beloved Meher Baba, and what he has allowed me to gather of his expressed wisdom. The rest of this volume contains chapters with fine points of the various faiths, as presented by contributors who live and breathe that faith. Therefore the "beads" (contributing authors) will share directly from their tremendous insight and give details related to their particular faith. My work here is just to skip a rounded stone over the surface of this mystical lake, and with each hop, may you enjoy a splash of ancient wisdom.

If you draw a small circle on a map of the world, you will see that most of the major world religions have originated in the heart of Asia. I want to draw attention to this fact, as these faiths were all born in an extremely small area of the world, they are all Eastern in origin. Now of course you can say there are aboriginal and other native faiths and religions, such as the indigenous Chinese, Japanese, Australian and Native American faiths. Because of the ample treatment those native faiths have been given elsewhere, we have decided not to include those beliefs in this work.

---

*This includes having read many spiritual volumes from all faiths, and my direct personal spiritual experience with Meher Baba. -LW

My close friend Haring Singh sent me a quote, while we worked together on this project, that he felt was very important, and I love it also: "Never before has the world needed a blessing of an interfaith song to every heart."[2] To me this means that now is the time for us to come together, with deep respect and honor for one another, regardless of faith and other cultural differences, to love simply for the sake of loving.

Let us look more closely at some of these Eastern cultures and faiths. We have Arabian, Persian, and Semitic faiths. Part of what we see right now in the East is that Hebrews and Arabs from all these different countries are mixed together. (They're incredibly closely linked, the Arabian, Persian, and Semitic cultures.) They're extremely interwoven in that their origin stories and their spiritual and philosophic views have influenced each other so profoundly it can be hard to know sometimes where the influence originated.

We're not going to learn about the ancient pre-Islamic faiths of Egyptian and other Near Eastern cultures, even though they are Eastern, because they've become almost entirely Islamic. This is not an anthropological study, rather a spiritual one, so we will focus on Islam instead for those regions.

Asia – China, Japan, Korea, and Tibet – again, we'll see more of Buddhism in those countries, and not so much of the pre-Buddhist faiths. We are grateful that our spiritual sister, Lopon Tsultim Wangmo, has devoted an entire chapter to Buddhism in this volume. Here are the faiths we shall discuss in brief now and then in detail as chapters in this anthology: Zoroastrian, Jewish, Vedic, Hindu, Buddhist, Jain, Christian, Islamic-Sufi[3], & Sikh.

What do we mean when we talk about cultures? We are really talking about people, their customs, their beliefs, what they like to do, what they like to eat, their vision, and their world view.

An important point that I want to make is that in the West we tend to separate our culture from our faith and from our government. Unfortunately, in recent times here in America, the government has drifted towards some fundamentalist ideals which concern many people as these extremes are proving to be quite dangerous. There's a lot of compartmentalizing that goes on in the West around culture. Often in the West "culture" refers to movies, plays, good food, literature, and more.

However, the problem with discussing Eastern cultures is that it's not so compartmentalized. There are countries where the faith, the religion, the government, the way they share about their creative arts, it's all in one category. It's not clearly divided, rather it is in one cultural category. A Sufi friend of mine reminded me, "In some Islamic countries, religious law is the law of the land." You can't really just call it culture, it's much more than culture.

Eastern faiths are sometimes extremely tightly woven into their culture. Just how many people are we talking about? In the near East there are about 140 million people, almost all Muslim. In the Middle East, about 160 million and, excluding Israel, they are almost all Muslim. In the far East, there are many different faiths, definitely not all Muslim. China has about 1.25 billion people. India now has one billion people. In the far Eastern countries there are almost three billion people. How many people live in America today? Somewhere around 300 million.[4]

America seems to be mostly Christian, however I believe it is difficult to know for sure. Let's say we have all different faiths here. We've obviously got a lot of Christians in this country, however we have a lot of Jews and Muslims and other faiths represented here. If 300 million people is an accurate estimate for the population of the USA, we can compare that to the population of the near East and the Middle East combined, and there's easily just as many people on each side of the Atlantic Ocean, with those in the east being mostly Muslims. So, it is important to put America in the proper perspective: we are just a part of the whole glorious tapestry of various faiths and cultures and we are not the predominant faith or culture. Again, we are not even speaking about the Far East yet.

The point is that we, in America, are definitely not the majority of the world, although as a country we frequently act as if we are. Neither are we the strongest faith in the world (as represented in pure numbers). Americans are simply an important part of what's going on in the world.

There are three billion people living in the Near, Middle and Far East combined. The population estimate of the world today is soon to reach seven billion people.[5] This means one out of every two people in the world lives in the East. Conservative estimates say there are five hundred million Muslims in Eastern countries at the very least (and this is a low estimate). There are over eight hundred million Hindus living in India alone. There are a lot of people out there with the faiths that we're going to learn about in this book. I hope this chapter may help put some things, such as our role on the world stage, into perspective.

Facets of One Diamond

You can say this in many different ways. All these different faiths are like facets of one diamond. The diamond is the Truth – it is knowledge, it is wisdom. Depending on which facet you approach it may look different: it may be cut a little bit differently, it may give a little bit different refraction, or vision. You can also say, "branches of one tree." While you can say it any way you want, it can be broken down into two main traditions:

1. Persian-Arabian traditions came out of the "fertile crescent" area of the Middle East[6] which count as one tradition for the purpose of this book.

2. Farther east, ancient India was known as Bharat. In fact the Indians today call it Bharat, they don't call it India. So we use Bharat to remember that India's not just the land of India today. There are other lands around it that were included in those tradition, and so that forms the second main tradition for this book.

In the Perso-Arabian traditions, Zarathustra was the first major Prophet. Abraham was also a prophet. From Abraham came two sons, Ishmael the first-born, and then Isaac. The Arab people look at Ishmael as the father of their people, and the Prophet Mohammed comes down from that tradition. Isaac was the father of Jacob (who is also known as Israel).

Historically, the "twelve tribes of Israel" start with the 12 sons of Jacob. These tribes over time became known throughout the world as the "Jewish" people. These tribes end up living in Egypt and then became Egyptian slaves. Of course, Moses was a great prophet who God used to free the Jews from their bondage in Egypt. Moses gave the Law from God and that was kept in the Ark of the Covenant. David became a king of Israel after the exodus from Egypt – not the first king, although some people think that. And then Lord Jesus also comes to us from that tradition.

When I say Bharat (the Hindi word for India) it actually includes the lands of India, Bangladesh, Pakistan, and Nepal. This is because the more modern countries have a recent independence, as the original country of India was carved up by the Europeans during the colonial period. Ancient India included all those lands.

The Bharat traditions of the original "Vedic" masters are extraordinarily old, as the Vedic scriptures predate the lives of Lord

Rama, Lord Krishna, and Lord Buddha. The Master Mahavir is featured in the chapter from Ameeta Vora on the Jain tradition. Master Shankara comes to us from the Vedic tradition. In addition we will learn about other "Perfect Masters" and saints.

If we consider a time-line we can see the historical perspective.* The Zoroastrian, Sufi, and Jewish traditions are exceedingly old. I use "BCE" before the common era (and ACE for after) which correlates to the Christian calendar. The two faiths, Christianity and Islam, are actually relatively recent arrivals on the world scene. Zarathustra was a prophet. Abraham, Moses[7], Jesus, they were prophets. Mohammed was a prophet. Which brings us to modern traditions, including the Baha'i, and these all come out of the Middle Eastern, what I call the Semite-Prophetic tradition. The Baha'i say that "Ba'ha ullah" was a modern prophet.[8]

What we call the Bharat-Avataric tradition, comes out of the lands, in and around, India. This Vedic tradition is so ancient that there are not accurate dates available for exactly how old it is. It is, undoubtedly, one of the earliest faiths we have on this planet. Some date the Vedas to around 4000 BCE. There was an oral tradition that wasn't written until thousands of years after the original gift of knowledge was given by those Masters.

The fact is that we don't really know when these early Vedic Masters lived, for one thing they were almost entirely anonymous writers, and then they did not seem to date their own writings. Meher Baba said that Lord Rama, the Hindu Avatar, lived more than 5000 years ago. With the Buddhist and Jain traditions, there is more exact dating – about 500 BCE. However, the Sikh tradition, founded by Guru Nanak, is more modern, as he was born in India in 1469 ACE. Lastly, we have Meher Baba and other modern mystics. In my last chapter, Modern Mysticism, I focus on these modern Masters:

---

* See Time-line Charts in Figures 1 & 2 on p. 42, in this chapter.

- Sadguru Ramakrishna of Calcutta and his chief disciple, Vivekananda
- Sufi Hazrat Inayat Khan
- Avatar Meher Baba

All four modern personalities are sublime examples of a life lived entirely for and with the Divine.

Zarathustra

This is the classical depiction of Zarathustra: wearing white and with the long beard. He lived in ancient Persia (what is now Iran) about 6000 years ago. Again, we simply don't know exactly when these people lived. Scholars are all over the place with dates for Zarathustra, and we know precious little about his actual life and his teachings. The gist of it was, "Have good thoughts, good words, and good deeds. Or, Think truly, act truly, speak truly."

A Zoroastrian is a follower of Prophet Zarathustra. He told the people at that time to worship "Ahuramazda," the wise lord, and he directed them to worship the formless, infinite God. He did not stress personal manifestations of God. He explained that God is formless and infinite, and he gave them a symbol of fire as a way to connect to Ahuramazda. That should not be misconstrued, as some people have done, to think that Zoroastrians are "fire worshippers." They do not worship fire. They worship Ahuramazda, the formless infinite God, and fire just happened to be an excellent symbolic representation to which they could wholeheartedly connect.

There is a beautiful Zoroastrian symbol named "Faravahar" (or "guardian angel") which depicts the prophet. It is one way of representing the Zoroastrian faith. It looks quite similar to some of the Egyptian art. As we have seen, these faiths and cultures are all very tightly knit. At times Zoroastrians use the symbol of

a fire brazier, with flames coming up. The "Zend Avesta" is the
Holy Scripture which records some of Zarathustra's words and
deeds. There is one prayer in particular, contained in the Zend
Avesta, which Meher Baba personally translated, because he was
raised in the Zoroastrian tradition.

Let us take a moment to receive these words of Prophet
Zarathustra:

> *In the name of God Almighty*
> *I praise and utter almighty God*
> *Full of glory – full of radiance*
> *All-knowing – preserver of all*
> *God of gods – King of kings*
> *Protector of all*
> *Creator of all things created*
> *Bestower of bounties and giver of food to all*
> *Lord of nature – almighty God*
> *The Ancient One – forgive us*
> *Bestower of grace – O merciful*
> *O omnipotent – O omniscient*
> *O Lord of all – O nourisher of purity.*

When I read this – by the way, I love this prayer – it sounds so
much to me like the God of the Jews and the way Judaism relates
to God, the formless infinite. It's so similar. The same types
of terms show up in the books of Moses: God of gods, King of
kings, Creator of all things created, Lord of Nature – almighty
God, Bestower of grace. These types of feelings and sentiments
are almost identical to what we see in Judaism.

The following figures show the relationship between faiths throughout time:

Figure 1 (below) "Prophet Zarathustra lived some 6000 years ago. His Master was a Hebrew ... Zarathustra was the greatest Sufi. He was the Father of Sufism, and its very foundation owes its creation to him. Sufism began with Zarathustra and ended with Muhammad." – Meher Baba (Aug. 1929), *Lord Meher*, p. 1196.

Figure 2 (right, top) We know from Ameeta Vora's chapter on Jainism, that Master Mahavir lived at the time of Lord Buddha. Mahavir was the 24TH master in that lineage, however Jainism as we know it today, is associated with Mahavir. Many would have dated Jainism starting before Buddhism.

Figure 3 (right, bottom) See following section on Abraham, Jesus, and Mohammed.

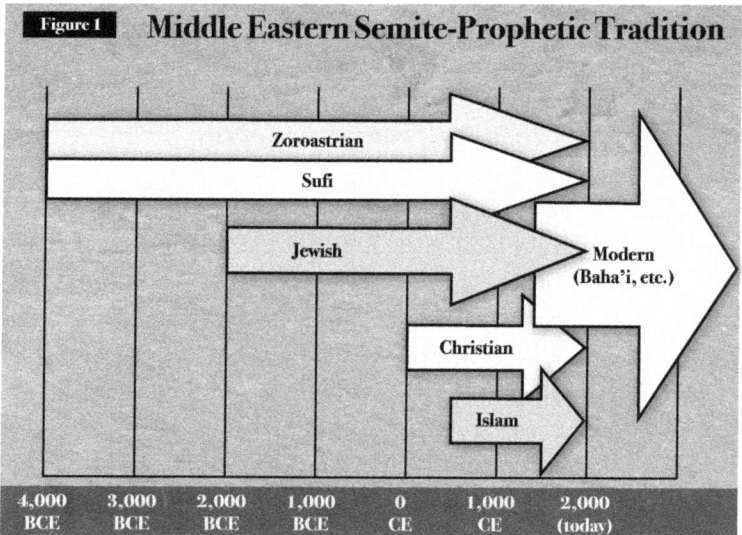

Figure 1 — Middle Eastern Semite-Prophetic Tradition

Figure 2 Far Eastern Bharat-Avataric Tradition

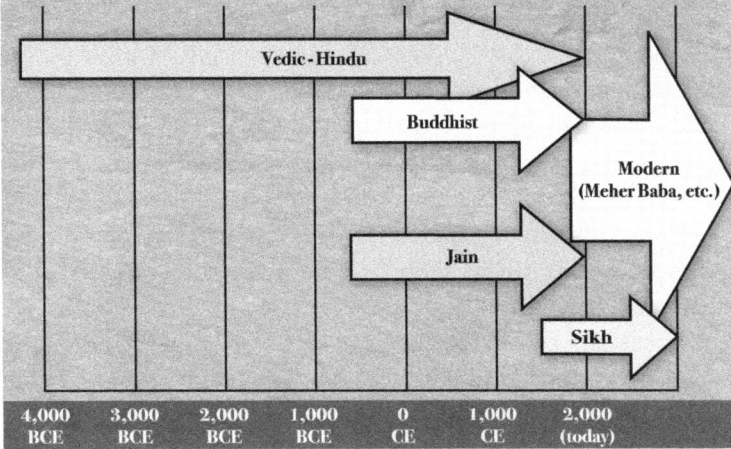

Vedic - Hindu

Buddhist

Modern
(Meher Baba, etc.)

Jain

Sikh

4,000 BCE	3,000 BCE	2,000 BCE	1,000 BCE	0 CE	1,000 CE	2,000 (today)

Figure 3 Prophetic: Heritage

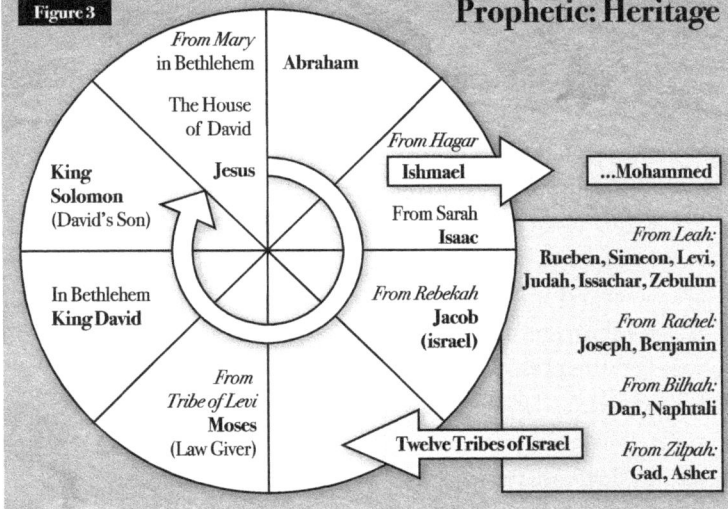

From Mary in Bethlehem

The House of David

King Solomon (David's Son)

Jesus

In Bethlehem King David

From Tribe of Levi Moses (Law Giver)

Abraham

From Hagar Ishmael

From Sarah Isaac

From Rebekah Jacob (israel)

Twelve Tribes of Israel

...Mohammed

From Leah: Rueben, Simeon, Levi, Judah, Issachar, Zebulun

From Rachel: Joseph, Benjamin

From Bilhah: Dan, Naphtali

From Zilpah: Gad, Asher

Abraham

The Old Testament tells us that the Prophet Abraham was born and raised in the ancient city of Ur, which would be located in Iraq, but it is no longer present. His life story is told in the *Bible's* book of Genesis. Shortly after Noah's flood we hear about Abraham, who is also mentioned as a prophet in the *Qur'an*, the holy book of Islam. In fact, the *Bible* also gives a genealogy of Abraham showing his direct descent from the Prophet Noah.[9]

Why is Abraham important? Because three of the major world religions look at him as their founder, or as the "root" of their faith:

1. Christians revere Abraham because Jesus Christ is supposed to be a direct descendent of Abraham. The family tree of Jesus in the New Testament shows that direct descent.[10]

2. In the Muslim faith, Abraham's first son Ishmael is the father of the Arab people, and there is a direct descent from Ishmael to the prophet Mohammed. Also, Abraham and Ishmael built the Ka'bah, a temple which is the holiest house of Islam, where once even the Jews used to worship alongside Muslims.

3. Jews, of course, because Abraham is the father of Isaac, and Isaac was the father of Jacob, and Jacob was the father of the 12 children whose offspring became collectively known as the twelve tribes of Israel.

So, there is an intensely strong focus on Abraham, which causes all these faiths to look upon him as their founder.

I've created a Prophetic Heritage chart which shows the heritage of prophets in the Eastern Semite tradition.* Abraham appears at one o'clock, and he starts the ball rolling. This gets a little complicated, but suffice it to say that Sarah thought she was unable to bear children. She gave her "maidservant" Hagar to her husband Abraham for the purpose of having a child. From Hagar,

---

*See Figure 3 on previous page.

Sarah's maidservant, Abraham's firstborn son Ishmael was born. The line of Ishmael continues to prosper over many generations, finally into the branch that leads to the birth of the Prophet Mohammed. From Abraham's wife Sarah, Isaac is born, and the name Isaac means "laughter," because Sarah laughed when she heard an angel say to Abraham that she would bear a son. Isaac and Rebekah became the parents of Jacob, and his brother Esau. Jacob married Rachel, as well as Leah.[11] From Rachel came two sons, and Leah had six boys. Looking further into the situation, Bilhah and Zilpah are the two handmaidens of Leah and Rachel, and Jacob had four more sons with those handmaidens. So, the twelve sons of Jacob started families of their own, and each family became a separate "tribe" over time, and they flourished. That's how the twelve tribes of Israel began.

In the Old Testament, God changed the name of Jacob to Israel, which means "Wrestles with God" or "Struggles with God."[12] The twelve tribes of Israel can also be interpreted as the twelve tribes of Jacob, because Jacob's name became Israel. To be an Israelite means to be from one of the twelve tribes of Israel. The chronicle of the Jewish people is a long one, and we have a wondrous chapter from Yaakov Weintraub dedicated to Judaism.

At one point in the epic history, the twelve tribes are all slaves in Egypt. By God's direct order, Moses delivers them from their bondage and then he gives them their laws, also directly from God. To learn how they became slaves in Egypt is beyond the scope of this chapter; please refer to the life of Joseph the son of Jacob, who was the first Jew to be taken to Egypt as a slave.[13]

The first five books of the Old Testament are called the Pentateuch, and they're commonly attributed to Moses as the author, according to Jewish tradition. So not only are the Ten

Commandments given by Moses, but if you read those first five books, you'll find many different rules, regulations, laws, do's and don'ts, stories and more, and all that is attributed to Moses. The Ten Commandments became a covenant between the Jewish people and their God, and these commandments were housed in the "Ark of the Covenant."

The Old Testament also contains a book named simply "Numbers," which counts the populations of all the tribes two years after the Exodus from Egypt, and there are quite a few souls in that total census. The tribe of Levi is the family from which Moses, his brother Aaron, and their sister Miriam come. At that time there were more than 600,000 people counted, but none of the tribe of Levi was counted, as they were told to become the priests of the "tabernacle of the Testimony." A tabernacle is a holy sanctuary, and they set up and tore down this tent (which housed the ark of the covenant) everywhere they went. Generations later, the ark ends up being in the care of King David. There is a time-spanning connection between Moses and King David through these sacred objects, the commandments themselves and their ark.

Jesus

King David had many sons, one of whom was Solomon. David was from Bethlehem[14], and in the New Testament you can find a direct lineage, father-to-son, between King David and Lord Jesus through Solomon, including a family tree from Solomon's children and their children which reaches down to Jesus. In fact, the New Testament shows Jesus' lineage going back even before David, all the way to Abraham. If Jesus was indeed born of a virgin, and Joseph had absolutely nothing to do with his conception (as the doctrine declares) then why would Christians take such great care to put Joseph's direct lineage going back to Abraham? The early Christians must have known that Jesus was a descendent of King David through his father, Joseph, and thereby fulfilled their own Jewish prophesy concerning the coming Messiah.

How much do we really know about Jesus? Even after centuries of scholarly study, there is almost nothing in the way of original source material. The oldest surviving texts are written in Greek, and no one believes that Jesus went around speaking Greek, so these texts are all translations. The earliest complete copies of the New Testament date to hundreds of years after the life of Jesus.[15] We should address Jesus as a Jewish prophet, because that's really what he was. The boy whom the world would call Jesus was raised as a Jew in the Jewish tradition. He never abandoned Judaism. On the contrary he lived in such a way as to bring his experience of God into this faith. The problems began when he started speaking in the way that the prophets speak.

Then he took the message just a little further. But Jesus gave original messages which were extremely close to those with which the Jews were already familiar, similar to other prophets in tone and depth of meaning. Jewish scripture abounds in the words of the ancient prophets such as Abraham, Elijah, Daniel, and Moses. These prophets of old said something like, "I have a message to give you from God, because God told me something that He wants you to know ... You're doing it wrong. I have the right way to do it." The Jews were familiar with this, because sometimes they'd get quite upset with this message and they'd kill the prophet. Later upon contemplating the message they would think, "Oops, he was right." And then they'd put everything that prophet ever said in a book with his name on it, with a foreword: "This guy had it right, but we didn't realize that at the time." This was a commonly occurring pattern in Jewish history.

Rarely would they say, during the life of the prophet, "Yes, this prophet is right on, and we're going to honor him." And then that prophet would live out his natural life, and make other prophets.[16] So you had all different types of situations. But Jesus came amongst the Jews as a prophet. By the way, his name wasn't Jesus either. Jesus is a Greek translation of a Hebrew name. His name was probably something like "Yeshua"* or "Yeheshua," akin to the modern Joshua.

Regarding the word, "Christ," this is also Greek for "The Anointed One," which is a translation of the Hebrew "Messiah." So, Jesus was a prophet, and in this tradition prophets are anointed by other prophets (or directly by God, as in the case of Abraham). In the case of Jesus, John the Baptist baptized Jesus in the Jordan River. This was the "anointing," which is one example of how one prophet creates another prophet.

According to the New Testament, Jesus referred to himself as the "Son of Man." Only once can I find a direct reference by Jesus to his claim of being "God's Son" and it is when he is being verbally abused and threatened by those around him, and he replies: "Why then do you accuse me of blasphemy because I said, 'I am God's Son?'"[17]

He was extraordinarily careful not to be too bold, and while he spoke of God as his father, and mentioned the Son of God, he never seems to come right out and publicly claim to be the son of God (according to Gospel accounts). He spoke of himself, saying, "I am the way and the truth and the life."[18]

Here is a New Testament story, one of my favorites:

> *He asked his disciples, saying, "Whom do men say that I the Son of man am?"*

---

*The name Yeshua is the root of the Latin transliteration of the Greek name "Jesus" and can be found in the merriam-webster dictionary at: *www.merriam-webster.com/dictionary/Jesus* Main Entry: Je∑sus; Etymology: Late Latin, from Greek Iesous, from Hebrew Yeshua; 1: the Jewish religious teacher whose life, death, and resurrection as reported by the Evangelists are the basis of the Christian message of salvation; called also Jesus Christ. See also: *en.wikipedia.org/wiki/Yeshua_(name)*

*And they said, "Some say that thou art John the
Baptist: some, Elias; and others, Jeremias, or one of
the prophets."
He saith unto them, "But whom say ye that I am?"
And Simon Peter answered and said, "Thou art the
Christ, the Son of the living God."
And Jesus answered and said unto him, "Blessed
art thou, Simon Barjona: for flesh and blood hath
not revealed it unto thee, but my Father which is in
heaven."... Then charged he his disciples that they
should tell no man that he was Jesus the Christ.*[19]

I put that part of the gospel of Matthew here because I think
it's important. Jesus is basically saying, "Okay, so the cat's out
of the bag, but do me a favor, just don't tell anybody, because I
have work to do, and don't spoil it. They'll figure it out later, who
I am, why I came. This will all be clear later. All right, everyone
clear?" I think that is very important. He didn't want people to
know too much about him during his lifetime.

Jesus was, of course, tortured and crucified by the ruling
Romans and Jews of the time. Apparently, Jesus "rose from the
dead." However, this needs more discussion, as it is a cornerstone
of the Christian faith. Jesus is now considered to be the Son of
God by Christians. Some "Messianic Jews" are still waiting for
their messiah, as they do not recognize Christ, as such, so they
are still waiting for their Anointed One. Jesus is also mentioned
in the *Qur'an* as a Prophet. Furthermore, there are legends in
India of a great prophet named "Issa" who came from another
land and settled in Kashmir, which is a northern state of India,
on the border of Pakistan.

This is an explanation about Jesus from Meher Baba*:

---

*Meher Baba is my Spiritual Master. –Laurent

What did Jesus really say? To the multitude he said,
"God is in heaven. Try to go there."
And to reach that end he said to overcome certain
temptations and sufferings.
To his followers he said, "God is everywhere.
Try to see him."
And he gave explanations to that effect.
To the close circle of apostles he said,
"God is in me, and in you too," and actually revealed
this to them. Why did Jesus say different things?
Owing to the time and the people, according to their
readiness to listen and understand.
What Jesus meant was to leave all and follow him.
That means to know him, see him, experience him.[20]

What I love about this quote from Baba is that he shows how a real master, like Lord Jesus, teaches the same message, but differently according to the needs of the group with which he is working at the time. Those who had ears to hear him more directly got a more direct message, and those who did not have ears to hear, got a more general message. This is perfect spiritual mastery, as it is all inclusive and guides according to the aptitude of the student. Our spiritual sister, Mary Esther Stewart, has composed a beautiful chapter which expounds upon her vision of Christianity, and a bit about Saint Francis which is quite inspired.

Mohammed

I found some Arabic calligraphy* which reads, "Mohammed is the Prophet of God"[21] and "God, Glory be to His Majesty."[22] In the West we know precious little about one of the greatest prophets, named Mohammed, which means "one praised." He lived in,

---

*See calligraphy in the Chapter Images section (images #12, 27, and 30).

and around, Mecca (and traveled all over Arabia) around 600 CE.
Mecca is a city which is the home of the Ka'bah, the temple built
by Abraham and his son Ishmael. Mohammed declared himself to
be the "Rasool Allah" or "Rasool-e-Khuda," which is translated
as "Messenger of God," or the Prophet of God. "Rasool" means
messenger or prophet. "Khuda" is a name for God in Persian,
and "Allah" is the primary name for God in Arabic.

Mohammed said, as a prophet, that he was receiving direct
instructions and revelations from an Archangel named Gabriel
(in Arabic "Jibreel"). This is the same Archangel who gave the
annunciation to Mary, the mother of Jesus 600 years earlier.[23]
Mohammed is in the same tradition of prophets, and both faiths
believe in angels, with the names of the angels being almost identical as well.[24] The revelations that Mohammed received from the
Archangel Gabriel were put into a collection which Mohammed
called the "*Qur'an*," which means the "Recitation," because
it was recited by Gabriel to Mohammed. Gabriel then ordered
Mohammed to recite this revealed material to all of the other
people (in the world). For the Muslim, the words in the *Qur'an*
are not the words of Mohammed and do not contain the life of
Mohammed. It is quite different, therefore, from the Christian
gospels. The *Qur'an* is not the Gospel of Mohammed; it is said to
contain divine revelations by Archangel Gabriel on behalf of God.
Because the Arabian people had no history of prophets, there are
many sections (surahs) of the *Qur'an* which explain the life and
work of the Jewish prophets and patriarchs, including Abraham,
Joseph, Moses, Jesus and Mary. The *Hadith* (pronounced ha-
deeth) is a collection of words spoken by Mohammed, the deeds
of Mohammed, basically his life and teaching as apart from the
contents of the *Qur'an*. These *Hadith* passages were not put
together by Mohammed, but by those who remembered what he

said and did. *Hadith* literally means, "the news," so if you want stories about his life, read the *Hadith*.

Mohammed told people not to worship those gods, so many gods, so many idols, as at that time the spiritual atmosphere in Arabia was highly pagan. Instead, he said, "There is no God but God," meaning Allah. "Not many gods, there is only one God." This message, understandably, met with quite a lot of resistance. The message from Mohammed was breaking traditions of the tribes of Arabia, and they were furious.

Mohammed never equated himself with God. He said, instead, "I am the Messenger of God," and the gist of his message was, You're doing it wrong. This is the way to do it ... and told them to listen to and obey God's message as given in the *Qur'an*. When the Arabian people in Mecca heard him speak, heard the contents of the *Qur'an*, and then saw that he was gaining a following, they tried to kill him. They sent one person as a representative from each of the Arabian tribes in Mecca, and they went to his house with the intent of assassinating him. Mohammed escaped, and with his followers lived in exile in the nearby city of Medina. He continued building a following, which grew so strong that eventually he entered into battles with Mecca. The Meccan army fought the army of Mohammed, and Mohammed's armies won. Eventually, Mohammed captured Mecca and over time his armies conquered the entire Arabian Peninsula.

After Mohammed captured Mecca by force, he made the Ka'bah the way he wanted it to be. First, he removed all the idols that had been set up in the Ka'bah. He cleaned all the walls in the Ka'bah, which had been painted with pagan murals of different gods and goddesses. So he personally cleaned out the Ka'bah, this sacred house built by Abraham and Ishmael. There is a phenomenal story that while they were cleaning it they asked

Mohammed, saying, "What about this?" And he looked, and there among the murals was painted on the wall Mary holding the baby Jesus. And Mohammed said, "Leave that, do not remove it." So he had deep respect for Jesus and for the Christian faith, as you will see if you read the *Qur'an*. In fact, Mohammed had respect for all faiths including Judaism, and it is common knowledge that one of his wives, Safiyya bint Huyayy bin Akhtab, was actually Jewish. *

Mohammed had many wives. Scholars seem to disagree on the total number throughout his life, but we know there were more than 10, and they brought forth six children, including two sons. Both sons died before reaching maturity. According to his own admission, Mohammed was most fond of his first wife, Khadija. She gave birth to their daughter, Fatima, who married his cousin and chief disciple Ali, and that's where the blood line of Mohammed comes from. Some say that Mohammed was most fond of Aisha, one of his last wives, but that discussion is for another chapter in another book. These two women are both considered the greatest wives, depending on whom you ask. This could in part be due to the fact that Aisha's father, Abu Bakr, became the first "Caliph" (a Muslim leader) after the death of the prophet.

Mohammed called his faith "Islam," which can be translated as "Peace with God, Surrender to God," or "Submission to God's Will." Mohammed expressly forbid in his faith any representations of the Divine, period. No idols, no pictures of God. In fact, it seems Mohammed didn't want people representing him in images either, so we have none. Although I have not read a specific *Hadith* that says this, it is a law in Islam. He told his followers to worship only Allah, the formless infinite God. This rule is almost identical to Judaism, which from the time of Abraham, does not allow the creation or worship of any artistic representations of

---

* Also see the excellent book, *Muhammad: His Life Based on the Earliest Sources,* by Martin Lings (Inner Traditions, 2006)

God. This was reinforced by God through Moses, when he brought down the Ten Commandments from Mount Sinai.[25]

Here's the opening section of the *Qur'an*, the "Fatiha" as it is called:

1. The Opening

In the name of Allah, the Beneficent, the Merciful.

[1] All praise is due to Allah, the Lord of the Worlds.

[2] The Beneficent, the Merciful.

[3] Master of the Day of Judgment.

[4] Thee do we serve and Thee do we beseech for help.

[5] Keep us on the right path.

[6] The path of those upon whom Thou hast bestowed favors.

Not (the path) of those upon whom Thy wrath is brought down, nor of those who go astray.[26]

That's a little bit of the flavor of the *Qur'an*. This is just an opening verse, not the real substantial message. It is fascinating to note that the *Qur'an* contains numerous stories of the Jewish patriarchs and prophets. Why? Because the early Muslims had absolutely no prophets in their heritage, none at all, only Mohammed. So the *Qur'an* honors and upholds the past Jewish prophets sent by God, as well as the Jewish people, including Jesus. Read the *Qur'an* and see for yourself, there are countless translations.

The *Hadith* contains the stories about what Mohammed (and his spiritual companions) said & did. Each item looks like this:

On the authority of Abu Hurayrah (Radhi Allahu Ta'ala Anhu) who said that the Mohammed, the Messenger of Allah (Peace be upon him and his family) said: "When Allah decreed the Creation He pledged Himself by writing in His Book which is laid down with Him: 'My mercy prevails over my wrath.'" It was related by Muslim, al-Bukhari, an-Nasa'i and Ibn Majah.[27]

The conscientious Muslim always gives a clear line of how the story came to us. They are meticulous about showing the source.

Now, I think this is an important little piece of Islamic scripture. Mohammed himself is saying: Allah wrote "My mercy prevails over my wrath." And then they say it was related by Abu Abu Hurayrah, Muslim, al-Bukhari, an-Nasa'I and ibn Majah. So they always give the detailed references in the *Hadith*, in the succession of how the story traveled through the generations.

That way you can say, "Oh, I like what this Ibn Majah guy says. He had good stories, they were accurate, he is reliable ..." Or whomever you trust you can work with that material. This was an oral tradition. And even when it was finally published in printed books, they first went to the oral tradition holders and asked them to repeat the *Hadith* they knew, that was what they trusted.[28]

So, the question naturally arises, Who do you trust? That was the flavor of the Semite-Prophetic tradition, but just an overview. The prophets speak with a certain tone. And the tone is, "I'm here to tell you what God has to say because he said it to me." The prophets didn't go around saying, "I am God." They said, "I know God really well, I talked to him this morning. He told me to tell you something." We have a tremendous chapter on Islamic Sufism from Karl Moeller, which explains much of Islam from the more mystical perspective of the classical Sufi period, 800 to 1200 years ago.

In Islam, a perfect spiritual master is known as a "Qutub." Qutub means the pivot, or the center, or axis, or the hub. This is because to a Perfect One, all things are equidistant. It is said that a Qutub experiences being "One" at the center of Creation, everything revolving around the real Self. Examples of such Perfect Masters are Kabir, Rumi, St. Francis,* and Hafiz, all of whom

---

*Meher Baba indicated to Don Stevens, in Myrtle Beach, S.C., that Saint Francis of Assisi, Italy, was the unique example of a Perfect Master in the West. -LW

have become somewhat well known in America through their poetry, and in the case of St. Francis, because of his relationship to animals. I must also mention the superb life of Qutub-e-Irshad Moinuddin Chishti, whose tomb in India is one of the greatest places of pilgrimage for a Sufi, and whose spiritual presence is still felt there by many.

I cannot bring myself to end this section without mentioning one of my personal favorite Sufis, whose life and work so obviously influenced all those around her and for many generations afterwards. Hazrat Rabia (of Basra) was perhaps the quintessential Muslim woman and her impact on Islam, both mystical and poetic, can hardly be denied. Rabia said, "May God steal from you all that steals you from Him."[29]

The Avataric Tradition

India's Bharat-Avataric tradition is experienced as quite a different flavor from what has been presented so far. The tone of these divine beings, the Spiritual Masters and Avatars, I interpret to be something like this: "Let's just cut to the chase. I am God. You don't have to read about ancient prophets, you can just talk to me because I'm God. I can help you to become God because I am perfection personified. I can make you perfect as well. I have attained Oneness with God. You also want Oneness? Come, obey me, and I will help you. You have to listen to my instructions. You must obey me, and when you completely surrender to me, you have my Grace. You have only to worship me, because I am God in Human Form."

This is the general tone that comes out of that tradition. It can be deeply unsettling for many people rooted in Western philosophical or religious traditions, where such talk would be considered blasphemy or madness. Other people seem to love it, as it is bold and fresh, and if it is true, it is here and now – completely accessible. For example, there are so many personality types with their different preferences, and while some people love the ice cream flavor, Rocky Road, others may prefer Swiss Chocolate Almond, yet they are both ice cream.

The Avatar is known to be God in human form – one who physically comes into this world and eventually passes away. A spiritual master is one who has made the journey through evolution, and involution, and after countless reincarnations finally arrives at the goal of Self-realization (Perfection). A saint is a spiritually advanced person who is still striving for Perfection. There are Avataric incarnations, which we'll explain more about shortly, such as Lord Rama, and Lord Krishna. Many also consider Lord Buddha to be the Avatar, and the chapter from Lopon Tsultim Wangmo will explain more about Buddha. Major incarnations of the Avatar become household spiritual names the world over.

There also seem to be "minor" incarnations of the Avatar, which is a little bit different. Special spiritual work is performed by such a minor incarnation, and yet when the figure disappears from the spiritual scene those left behind may scratch their heads in wonderment, saying, "Wow, what was that all about? What just happened here? He did what? What did he say?" However, most of humanity never really comes to know too much about this incarnation. For the special few who are deeply interested in spirituality, their work is known to be matchless. For example, Shankara gave us a tremendous push specifically regarding the Vedic path in India. Also, Shivaji was matchless, as when the Moguls were invading India, pushing Islam through the land, Shivaji lived in the central part of India, in Maharastra. He battled the Moguls and stopped the invasion with his armies, and thereby the Muslims did not overrun all of India, just the northern parts.

After that work was completed, he left the stage. Meher Baba indicated that both were minor incarnations of the Avatar. Like the movie, *It's a Wonderful Life*, we will never know how the life of Shivaji really did change the course of history. But for whatever reason, that was his "God given work."[30]

Let us consider as well that we have masters and saints, some of whom we may have heard about, and some of whom I am sure we have not. In India, if you're a Hindu, you call such a perfect spiritual master a "Sadguru." The term "sat" meaning true, or truth. A guru is a teacher. So "Sadguru" means an authentic teacher of the highest order. These are extraordinarily difficult to find and, as we know, there are so many imposters.

We have a splendid example in the Jain tradition, Sadguru Mahavir, about whom we shall learn more in the Jain chapter. Then we have Guru Nanak (the most excellent Sikh Perfect Master), whose "dharma" we'll hear about much more in depth from Haring Singh Khalsa in his chapter. We have the matchless example of Sadguru Ramakrishna of Calcutta, about whom Kelly McCabe will share in depth and detail in his chapter, as he was a monk in the Ramakrishna Order in India. I shall write just a little in my final chapter on Modern Mysticism about Ramakrishna and his chief disciple Vivekananda.

Then we have some modern Perfect Masters: Shirdi Sai Baba (who should not be confused with the afro wearing "Sathya Sai Baba" of today). We can learn about the great Sadguru Narayan Maharaj of Kedgaon, India and the female Perfect Master, Hazrat Babajan, who settled in Pune, India. Babajan had a special spiritual duty to perform for Meher Baba, as we will see in the chapter on Modern Mysticism.

In addition, there are a number of saints (past and present) to be considered. Lady Mirabai was a great Hindu saint who loved

Krishna more than life. Although her lifetime was hundreds of years after Krishna lived, still she fell in love with her Lord Krishna. Anything is possible with God. We will also hear about Hazrat Inayat Khan, who is known for bringing Sufism to the West. You can learn about Sri Aurobindo, and Kirpal Singh, and so many more not to mention the innumerable gods and goddesses in the Indian traditions.

What is an Avatar
Meher Baba gives the following explanation:

> *It is very difficult to grasp the entire meaning of the word 'Avatar.' For mankind it is easy and simple to declare that the Avatar is God and that it means that God becomes man. But this is not all that the word 'Avatar' means or conveys.*
> *It would be more appropriate to say that the Avatar is God and that God becomes man for all mankind and simultaneously God also becomes a sparrow for all sparrows in creation, an ant for all ants in creation, a pig for all pigs in creation, a particle of dust for all dusts in creation, a particle of air for all airs in creation, etc. for each and every thing that is in creation.*[31]

According to Baba, as an Avatar not only does God become a man for the benefit of mankind, but simultaneously God becomes a sparrow for every sparrow in Creation, and an ant for every ant in Creation ... A pig for all the pigs in Creation. A particle of dust for all dust in Creation. In other words, for each and every thing that's in Creation, God is manifest as that to help everything move closer to the Truth. This is pure mystical revelation. I will explain more about the concept of Avatar in my chapter, Modern Mysticism. (See the section, The Ten States of God.)

Lord Rama

Here are some classical cases of Avatars throughout the history of India. Rama lived more than 5000 years ago, and he was raised in the capital city, Ayodhya, in Kosala kingdom, which was a northern province of ancient India. Rama's father was also a king, so Rama was one of four princes. He was trained as a warrior, and he became the greatest archer of all time. Said Ramakrishna to his devotees about Lord Rama: "Ordinary people do not recognize the advent of an Incarnation of God. He comes in secret. Only a few of His intimate disciples can recognize Him. That Rama was both, Brahman Absolute and a perfect Incarnation of God in human form, was known only to twelve rishis."[32]

Ramakrishna of Calcutta was a living Perfect Master, who revealed secrets about the lives of the Avatar. He said that only twelve "rishis" or sages recognized Lord Rama as the Avatar during his physical lifetime. Rama was married to his beloved Sita, and she bore two sons (that is a long story). Before those boys were born, Sita was kidnapped by Ravana, a "demonic" figure. The story of Rama is an epic saga of his battle against Ravana to get Sita back. The modern island country of Sri Lanka is where Ravana had his fortress, and where Sita lived in captivity. Lord Rama, aided by the "Monkey" and "Bear" armies of India, fought a great war against Ravana and his army. Lord Rama was victorious, and he became the King of Kosala.

According to Meher Baba, Lord Rama also had spiritual masters, as his father-in-law, King Janaka, was a Perfect Master. Rama's chief disciples were his brother Lakshman, and his favorite monkey, Hanuman, who's known now as the "monkey god" in Hinduism.[33] I have to note here that we have almost nothing in the way of words from Lord Rama, in that he didn't seem to write anything and what we know of anything he spoke is passed down through thousands of years of oral tradition before it was committed to writing in the form of rhyming couplets in Valmiki's poem *Ramayana*. No one believes that Rama went around speaking in rhymed couplets, so we have in this case a spiritual message given to the world primarily through dramatic action. If you want to read about the life of Rama, and find out the fate of Sita and her two sons, Kusa and Lava, read his story in the poem *Ramayana*, by Valmiki. You will not be disappointed.[34]

Lord Krishna

The story about the life of Krishna is the *Mahabharata*.[35] It's ironic that he is not the main character, which may strike the Western reader as odd, but his story is in there. *Mahabharata* is an unusual story; it's magical, wonderful and lengthy. In the heart of *Mahabharata* is Krishna's dialogue with his chief disciple Arjuna, and it is called the *Bhagavad-Gita (Song of God)*.

So basically, Arjuna was having a nervous breakdown. And Krishna had to pull him out of this funk in a major hurry. Why? Because they were all about to go to war. All the warriors were lined up, literally, one side against the other, & Arjuna says to Krishna in the middle of the battlefield, "I just can't do this." In the *Bhagavad-Gita,* Krishna, as the master therapist, brought Arjuna a few steps closer to the Truth, and they fought together. Lord Krishna said to his chief disciple Arjuna:*

> *He who works for Me, he who looks upon Me as his*
> *goal, he who worships Me, free from attachment,*

---

*As told in the *Bhagavad-Gita.*

*and who is free from enmity to all creatures, comes to
Me, O Pandava.* *

This quote is an expression of the Avataric tone which I explained
earlier. It can be compared to the tone of Jesus, or of Buddha.
There are similarities and differences, but we are not getting into
that here. We know from Valmiki that Lord Rama said almost
nothing in the way of public spiritual discourse during his lifetime; at least we have no Rama discourses passed to us in the oral
transmission. Whereas Lord Krishna gave a tremendous amount
of experiential wisdom directly to Arjuna, and that transmission
has been preserved in the scripture known as the *Bhagavad-Gita*
(Song of the Lord). As far as we know, Krishna did not write at all,
and we have only versions of what he said, based on those who did
write at that time such as Master Vyasa, and others. Thom Knoles
comes from the Vedic tradition of Vyasa, and Shankaracharya,
and we are honored to have a chapter from him as a Bead.

Meher Baba said about Krishna:

> *Krishna proved to Arjuna, who was his devotee,
> that his apparent bringing about of the physical and
> mental annihilation of the vicious Kauravas was for
> their spiritual salvation. Perfection might manifest
> itself through killing or saving according to the spiri-
> tual demands of the situation.* [36]

When Baba mentions, "Kauravas," that means the leaders
of the army against which Arjuna and his brothers were fighting, with the help of Lord Krishna. Many people don't like what
Baba is saying here. Many simply cannot hear that killing can be
spiritually the best thing for the situation, it just goes against so

---

*When Krishna says, 'O Pandava,' he is acknowledging Arjuna as one of the five sons
of the great Indian ruler Pandu. When Krishna says, "... comes to me" this signifies
a spiritual event of self-realization. –LW

many "spiritual" grains, and stereotypes of meditating monks and nuns with hands folded in prayer. But Krishna told Arjuna directly and strongly that it was time to kill, and ordered Arjuna as his disciple to kill the enemy. That said, it is also true that Krishna apparently gave Arjuna a spiritual experience (there on the battlefield before the war started), wherein it was revealed to Arjuna that there is no real-death in being killed during war, because of reincarnation, and the eternal soul, and the only real-death is the death of the ego, when it merges into the Divine.

Nonetheless, to those looking on it was an awful war with much killing and sorrow. Spirituality is not always rainbows, puppy dogs, butterflies and hugs. It's not always sweet and peaceful. There are many different facets to the spiritual gemstone. There are countless different aspects of God. In this case, there was a giant war in India. The two ruling families killed each other, and Arjuna's army (the army of the Pandavas) aided by Lord Krishna defeated the Kauravas. To learn the details of the life of Arjuna and the role that Lord Krishna played before during and after that war, read the *Mahabharata*, and you will be astonished. Krishna was never married, as far as we know, but his Beloved was a woman named Radha.

Lord Buddha
Buddha gave us "Four Noble Truths," and the fourth Noble Truth is his path to enlightenment. The Truths are "The Noble Truth of Sufferings," being born into a physical body, aging, being sick, and dying – these facts all constitute sufferings. "The Noble Truth of the Cause of Sufferings," asks what causes these sufferings in the first place? Buddha's answer is that craving, wants, desires are the cause of sufferings. "The Noble Truth of the End of Sufferings," means how do we get past suffering in life? We

renounce the cravings, desires, and multifarious wants.

Lastly, there is the "Noble Truth of the Path," in which he brings forth his "Noble Eightfold Path," summarized as:

1. Right views: Truth
2. Right intentions: Away from selfishness
3. Right speech: True and kind (non malicious)
4. Right conduct: No killing, no stealing, etc.
5. Right livelihood: Proper earning of one's living
6. Right effort: Vigilant wholeheartedness
7. Right thoughts: Non-complacency
8. Right state of peaceful mind

These are the points for properly following the path leading to the end of sufferings. With this Noble Eightfold Path, Buddha says we can attain the same enlightenment that he achieved.

Conclusion

My aim was to provide you a tiny taste of these ancient mystical traditions, like that tiny spoon they give you at Ben & Jerry's Ice Cream, when you want to try a new flavor, but are not ready to commit to a whole cone. May this opening chapter serve as a single thread of truth running through all the sacred beads that are gathered together in Oneness. I think this Oneness is tremendously important because it gets back to the facets of one diamond. All these different faiths and cultures, naturally they all worship the God that they've come to know and believe in. It's not that they are all different gods, it's just that the God, the diamond, has different facets (or aspects), and some people relate more easily to one aspect than another. This is simple human nature in that we have different personality types. It has been said there are 12 distinct ways (or styles) of learning. Some people say there are 12 human archetypes, or personality types, as seen in the zodiac of astrology, and in the 12 disciples of the Christ. Some may gravitate toward one more than to another. In the same way, it appears that there are many revelations of this One God. To say one is true and the others are false is a mistake, and this book will not engage in a theological or philosophical debate. Instead, this book is an invitation to honor these spiritual paths, and Divine revelations, in a respectful and thoughtful way.

If this sharing from my heart contains mistakes, it is simply due to my spiritual ignorance, and a failure to perceive the deepest truth. And if anything that I have shared sheds any light at all, it is entirely due to the grace of my Beloved Master Meher Baba, who has blessed my life with his divine love and taken me by the hand out of the depths of ignorance towards his light.

One of Meher Baba's last acts while living was to have the following quote from the glorious Qutub Hafiz read aloud at his bedside, by a longtime Persian disciple of his, just hours before passing away:

> *Befitting a fortunate slave, carry out every command of the Master without any question of why and what. About what you hear from the Master, never say — it is wrong — because, my dear, the fault lies in your own incapacity to understand him. I am the slave of the Master who has released me from ignorance; whatever my Master does, is of the highest benefit to all concerned.*

According to Bhau Kalchuri, in silence Baba then, "bowed with his hands and gestured in respect, 'Khuda Hafiz!'" This can be translated from the Persian as "May God protect you."[37]

Sunrise, overlooking Hyderabad, Andhra State, India, from near Meher Baba's "Manonash Cave."

CHAPTER THREE

Among the Sleeping:
Sufism Within and Without Islam

Karl Moeller

K NOWING FULL WELL I HAVE NOT THE WISDOM for this task, I undertake it and call upon al-Razzaq, Allah The Sustainer.

Introduction

> *Any sufficiently advanced technology is*
> *indistinguishable from magic.*

British science-fiction author, Arthur C. Clarke, wrote this in 1961. He was right. Recent scientific and lay writing on quantum physics utilizes terms such as multidimensionality, quarks, particle/wave duality, link theory, and Planck's constant. Close reading reveals that cutting-edge physics denies the existence of time and the reality of physical matter, the latter being a mere series of improbability curves. Physics may as well be magic. One would not expect a reader to instantly grasp what can take physicists a lifetime to master. However, over time, even an interested layman may, through repetition and multiple examples, get a mental glimpse of the unlikely reality.

But the subject is Sufism. What is Sufism? It is a guided mystical path, a course of training, predicated on the concepts that mysticism is a science, and that spirituality can be systematically unveiled in those with the right potential for love. Sufism's 'classical' period was 1200 to 800 years ago, on the far side of

67

the planet, in a culture much different from the modern, postindustrial West, lived by Muslims speaking or writing in Arabic or medieval Persian or Turkish, describing human experiences quite alien to ours – it may as well be science fiction or quantum physics.

However, in all these efforts, we are trying to use words to describe something far more complex than quantum physics. Persons far advanced on the Path might argue that Sufism and quantum physics are one and the same, except that the Sufi ascribes infinite consciousness to the universe and its Creator, while the best the physicist can do is hold up an 'uncertainty principle.'

This chapter will present Islamic and Sufi concepts along with their original Arabic or Persian terms; just as a physicist finds it impossible to totally avoid his discipline's jargon, so must those interested in Sufism begin to learn the terms that practitioners actually employ.

Included Discussions

1. The Prophet Muhammad and the history and spread of Islam.

2. Muhammad's own spiritual practices, which inspired the early Sufis.

3. Famous Sufi orders and their founders.

4. Sufi poetry and teaching-stories written over the past 1400 years, which attempt to describe the inner states of realization.

5. Apparent practitioner miracles.

6. How Sufism is based on and interrelates with Islam.

7. Using strained metaphors, teaching stories and quotations from 1400 years of Islam and Sufi tradition, the goal here is, like a pointillist painter, to create a recognizable outline of Islamic Sufism with at least a little detail right there in the middle. We

are, in the end, simply confounded by our conditioning, lack of like experience, by the use of imperfectly translated words in a different language from the original practitioners, and by the ineffable quality that defines the Sufi.

Any discussion of Sufism is further complicated by the fact that words are themselves metaphors, mere stand-ins for the real thing or experience; the meaning derived from reading a sequence of words is utterly dependent upon the experience of the person reading them.

Surrender

If the term applies to those who systematically attempt to live so as to invite God into their beings, then Sufis state that there have always been Sufis. There are records going back centuries before Christ, indicating there were active groups of dedicated Zoroastrian mystics. The Essenes have been referred to as a mystic brotherhood. The *Gnostic Gospels*' Acts of John describe a Dervish-like dance at the Last Supper, with Jesus in the middle leading a call and response litany.

However, for over 1200 years, Sufism has been defined by and seen as an extension of traditional Islam. The terms and methods are inextricably Muslim. Islam is the exoteric religion. Sufism is mysticism, esoteric practice in an Islamic wrapper. Islam literally means 'surrender,' to the will of God, or Allah. In the West, we tend to associate surrender with subservience and have lost touch with its hidden power.

The only places in the West available to the public where surrender is ever discussed is in the process of substance abuse recovery in the various 'Anonymous' groups. This is an interesting parallel since advanced Sufis consider the bulk of mankind to be addicted to their hypnotized and spiritually asleep state. Similar to an AA group, the would be Sufi also has to system-

atically surrender to the Higher Power, making amends, and
'recovering' from the 'sleep' state, gaining the inner sight of
which some are capable.

Surrender creates an empty space within the psyche which
allows us to experience the power of our true Self without being
overwhelmed or inflated. Sufi practices are designed to help man
to surrender, and to realize that man can become infinite, that we
are not contained by the limited horizons of the mind and ego.

In the Sufi view, the practice of systematic surrender begins
with an understanding of Islam, study of the *Qur'an*, and absorbing the ongoing impact of the life and example of the Prophet
Muhammad.

Islam
Within Islam, there are Five Pillars which are the framework of
Muslim life: testimony of faith (Kalimah), prayer (Salat), concern
for the needy (Zakat), self-purification (Sawm, Ramadhan), and
Hajj, the pilgrimage to Mecca, for those who are able.

There are also clear guidelines of behavior for the Muslim
believer, in order of severity of consequence in the next world.
However, these all refer to external, observable behavior, which
may or may not be accompanied by genuine personal change or
even belief. Or, one may scrupulously follow every one of these
guidelines, while being motivated by nothing more exalted than
a fear of Hell.

Muslims are expected to follow not just the words and actions
of the Prophet Muhammad (the 'Sunna'), but also to attempt to
attain the states of his being, his states of the heart, such as god-
fearingness (taqwa), mercy (rahma), reliance (tawakkul) upon
Allah, humility, sincerity, and many others. Sufis believe these
states are desirable, not because of fear of Hell, but because the

Prophet Muhammad was 'insani kamil' – the Completed Man, the best and most lovable of men, the most worthy of honor and emulation, and he carried the words and decrees of an irresistibly lovable God.

Exact instructions on how to achieve these surrendered states of the Prophet's are not in the *Qur'an*, nor in books of Islamic jurisprudence, because unlike prayer, gifts to the poor, or fasting, there are no hard and fast guidelines, universally applicable, for each soul, no single recipe for enlightenment.

Hadith, the authenticated utterances of the Prophet, and many *Qur'anic* verses illustrate repeatedly that not only must a Muslim do and say certain things, but must also change internally, become something new, must clean his or her heart. These changes may only be acquired with considerable, right-minded effort, termed 'purification' in many places in the *Qur'an*:

He has succeeded who purifies himself. (87:14)

But the *Qur'an* tells the Muslim only that change is obligatory; it does not say specifically how. This is where the example set and internal states experienced by the Prophet become crucial to understanding the methods and goals of Sufi training.

Systematically bringing about this change in the individual is the aim of the Islamic science of Sufism.

The Prophet's Example

The Prophet Muhammad is seen by all Eastern, traditional Sufi orders as the Gnosis of Reality, 'marefat-e-haqiqat', or the Complete Man, 'insani kamil'. Born Muhammad ibn Abdullah ibn Abdul Muttalib ibn Hashim, he lived from 570 to 632. The Prophet and his close associates, the Companions, exceeded all requirements in regard to prayer and devotional practices. All through his life, he kept long night vigils and often practiced voluntary fasts. He never ate barley bread, which was a staple at that time, on three consecutive days, and he never ate wheat bread, which was considered a luxury. One of his favorite sayings was, "Poverty is my pride," and this saying came to be quoted in every manual of Sufi doctrine, making the rule of poverty a basic characteristic, at least theoretically, of Sufi life.

Going back to antiquity, the prevalent model of a mystic is one with a quiet, modest, retiring demeanor, vegetarian, dressed implausibly, head in the clouds, impractical, residing in a monastery or a cave, in order to eliminate distractions and temptations from the noisome outer world. History does indeed show various Sufi monasteries around the Mideast and East. But a quatrain from the Sufi poet Hafiz tells us:

> *Come to the tavern*
> *Drink the wine*
> *Go not to the cell-squatters in the monastery*
> *For their deeds are dark.*

The Prophet did, at age 40, spend time in meditation in a cave near Mecca, ending with a visit from the Angel Gabriel ('Jibreel' in Arabic), who said, "Rise, for thou art the Prophet of God. Go forth and preach in the name of thy Lord. Your God is merciful." After this mystical experience, Muhammad left the cave, but he was visited by Jibreel many times in the next 23 years.

The Prophet Muhammad was an orphan, then a successful trader, husband, father, widower, legislator, educator, warrior, & general. The Sufi, whether in the East or West, may be involved in literally any profession, meeting his or her societal & familial obligations, all the while maintaining inward detachment from the role. There is a Sufi saying, "Be in the world, not of the world."

The Qur'an
A Muslim believes that the book known as the *Qur'an* is the word of Allah revealed to Prophet Muhammad. The *Qur'an* was dictated to the Prophet by the Angel Jibreel on various occasions throughout his lifetime to answer questions, solve problems, settle disputes and to be man's best guide to the truth. The *Qur'an* was revealed in Arabic and is still in its original, unchanged state today. One who has memorized the *Qur'an* may carry the title 'Hafiz'.*

A Muslim also believes in a clear distinction between the *Qur'an* and the Traditions, '*Hadith*' of the Prophet Muhammad. The *Qur'an* is the word of Allah, dictated to Muhammad, meant for all mankind. *Hadith* are the traditions of Prophet Muhammad (i.e. his teachings, sayings, and actions). The 'Sunna' are the practical interpretations of the *Qur'an*. The *Qur'an* and the Sunna of Prophet Muhammad are the primary sources of knowledge in Islam.

Hadith and Sunna of The Prophet
Hadith of the Prophet Muhammad have come to us in various forms, describing his sayings and his deeds and approval or disapproval of various actions or events. Looser interpretation of the term also may include narration by or about the Companions and Successors of the Prophet. Together these various texts are referred to as the Sunna, describing essentially how the Prophet lived his life.

Since *Hadith* literature is the other arm of Islamic thought, the rapid growth of Islam in the two centuries following the death

---

*The word Hafiz means "protector," as one who has memorized the *Qur'an* is considered thereby to be a protector of the faith. –LW

of the Prophet understandably challenged Islamic scholars with two tasks:

1. To preserve this knowledge
2. To identify and classify the body of *Hadith* as to accuracy.

Thus the exacting science of *Hadith* evaluation and attribution came into being, the 'Isnad', a subject beyond the scope of this chapter, and your patience.

However, there is a special class of *Hadith*, called '*Hadith Qudsi*'. These are post-Qur'anic revelations from Allah related by the Prophet. Unlike the Prophet's comments on events or spirituality, these are received as if they were part of the *Qur'an*.

Early Sufis

Prior to the 8TH century A.D., Sufism was very much an internal, personal process. Following the example of the Prophet Muhammad, certain ascetic-minded Muslims began very rigorous self-training, making devotional prayers and solitary nocturnal vigils an integral part of their lives.

Famous mystics of this period were Malik ibn Dinar and Muhammad ibn Wasi. Malik ibn Dinar who believed it was permitted to own land and be independent of men, while ibn Wasi believed it was better to not know where one's next meal would come from. A famous woman saint of the time, Rabia al-Adawwiya, elaborated on the Qur'anic theme of trust in God, through ecstatic songs and poems, stressing purity of heart and the inner life. It is said that she used to kneel a thousand times daily saying,

> *I ask for no recompense but to satisfy the Almighty God.*

She also stated,

True devotion is for itself: not to desire Heaven nor to fear Hell.

This last is an important point, because devotion driven by fear is not devotion at all. Yet Suhrawardi states,

Fear and hope are both necessary to prevent bad conduct.

The first mystic orders began to develop in the 2ND century following the Advent of the Prophet, the 8TH century A.D. The doctrine of annihilation (Fana) of the false self (Nafs) into Allah had taken root. This is the beginning of a science of spirituality.

The nafs is the root cause of human suffering and confusion and the enemy of individuation. It is the never satisfied, busy, tricky, fidgety monkey in a cage.
 – Suhrawardi

Sufis are fond of characterizing the uncontrolled nafs as an animal. It is more appropriate for the man to ride the donkey, than for the donkey to ride the man. In the Mathnavi (Masnavi, or Mathnawi), Rumi tells the story of a bull who lived alone on a verdant island. Each night the bull would worry anxiously about the grass, since he'd eaten so much, what would he eat upon the morrow? Each morning of his life, there was plenty of grass to eat, but each night in the dark, unable to see the grass, he would start worrying again.

LEVELS OF THE FALSE SELF/EGO Following is a short list of these levels of the false self/ego as defined by the Sufis.*

- *Commanding Nafs (Nafs-i-Ammara)* In undeveloped man, this is the mechanism which drives one to indulge primitive satisfactions;
- *Blaming/Accusatory Nafs (Nafs-i-Lawwama)* When conscience is awakened, one cannot ignore certain matters of the heart;
- *Inspired Nafs (Nafs-i-Mulhama)* One raises one's sight to things spiritual and begins to live the ideal;
- *Tranquil Nafs (Nafs-i-Mutmaina)* One continuously contemplates the beauty of the Divine;
- *Satisfied Nafs (Nafs-i-Radziyya)* One accepts all that existence brings, remaining detached from other than Allah;
- *Satisfying Nafs (Nafs-i-Mardiyyah)* One has arrived in a stage which is pleasing to Allah;
- *Purified Nafs (Nafs-i-Safiyyah, or Nafs al-Kamila)* One has no desire but is absorbed in the Truth – 'haqq.'

There is a *Hadith* of the Prophet that when the Muslims returned from the battle of Uhud, the Prophet said to them, "We are back from the minor battle and we are approaching the major one." They asked him, "What is that major jihad, O Messenger?" He replied, "Fighting against the ego (nafs)." This *Hadith* clearly shows the superiority of 'jihadun nafs' (the struggle with the ego), which is the main aim of Sufism.

The Sufis are saying, loud and clear, that there are worlds and layers of development – even the possibility of divinity. This spiritual practice of surrender, scouring out of oneself, making room for the Divine, led the famous Sufi al-Bistami to ecstatically proclaim,

---

*This list traces the evolution of the Self from cruelty to compassion and may be described as stations on the path, or 'maqam.' The name of the nafs changes according to its function. Also, it seems to represent the process of recovery, as defined by modern psychotherapy.

Praise is to Me; how great is my majesty;
I am your Lord.

and also,

My banner is greater than that of Muhammad.

These outrageous statements were explained away as 'non-responsible' and 'made in a state of God-intoxication':

> *A person who is in a state of ecstasy should not be*
> *rebuked for what he may utter in his ecstatic state.*
> –Subayhi

The early orders, and all that followed them, shared a characteristic: spiritual seekers clustered around an acknowledged teacher, following his example and absorbing the outward (adab) and inward (ahwal) states, in the same way that the Companions of the Prophet were changed by keeping company with him. Students of Sufism, 'murids', benefit profoundly from associating with a particular 'murshid' – teacher or master – a pattern which continues to the present day.

To summarize the purpose, message, and methods developed by the early Sufis:

- The *Qur'an* described following the example of the Prophet Muhammad as 'purifying' for all mankind, and membership in a Sufi order reflects this same method and purpose.
- The heart states of Muhammad are not committed to books, but communicated from the knowers ('arifin) to students.
- Because of the complexity of the task of surrender and spiritual growth, and the myriad beginning states or starting points

of murids, the only effective method of transmission of this
spiritual science is the personal example of a living master.

Sharia, Islamic Law

Together, the *Qur'an* and the 'Sunna' are the basis for the religion
of Islam. Sharia adds the use of interpretations of Muslim jurisprudence to the *Qur'an* and Sunna. While Sharia may be taken as
a set of ethical guidelines, in some Islamic countries Sharia is the
actual rule of law. Since an inner as well as outer understanding
of the letter and spirit of the Sharia is seen as crucial, Sufi and
jurist Ibn al-Arabi once stated that the only jurist or 'faqih' (one
trained in jurisprudence) or 'Ulema' that could serve well was a
Friend of Allah, a waliullah (Sufi) who was also trained in ethical thinking. But Ibn al-Arabi's standard for religious jurists has
seldom been met. There is a *Hadith* of the Prophet:

> *Whoever among you outlives me shall see a vast
> dispute.*

Man being man, there is always the danger of turning religion
itself into a idolatrous net which insulates the practitioner,
worried about legality of this or that act, from any possibility of
experiencing the Divine. Within the Islamic tradition, the cure
for this is Sufism.

Sufism and Sharia

In addition to the visible order structure of murshid – murid
relations and Sufi practices, the Sufis introduced a concept
called "The Preserving Saints," which holds that the world is
kept intact thanks to the existence of a network of corporeal or
invisible saints of different ranks.

These are some rungs of this spiritual ladder: 'Awtad' or pegs, people who can communicate with Perfect Masters across space and time. 'Abdal,' or successors, can appear and disappear anywhere on earth. Next are the 'Am'aid' or pillars, and all of these connections terminate in a being, the 'Qutub,' which is the pole or axis around which the whole universe rotates. If not for this structure, the Sufis believe the universe would go to pieces.

A special place in this spiritual hierarchy* is occupied by al-Khidr ('Khizr'), the Green Saint, who some say is immortal, or possesses the water of Life, and whose function it is to guide those in need, those without access to a living teacher. Some traditions say that al-Khidr is the prophet Elijah from the Old Testament. Many eminent Sufis claim to have received knowledge directly from al-Khidr. He is deemed to be a special 'Servant of God' as described in the *Qur'an* Sura 18, where he is described as spiritual guide to Moses. Sufi lore also indicates that Saint Francis benefitted from contact with al-Khidr.

One of the main tenets of Islam is the Kalimah, the statement 'La ilaha illa Allah,' "There is No God but Allah." Within Islam, this monotheist concept is called 'tawhid' – to believe that there is no partner to Allah in His being and in His attributes. Alternatively, a major sin within Islam is called 'shirk.' Shirk is defined as putting anything, or anyone, on a level with Allah. Divinity cannot be given to Man, including the Prophet, who was known as the Messenger. As Man is slave to Allah, believing that Man can become divine is considered shirk.

Contrast this to the concept of The Preserving Saints and reverence and belief in both the Qutub and al-Khidr, and we have now arrived at the point where some Sufi beliefs and statements appear to constitute heresy.

---

*The online Webster's Dictionary has this as the first definition of hierarchy: "A division of angels."

In Islam, though there is not officially an intermediary between the Muslim and Allah, the jurist class, the Ulema, condemned some of the early Sufis and their practices as 'innovations' and therefore suspect, if not outright heretic. A famous Sufi, Mansur al-Hallaj, was executed in Baghdad for consistently stating, 'Ana al-Haqq,' "I am the Truth."

He was also notorious for insisting that Jesus had been a Sufi master, which somehow labelled Hallaj as a secret Christian, and therefore a 'kaffir,' or unbeliever, even though both the *Qur'an* and various *Hadith* repeatedly honor Jesus and Mary. Dhu-Nun al-Misri, the Egyptian, credited with classifying the stages of spiritual development, was charged with heresy by the Ulema in Baghdad in 854 A.D.

Early Sufi masters al-Junayd and al-Ghazzali did much to legitimize Sufi practice. Muhammad al-Ghazzali, around 1095, wrote several works which managed to reconcile intellectual, traditional Islamist, and Sufi mystic elements. Al-Ghazzali erased many of the objections that orthodox Islamic jurists had to the Sufi orders, by reinterpreting *Qur'anic* verses and pointing out the interior meaning of many of the sayings of the Prophet, the *Hadith*. For example, there is a *Hadith Qudsi* where the Prophet explained that Allah has stated:

> *When my Slave becomes My beloved, I become his ears through which he listens, his eyes through which he sees, his hands by which he holds, his feet by which he walks. When he pleads to Me for anything I definitely bestow it on him. When he seeks refuge in Me from any bad deed, then I definitely save him from it.*

The *Qur'an* contains instructions suitable to man with varying levels of spirituality. It satisfies those who are content with merely exoteric practices, but also contains the deepest and most profound esoteric meaning for those who desire a closer, more mystical relationship with God. One *Qur'anic* verse which is a favorite of the Sufis is,

Allah is closer to man than his own jugular vein.

To this day there is still shouting from those who believe the science of Sufism to be "bid'aa," a reprehensible innovation, clearly involving saint worship and 'intermediaries' between man and Allah and therefore is shirk and outside Islam. Sufis consider those people to be externalists and primarily concerned with appearances, not the cleanliness of their own souls.

However, this fundamentalist anti-Sufi attitude is far from universal. Many Muslim communities around the world have historically, and to this day consider membership in an order to be a normal part of life. Traditional Muslim Sufis are very devout and adhere closely to Islamic law as defined in the *Qur'an* and *Hadith*, considering this activity the starting point, not the ending, of their spirituality. Rumi, founder of the Mevlevi Sufi order, wrote:

> *I am the slave of the Qur'an for as long as I am*
> *living. I am dust on the path of Muhammad, the*
> *Chosen One.*

Silsila Concept
The Arabic word 'silsila' means 'chain,' or continuity of personal transmission of esoteric knowledge. A Sufi student is initiated

into an order by a Sufi master. The master's authority has been passed to him by a previous master, through the investiture of the traditional mantle of authority, symbolized by the presentation of a cloak of patched cloth, or khirqa. This initiation is supported by the chain of lineage going back through all the previous masters to the Prophet Muhammad, from whom the authority to instruct in the esoteric doctrine originated. Even today, this is the general practice of all the recognized Sufi orders. Each Murshid can present a written list of his spiritual lineage, going back to the Prophet and the Angel Jibreel (Gabriel). Who is on these lists? There is a *Hadith* from the Prophet which states,

I am the city of knowledge and Ali is the door to it.

Ali was the son-in-law of the Prophet, and was one of the first Muslim converts. Because of his courage as a very young man, Ali is known as the Lion of Islam. Ali had four Khalifs, or lieutenants: Hassan, Hussain, Kumayl, and Hassan Basri. The first formal Silsila was founded by Abdul Wahid bin Zayd who was a Khalifa of Hassan Basri but also received a khirqa (robe of initiation) from Kumayl. Bin Zayd passed away 171 years after the Prophet's Hijira to Medina, or 793. (Rabia al-Adawwiya, mentioned earlier, also known as Rabia al-Basri, was a contemporary of Hassan Basri.)

Sufi Orders
So we see that the earliest Sufi orders began very close to the Prophet's lifetime, with knowledge and instruction communicated from him to Ali, and then from Ali personally to the various Khalifs. There are 14 main and formal Silsilas, or orders. All of these originated from Ali. Later, these orders expanded

into more than 40 separate groups. Each order has at all times a 'Shaikh-ul-Mashaikh', or living leader.

There are two main branches of Islam, the Sunni and the Shia. When the Prophet Muhammad passed on in 632, there was dissention in the Muslim community regarding whether he had designated a successor. Some of the Companions believed he had clearly stated that Ali, his son-in-law and nephew, should be the leader, or Imam. Tradition, however, swayed the majority of the community, and Abu Bakr, an old friend of the Prophet's, was elected as the first Caliph, first leader of the Sunni movement. The other group believed that Ali and the family and descendants of the Prophet were his legitimate temporal and spiritual successors. This group is known as Shi'ati Ali, the supporters of Ali, or the Shia. An individual in this group is a Shi'ite. Estimates of Shia among Muslims worldwide range from 15 to 20 percent, concentrated mostly in Iran and Iraq.

A sorry series of events occurred in the Muslim community within thirty years of the Prophet's death; attempted and completed assassinations, all the way to open warfare.

Just as there are Sunni and Shia Muslims, it follows that there are Sunni and Shia Sufi orders. Shia Sufi orders such as the Nimatullahi have Hazrat Ali in their written Silsila, immediately following the Prophet. Surprisingly, all the Sunni orders do as well, except the Naqshbandi/Haqqani, who mention the first Caliph, Abu Bakr, not Ali, in their written Silsila.

With this exception, it is clear then that 1400 years of both Sunni and Shia Sufis consider that Caliph Ali was given something not given to the other Companions, something vital to the spiritual development of man. Yet the vast majority of Sufi orders say, "We are Sunni," (i.e. religious followers of the way of Abu Bakr).

Here is the beginning of the Silsila for the Chishti Order,
(Sunni):
Hazrat Jibra'il (the Angel Gabriel)
Hazrat Khwaja Muhammad Rasul Allah (The Prophet)
Hazrat Khwaja 'Ali Wali Allah (4TH Caliph of Islam, Ali)
Hazrat Khwaja Hasan Basri (Ali's Khalif)
Hazrat Khwaja 'Abd al-Wahid bin Zayd (founder of 1st order)
Hazrat Khwaja Fuzayl bin 'Iyaz.

Here is the beginning of the Silsila for the Naqshbandi Order
(Sunni):
Muhammad ibn Abd Allah (The Prophet)
Abu Bakr as-Siddiq (1st Caliph of Islam)
Salman al-Farsi ('The Persian', a Companion)
Qassim ibn Muhammad ibn Abu Bakr (grandson of Abu Bakr)
Jafar as-Sadiq (6TH Shi'ite Imam)
Tayfur Abu Byazid al-Bistami (originator of term 'Fana')

A Sufi order grows from the personality and training methods
of the founder of the order, the original Shaikh. The orders also
take on the characteristics of the people involved in them; there
is a huge difference between the methods of the quiet, sober,
deadly earnest Naqshbandis of the Middle East and the wild,
exuberant Rifai of North Africa. The goal is the same, however
– annihilation of the false self into Allah. The visible effect is to
reach a state of inner equilibrium where no importance is attached to either praise or blame, failure or success.

The Heart
A Muslim's five times daily prayers, Salat, involve certain recita-
tions and prostrations in the direction of Mecca. These recita-

tions and prostrations are called Rakats, and are meaningful to the Sufi in part because this prostration is the only time one's heart is above one's head.

But a passive, in pain being with a broken heart is useless to Sufi order or to themselves. The murshid has the delicate task of slowly breaking the lifelong accretions around the human heart without causing permanent, debilitating emotional damage to the student, allowing them to love fully, freely and intuitively.

Love is both the message and the method of imparting the message. Since Sufis allude to nonverbal and distant communication between practitioners, the outsider must imagine the attunement, alignment and intuition necessary between these people for any sort of reliable connection or message passing. The hidden, unspoken and unseen connection between an advanced murshid and murid (or 'mutawassit') well along in the work can only be discussed in terms of Love. This direct transmission is called 'tawaj' by Naqshbandis.

This heart-to-heart 'rab'ta' (rabita) is also called tassawur-I-shaykh, 'blending with the Shaykh'. It is a non-romantic but burningly intense love between murid and teacher, love that the murshid attempts to transfer higher in the Silsila – the murid's Fana-fi Murshid becomes Fana-fi Shaikh (the founder of the order), then to the Prophet, then to the goal, to Allah.

Look at the same issue from the reverse angle. Assume that a murid misses an important signal or direction transmitted from the murshid. Since the murid missed it and therefore did not act upon it, there is no sense of having failed at a task, since each task actually begins by perceiving it. A very subtle and ultimately kind filtration system.

Rabita or tawaj may also exist between advanced Sufis, regardless of order, location, or time. The Sufi asserts that the founders of the orders may still be contacted directly. Taking this further, Suhrawardi and the Shia Sufis of Iran, the so-called Isfahan School, discussed and prepared for sudden illumination from above, by systematically purifying themselves. This science of direct cognition or, "knowledge by presence" is called by them 'ilm al-huduri.'

While it is relatively simple to mention and define states, methods, teachers, orders, and to call Sufism the 'science of spirituality,' the dimension of Love is necessarily far more difficult to access, understand, and explain. Disciples come for knowledge, devotees come for Love. It is better to come for Love.

The True Teacher

A murshid, or pir, or shaykh, is not the founder of an order. He has risen through the ranks, as khalifa, or lieutenant, has received the khirqa, or mantle, from an acknowledged murshid, and later may be granted permission to take murids and begin a branch of the order, if he so chooses and conditions are right. At that point that person is referred to as Murshid, or teacher.

There are in fact formal qualifications for a murshid. Most Sufi orders have the tradition of a written 'license to practice,' called 'ijaza nama.' The ijaza nama specifies the duties and responsibilities of the murshid as given by his own Shaykh, plus one or more complete silsila records (depending on how many orders to which the new murshid belongs) – tracing the spiritual lineage back to the Prophet and (with noted exceptions) to Caliph Ali. Simply having the license does not mean the bearer is a perfected teacher, a 'kamil shaykh.' A kamil shaykh is considered to possess:

• *Knowledge* of the Sharia, Qur'an, *Hadith*, and Islamic jurisprudence;

- *Expertise* in the rites and rituals of his particular order;
- *Practical knowledge* of the stations – maqqamat – that mark the progress of a murid;
- *Personal experience* with the stages of Fana, annihalation of the false self;
- *Continuous inner bonding* – rab'ta – with his own murshid, and with the founder of his own order, and with the Prophet Muhammad.

Some would-be students of Sufism are not aware that their motives include the wish for exotic, unusual experience, or are motivated by what can only be called spiritual greed. The teacher must provide a real context in which each murid can grow at his or her best pace. The teacher is not there to provide psychotherapy to the murid, but to adjust and open perceptions far beyond psychotherapy's scope. The teacher must be able to diagnose the stage of the pupil, and the learner must come to the stage where he can accept this without resentment or pride. Beyond this, the true murshid strives to make himself irrelevant – except in inner connection – to the murid.

Rumi says, "Wool, through the presence of a man of knowledge, becomes a carpet. Earth & stone may become a palace. The presence of a spiritual man creates a similar transformation."

Alchemy, in other words. Base materials become fine, and useful. But how to recognize the true teacher? The proof of the teacher is in the quality, nature, and accomplishments – the refinement of heart and mind – of the students. The Sufi master ibn al-Arabi stated, "People think that a teacher should display miracles and manifest illumination. But the requirement in a teacher is that he should possess all that the disciple needs."

Because spirituality works & expresses on the intuitive level, the opportunities to choose poorly are many. While one would

hope that the Silsila and investiture ceremonies and even posses-
sion of an 'ijaza nama' would eliminate them, there are as many
false teachers in Sufism as in other spiritual disciplines, which
is compounded by the Sufi's disregard for externals.

A seeker may encounter a false teacher who takes pains to
look and act the part, and therefore appears genuine, while a
kamil shaykh with real knowledge is avoided, because he does
not match the seeker's immature idea of how a spiritual teacher
should look and act. Many teaching-stories involve a teacher
acting in a non-spiritual or irreligious manner, scaring off the
unready. This process frees the genuine master of the task of
dismissing indiscriminating, incapable would-be murids; misled
by externals, these people dismiss themselves in advance. An
elegant system.

Murid-Murshid Pact

Love is both the door and the key to the door. Someone first
encountering Sufism by reading would imagine that its prime
reason for existing is to train new Sufis.

There is in fact a formalized relationship between the teacher,
known as a Murshid, and the aspirant, called the Murid, as well
as a course of study. While these connections may last a lifetime,
it is also possible that an individual may require exposure to
other teaching methods in different areas of the world. Travel
and apprenticeship have historically been part of the Sufi Way.
Because of special training, the aspirant's inner states are readily
apparent to the advanced Sufi.

Sufism utilizes a codified, systematic gradation of the various
stages of spiritual development. These terms and definitions
are usually in Arabic, and may be expressed in varying degrees
of Fana, meaning absorption or obliteration. The duty of the

student is to obliterate the Nafs, or false self, into the Murshid. This state is called 'Fana-fi Murshid'. Then the aspirant is handed up the chain to the founder of the Sufi order in which the Murid is enrolled. This state is called 'Fana-fi Shaikh'. Final states are known as 'Fana-fi Rasul', absorption into the Prophet Muhammad, then 'Fana-Fillah', into Allah, the Creator.

As Allah is pure light and energy, without preparation and the guidance of an (illumined) teacher, any touch of that true Reality (haqiqa) would drive a person of ordinary consciousness insane. There are in fact in the East some persons known as mahdzubs or masts, who have in a sense gone too far too fast without guidance, and are absorbed in Allah and have withdrawn or are unable to perform normal social functions. By Western standards they would be considered insane. Because of this, Sufi training systematically creates heavier and heavier emotional and mental circuitry, so the practitioner may participate in this world without being overwhelmed by a higher plane of consciousness.

The connection between the student and Murshid is all-important, and each has a set of obligations or duty toward the other.

Duties of the Murid
It is said that human beings utilize only about five to seven percent of their estimated mental capability. Because Sufism is, in one dimension, the science of developing higher human functions and consciousness, it requires candidates with extraordinary aptitudes coupled with a humble inner demeanor.

However, it should be acknowledged that would-be murids may appear before a murshid in a very imperfect, incomplete state. If they have that spark within them the teacher can, in time, help them transform into genuine students with real capabilities, balanced beings, and paradoxically having no greed for spiritual, exotic experience or special powers. Life's requisite leveling or grinding away of undesirable blocking traits is normally, even naturally, seen as misfortune, events to be avoided. These are the very experiences which work on the nafs and are therefore embraced by the aspirant. So we are told.

In Kitab adab al-Muridin (A Sufi Rule For Novices), Suhrawardi says, the first duty of a student of Sufism is that the student must make himself inwardly clean. This means he must be able to operate without the distorting effects of anger, greed, envy, and so on, which are regarded by Sufis as prehuman; monkeys and other animals exhibit all of these qualities on occasion.

The second duty is to have worldly interests, but to do one's best to not be attached to the results, and reach a state where apparent success or failure are truly seen as equal. Sufis say the proper attitude is "In the world, not of the world."

The third duty is submission to the murshid as part of a contract of mutual and total respect. Knowledge cannot be gained except in an attitude of humble openness.

Another duty is to follow a course of study prescribed by the murshid in the order recommended. Another is to understand the relative ranking of the various studies and to know the connections, so one doesn't concentrate on the irrelevant. And another duty of the student of Sufism is that the aim should be self improvement, not visible power or influence.

Teaching Methods — Zikr
The Sufis live with an ever increasing awareness of God. One aspect of this awareness is the practice of Zikr. (sometimes spelled 'dhikr'), means 'remembering God,' by pronouncing one of Allah's 99 names or attributes or by uttering a number of

recognized formulae. The Murshid usually assigns a phrase and a number of required repetitions.

The *Qur'an* repeatedly admonishes believers to celebrate the praises of God and to do this often. Some Sufis (notably the Naqshbandi) do constant 'wazifa,' which is the internal, silent repetition of Zikr phrases. The following verse of the *Qur'an* reveals the significance of Zikr:

> *Recite that which has been revealed to you of the scripture, and observe prayer. For prayer restrains one from lewdness and iniquity, but remembrance of God is the greatest virtue. 29.45*

In a passage of the *Qur'an*, the importance of Zikr is emphasized to such an extent that a response from God is assured:

> *Therefore remember Me, and I will remember you. 2.152*

A *Hadith* in support of the practice: "Allah did not listen to anything as He listened to Zikr recitation by a prophet with a nice voice." Sufis take the word 'remembrance' in the *Qur'an* to mandate the practice of Zikr.

The First Kalimah
The 'Kalimah,' the basic Islamic statement of belief, is:

> *'La ilaha illa Allah wa Muhammad ar-Rasul Allah.'*
> *"There is no God/deity but Allah and Muhammad is his messenger."*

The phrase 'La ilaha illa Allah' is one of the most commonly used phrases in Zikr. This phrase consciously affirms there is no deity besides Allah. On the surface this means to beware of idols, false prophets, money, prestige and power, but taken farther – and the Sufi always takes it farther – to deny one's own ego (justifying the Fana process of Nafs-obliteration), and denying the apparent supremacy of physical reality. This is what Hindus and Vedantists refer to as Maya, the illusion of physical reality – and the illusion of time. Quantum physics has also questioned the existence of time and physical reality. Albert Einstein (1879-1955), physicist and mathematician, said: "The difference between the past, the present and the future is only a persistent illusion." However, once one has negated everything except Allah, how can we possibly reach Him?

The last section of the Kalimah, 'Muhammad ar-Rasul Allah', "(and) Muhammad is the Prophet – or messenger – of Allah" kindly tells us that the Prophet Muhammad is the conduit or connection to Allah – the Prophet is the available bridge between the tangible and the intangible.

Therefore, learning and living the states the Prophet experienced is the goal of the Sufi teaching and the purpose of the orders. This is expressly why each major order is so conscious of of its silsila, the chain of personal, living transmission of knowledge and experience, going back to Caliph Ali and the Prophet.

Teaching Methods – Sama
The term 'sama' means 'hearing' or 'audition.' Two of the orders, the Mevlevi of Turkey, and the Chishtis in Pakistan and India, utilize a combination of Zikr, music, and dance to create the possibility of creating a 'Hal' state for the participants,

which may include visions and loss of normal consciousness. In Suhrawardi's, *A Sufi Rule For Novices*, Sufi master Junayd defines Hal as:

> *... a form of inspiration which comes down to the heart but does not stay in it permanently.*

The murshid or shaikh connects the state and aspiration (jam al-himma) of the listeners and dancers with the energy of the musicians, and may grant the experience.

However, knowing how easily the human organism can become addicted to the unusual, the exotic, some teachers discourage repeat experiences:

> *If a novice is attracted to sama, you can know there is still in him a remainder of falseness.*
> – Junayd

Teaching Stories

Sufi murshids have traditionally used teaching-stories as a part of the process of awakening the student. Study of these stories can lead to an intimate knowledge of cause and effect in the practitioner. While many of the stories have an obvious moral, for example, or a clever twist of logic which the acute reader may appreciate, it is held that many of these stories, considered in proper order and at appropriate length, will help the snail leave its shell. There is a Sufi aphorism, Al mujazu qantarat al-Haqiqa – "The relative is a channel to the Truth."

George Bernard Shaw said, "When a thing is funny, search it for a hidden truth." Mullah Nasruddin is an internationally known mythic figure, the Fool of God, used in many Sufi teaching-stories. These often uncover unconscious assumptions in the listener. Sometimes the logical fallacy in the story is meant to shock the listener into a different mind-space.

A MULLAH NASRUDDIN STORY: As a young man, Nasruddin went to his shaykh asking him for advice and blessings. The old sage said, "I will offer you some words of wisdom that will provide you with a source of guidance for the rest of your life, if only you know how to use them." Nasruddin nodded eagerly. "Always remember," the shaykh said sagely, "life is like a fountain."

Nasruddin pondered the shaykh's words carefully. Thirty years later, he received a letter informing him that his teacher was on his deathbed. Knowing that this was his final chance to see his shaykh, Nasruddin rushed to his beloved teacher's side. "Mawlana," began Nasruddin with a heavy heart, "I have but one question to ask of you. For over three decades now, whenever I fell upon hard times, or was sad or confused, I thought about the phrase you passed on to me, and it has helped me through many difficult times. But to be perfectly honest, I have never entirely grasped its implications nor fully understood its meaning. Now that you are about to enter the realm of truth, tell me, my dear teacher, why is life like a fountain?"

"Alright, alright," replied the old man wearily, "so it's *not* like a fountain!"

ANOTHER NASRUDDIN STORY: Once Nasruddin went to a garden and climbed an apricot tree. The gardener observed this and asked him, "Why have you climbed my master's tree?" Nasruddin answered, "I am a nightingale, and for nightingales climbing a tree is not a sin." The gardener said, "Then please sing so I may listen and enjoy." Nasruddin started to sing in his hoarse voice. The gardener asked him, "Why would a nightingale sing so badly?" Nasruddin replied, "A nightingale which eats raw apricots will never sing better than this."

AND ANOTHER NASRUDDIN STORY: Nasruddin used to stand in the street on market days, to be pointed out as an idiot. No matter how often people offered him a large and a small coin, he always chose the smaller piece. One day a kindly man said to him, "Nasruddin, you should take the bigger coin. Then you will have more money and people will no longer be able to make a laughing stock of you." "That may be true," said Nasruddin, "but if I take the larger coin just once, people will stop offering me money."

ANOTHER STORY (ILLUSTRATING AN UNCONVENTIONAL ESCAPE): An Iranian Sufi shaykh was a rather handsome man and many women were interested in him. A certain woman tried everything she could think of to draw the attention of the shaykh, but he was not in love with her. Then she had him kidnapped. When he was in her power, he said that he would marry her. But first, he wished to use the bathroom. The woman allowed him to go. He returned after shaving not only his beard off, but also his eyebrows and all the hair on his face. She was disgusted with his appearance and let him go.

A FABLE (NOT NECESSARILY FUNNY): Once upon a time, there was a country with a very strange custom. Any man could become king, but only for five years. At the end of that time soldiers would come, tie the king up, take him to a certain wild island full of fearsome beasts, and leave him there.

So king after king for generations had parties, married many women, indulged themselves completely, and were very happy. Until the five years were up. Then off they were carried, crying and screaming, to the island of wild beasts.

Then one day a young man volunteered to become king. But this young king was different. Instead of squandering the country's wealth on parties, or marriages, he enlisted farmers to journey to the island and clear some land. He hired hunters to kill many of the wild beasts that lived there. He employed builders to create a small village at the edge of the farmland. And toward the end he sent his family to move into this village.

At the end of five years he was packed off to the island, not screaming and crying, but with a wide smile upon his face.

Teaching Methods – Poetry

Sufi poetry was not written as entertainment. Read in the original Persian or Arabic by a prepared student of mysticism, the best Sufi poetry can help the murid's spiritual progress. Most of the imagery and metaphors come from the Persian character. As beauty (jamal) and majesty (jalal) usually accompany one another, Rumi often mentions the thorn with the rose.

The wine is the intoxication of divine Love (jadhba). This image is used deliberately, in an abstinent Muslim society, to make it clear that the absorption of the dervish in Allah is not simple emotionality. Drunken men tend to dance, as in the Mevlevi Sama, so the wine and the dance go hand in hand. The tavern is the world, and yet wine is readily available in the tavern.

> *A drunkard wasted away on Love's way*
> *His sweet drunken slumber*
> *Is profoundest prayer.*
>   – 'Iraqi

Upon that station that lovers,
With her lip in mind, drink wine,
Uncouth is the drunkard conscious of himself.
　　　　　　　　　　　　　　　　–Hafiz

None but the drunkard knows
The tavern's secrets —
How could the sober understand
The mysteries of that street!
　　　　　　　　　　　　　　　–'Iraqi

A recurring theme in Sufi poetry and teaching is the 'treasure in the ruin,' sometimes the 'Tavern of Ruin' – Kharabat. The message is that you must ruthlessly tear down your house, or the tavern, to the last stone, because there is a treasure in the foundation. This metaphor represents the gradual eradication of the false self, in which all external attachment falls away, leaving the treasure, a surrendered, winged heart.

Famous Sufi poets include Fariddudin Attar, Hafiz, Jami, Jelalludin Rumi, Saadi of Shiraz, Fakhr al-Din 'Iraqi and Shabistari. Finding readable translations which have not been drained of the essence is a difficult but extremely rewarding task.

Baraka

Baraka is not actually a teaching method but a product of directed Sufi work. Depending upon circumstances, or those involved, baraka may be perceived as a blessing, or energy, or benefit, or message, or personal power, or charisma. The Sufi order is in one sense a channel for baraka. Its manifestation may be invisible to a conditioned mind, accustomed to expect near immediate results for effort.

A STORY FROM RUMI: Two beggars came to the door of a house, asking for bread. One was immediately given some bread, and went away satisfied. The second was kept waiting, and waiting. Why? The first beggar was not greatly liked, and was given a small piece of stale bread. The second was made to wait while a fresh loaf of bread was baked for him.

This kind of story illustrates the temporal and causal disconnects which make a conditioned mind assume that nothing is happening, because the real activity is not apparent to him.

A STORY FROM MASTER FARIDUDDIN ATTAR (IN HIS MANUSCRIPT "RECITALS OF THE SAINTS"): The great Sufi Habib Ajami, when he went to a river to wash, left his coat upon the ground. Hasan of Basra was passing by and saw it. Thinking that someone should look after this property, he stood guard over it until Habib Ajami returned. Hasan asked Habib whom he had left looking after the coat. "In the care," said Habib, "of him who gave you the task of looking after it!"

Intercession

Sufi literature is peppered with miracle stories in which the founder of an order, or some murshid or shaikh, benefits a person or community indirectly or by spiritual or magical means. Among Sufis, a part of the process is often a visit to a tomb-shrine, perhaps the founder of the order, or another venerated by the order. These tomb visits, called 'ziyarat,' have an effect in direct proportion to the spiritual intention of the visitor, and should not be confused with Hajj, the major pilgrimage to Mecca, a required rite performed at a fixed time each year.

The question naturally arises, "How is this issue treated within the Muslim community? What is the attitude towards the supplication to a pious person, and why is this not considered 'shirk'? If the resulting benefit appears to be supernatural in origin, why is it not considered witchcraft?"

There are three *Hadiths* from the Companions about the actions & life of the Prophet which serve to 'normalize' the situation:

1. `Uthman ibn `Abdullah said: "My wife sent me to Umm Salama (one of the Prophet's wives) with a cup of water in which to dip a lock containing some of the Prophet's hair. Whenever a person was suffering from the evil eye or an illness, they would send her a vessel of water (for this). I looked into (it) and saw some red hairs."*

2. Abu Musa related that, "The Prophet called for a vessel of water, washed his hands and face in it, spat a mouthful of water back into it and then said to Abu Musa and Bilal, 'drink from it and pour the rest over your faces and chests.'"

3. Mahmud ibn Rabi` said that, "When the Prophet performed his ablution, the Companions almost fought over the excess water."

Each of these *Hadith* demonstrates that it is permissible to obtain blessings through someone who is closer to Allah than oneself. Because of the Prophet's personal impeccability, there was no taint of 'shirk,' in that he did not consider that the blessings emanated from anywhere or anyone except Allah. And because the channel for these blessings was the Prophet himself, Muslims continued the tradition of seeking blessings through awliya (saints).

Seeking the blessing from a saintly person is not the same at all as worshipping them, a distinction that is not always clear among detractors of the Sufi orders.

---

*The Prophet was redheaded, or somewhat so. –LW

Among The Sleeping
The Real Work may not be educating junior Sufis at all. While the Sufi Work depends on a populace of evolved practitioners, teaching is by no means the most important function of the Sufi hierarchy, historically or in the present day.

One favorite *Hadith* of the Sufis is, "Human beings are asleep, and when they die they will awaken." This *Hadith's* apparent meaning is that all will become clear upon our death. A deeper meaning is that the mass of mankind is in a deep hypnotic state in which physical reality is all, intuition is seen as unreliable, security equates to a large family and/or money in the bank, and religion is an obligation, necessary for social standing.

The Prophet also said, "Die before you die," which opens the possibility of awakening to our true nature and relation to the Creator while still alive. The Sufi considers that 'sleep' mentioned in the *Hadith* (above) is the deep illusion resulting from the Real Self being obscured by the False Self. The 'death' is the death of the False Self, or Nafs. The Sufi Hakim Sanai wrote,

> *Everyone in the ordinary world is asleep. Their religion — the religion of the familiar world — is emptiness, not religion at all.*

While Sufism does indeed aim to assist the properly motivated and capable human to awaken, i.e. training of murids, it has a parallel and deadly serious purpose. Earlier, certain spiritual personages were mentioned, the Awtad and the Abdal. The number of these people vary, and they are assigned to specific locales, depending on the area's history, population, and overall state of spiritual readiness. They may or may not reside in the area for which they are responsible. They have specific duties. We may say that in addition to helping members to rise, the Sufi Work

includes two other main phases:
- Absorption of the negative emanations from entire sleeping populations
- Distribution of positive emanations from Allah to those sleeping populations.

This leads to an outrageous statement – without this absorption of "evil" and dissemination of "good" performed by the corporeal Sufi orders along with the hierarchy of Sufi Preserving Saints, humanity would have ceased to be long ago. In that sense advanced Sufis benefit everyone in the world, whether they know it or not. These self-sacrificing advanced beings deserve our deepest possible gratitude. This is a secret that is concealed by its very improbability.

My Story

The man I will refer to as Abdul Samad (slave of the Eternal) and I worked for the same Dearborn, MI automotive company starting in 1972. I was 22, a musician, a recovering hippie, deeply infected by the Beatles and the lure of the Mystic East. My reading then included Paramahansa Yogananda and A.C. Bhaktivedanta Swami Prabhuprada (founder of ISKCON) – and I recall playing ragas endlessly on the stereo. About the time I met Samad, I had discovered a new direction, Gurdjieff and Ouspensky. Samad was a Pakistani engineer, in the US on the equivalent of an H1B visa, going to university and working full time. He'd brought his wife and young son along. He read the Gurdjieff along with me, heavy going indeed, and we had many happy lunches in the shadow of the Ford Rouge auto plant, discussing various forms of spirituality and eating his wife's spicy goat meat samosas.

Over time we moved on to Idries Shah's books, a wonderful introduction to the history and development of Islamic Sufism.

We both became interested in Chishti Hazrat Inayat Khan's

and Samuel L. (Sufi Ahmad Murad) Lewis' books. Lewis' various initiations by India and Pakistani Chishtis, Qadiris and Naqshbandis in his various visits to India in the early 1960s fired both our imaginations. Finding an American who had been initiated this deeply into the heart of Sufism was very exciting.

After several years of friendship, I gradually discovered Abdul Samad and his wife were longtime murids of a famous Chishti murshid in Karachi, Pakistan, Mohammed Jamil Arifi Sahib, 'Sarkar' to his followers. Sarkar had evidently been initiated into ten separate Sufi orders. I had some extraordinary dreams, and dreams are especially meaningful to Chishtis. Abdul Samad encouraged me to write them down and send them to Sarkar. The message came through: "clean your heart."

Over the next several years, Abdul Samad was able to travel back to see Sarkar multiple times. In 1976, I was honored to be a witness to Samad's naturalization ceremony: he became an American citizen. He also earned two doctorates – engineering and physics – in those same years, and went to work for one of the Big Three American auto companies. I spent many evenings at his house, discussing practical spirituality, Islam, and listening to Qawwali records.

In the summer of 1977, Samad and I visited Lama Foundation in northern New Mexico, where Alpert's, *Be Here Now,* and Pir Vilayat Khan's, *Toward The One,* were published, and where Samuel Lewis' maqbara (grave) sits in a clearing in a pine forest looking over the Rio Grande valley. At that time Abdul Samad told me he had been made Khalifa, able to start a branch of the Chishti order in the USA, should that be necessary. He had been initiated into at least four Sufi orders that I know of – Chishti, Qadiri, Naqshbandi, and Suhrawardi. * Six months later, Abdul Samad, having given me a Sufi name, instructed me to travel again to Lama, in the winter months when visitors were not al-

---

*The Suhrawardiyya is a Shiite order.

lowed. I did so, and since the Lama residents remembered my visit with Abdul Samad, they allowed me to stay at Lama for a while. I again visited Sam's grave on that mountainside and had an unusual experience; I could have found the gravesite with my eyes closed, like knowing where a hot stove is in a cold room. The snow had melted back about 20 feet in all directions. Later that day, looking out over the Rio Grande valley, there was another experience of profound gratitude and melting-of-the-heart.

Back in Detroit, I met some area Sufi Order USA followers of Hazrat Inayat Khan – and later visited the Abode of the Message in New Lebanon, NY, where I met Pir Vilayat several times. Oddly, I perceived more baraka from a dead Sam Lewis than a live Pir Vilayat.*

Abdul Samad does not have an active circle; he is one of the hidden ones. After a visit to Pakistan, he said he had, by his murshid's grace, 'graduated' to full murshid status. There is an enormous Mideastern population in the Detroit area, primarily in and around Dearborn. In 1979 and 1980, I studied Arabic for about 18 months. I also attended a Dearborn mosque for some time. This did not last. I was as out of place among *Qur'an* pounders as I'd have been among *Bible* beaters. During that period Samad told me my Arabic sounded Syrian, which made sense, as my instructor was a Syrian.

However, desperate for change and more sun, I made plans to leave the Detroit area in 1982 without his permission. Also, to be perfectly honest, I hadn't kept my pants zipped according to instructions. About that time, Sarkar passed away. The story Samad told me was that Sarkar was sitting in circle with his followers. He leaned over and whispered to his eldest son, " ... time for a change of weather," and died instantly.

There in Detroit, Samad told me that since I wasn't following

---

* Pir Vilayat was the son of Hazrat Inayat Khan.

the rules I could not play the game, that I should no longer consider myself affiliated with the Chishti-Qadiri orders, and that I
should not ask for help from Sam Lewis or Inayat Khan. He did
challenge me to find the local spiritual chargeman for the area
where I would settle. I took that instruction quite seriously.

My travels took me around the USA where I reconnected
with my future wife and settled in Arizona where she joined
me. For 14 years, I had no contact with Abdul Samad. He called
me in 1996 and invited me to travel with him to Ajmer, India,
home of Khwaja Moinuddin Chishti's tomb-shrine, or dargah.
This invitation led me to believe I had in fact cleaned my heart
sufficiently to pass muster with the Sufis. However, I stupidly
declined the invitation, choosing instead to invest six months in
a disastrous venture into the film business, where I crashed on
a Harley, coming back home with a smashed knee, on crutches
and oxygen.

In 2001, Abdul Samad wrote me again, inviting me to India.
I again declined, not wanting to be a hypocrite and pretend to
be a dutiful Muslim Sufi. Heading off to Ajmer alone, Abdul
Samad subsequently wrote me a series of God intoxicated letters
in which he referred to me by the Sufi name he had bestowed on
me years before. Over the next couple of years, he kindly made
substantial suggestions and revisions to this article on Sufism
via email.

In 2006, Abdul Samad's daughter came through my town,
and she had dinner with my wife and myself at our home. She
calls me Uncle Karl, which makes sense, in that her father is
my dear brother. The next year, Spring of 2007, I traveled back
to Michigan to bury my father's ashes in the family plot. Now
retired, Abdul Samad invited me to his home twice for dinner.
He showed me Sarkar's picture for the first time, indicated he
was in regular contact with Sarkar (remember Sufis consider

that the adept may be contacted regardless of time or space) and discussed his last visit to Ajmer. He now stays with Moinuddin Chishti's own descendants, keepers of the famous dargah, when he is in Ajmer, at the heart of the Chishti Order. He told me some amazing stories of staying up all night in the courtyard outside Khwaja's tomb. There has been no contact since that visit.

Questions & Answers:

WHAT DOES SUFISM MEAN? Sufism is the Science of erasure of self into the Creator, and alignment with His will. Sufism is also the Path of the Heart. Mankind is in a deep sleep or dream; Sufism consists of the individual waking to the true Reality and to our true divine nature.

WHAT DO SUFIS BELIEVE? The Sufi Work has existed in every age of man. The Sufi orders and their energies exist today. Communication between Sufis is possible without physical presence. A developed Sufi creates something permanent which continues after death. Therefore, the founders of each order can still be contacted directly, and visits to the tomb of a founder are often recommended. Practitioner miracles are a byproduct, not the goal, of higher consciousness.

ARE THERE SUFI PLACES IN THE WORLD? Sufi organizations come into being for specific work & may dissolve when the work is completed. Sometimes the burial places of the founders of various orders – such as Abdul Qadir Gilani in Baghdad, Iraq and Moinuddin Chishti in Ajmer, India – have active groups nearby.

WHO WERE SOME SUFIS THAT WERE GENUINE? Some Sufis are 'mashhur,' or well known, and some are 'mastur,' secret, or hidden. Many effective Sufis were/are hidden and are not teachers, and therefore unknown. Names (there are thousands) but the most prominent are those who were ordered to, or who willingly took on the teaching role, and thus were the nuclei of the orders mentioned in this document, such as Abdul Qadir Gilani, Bahauddin Naqshband, Suhrawardi, Maulana Rumi, Moinuddin Chishti.

WHAT DOES 'GENUINE' MEAN? It means participating in a living chain of personally transmitted knowledge and wisdom; it means attracting murids with the ability and willingness to surrender, and an illumined murshid to effect the change. Because of these rigorous requirements, the chances are good of encountering, not an active, living order, but rather an ineffective remnant cult.

WHAT DOES SUFISM HAVE TO OFFER PEOPLE IN TODAY'S SOCIETY? If you mean fast-paced, postindustrial Western culture where money is the true religion, where the individual is redefined as a consumer, creature comforts are all important, and three generations of television have conditioned people to expect a positive resolution of every dilemma within a half hour, then the regretful reply is 'not much.' People so deeply conditioned are not suitable subjects, too deeply 'asleep' for Sufism's course of study.

Real understanding and growth takes a lot of consideration and reflection, and requires unprecedented cooperation between the head and the heart, as well as an accomplished guide. No one can perceive the will of God alone. Most human pursuits and characteristics may be defined in terms of a statistical bell curve – intelligence, empathy, strength, etc. A characteristic of any bell curve is that high functioning people are very much in the numeric minority, out there on the thin right end of the curve. If Sufism is considered an effective path to the final stage of human evolution, it requires remarkable subjects, subjects with real capabilities and paradoxically humble attitudes. It is decidedly not a message for the masses.

CAN SUFIS PERFORM MIRACLES? Enough stories exist to indicate the answer is "yes, on occasion," or "yes, of necessity." There are two levels of paranormal experience occasionally encountered among Sufis. One is 'firasat,' or intuitive insight, often cited in murid-murshid relations. The other is the outright miracle, 'karamat.' However, the advanced Sufi would not consider either of these to be a miracle, but rather a necessary occurrence in accord with the wish and will of Allah. If the occurrence seems to violate laws of time and space, the Sufi would invite the observer to consider who created these so-called 'laws.'

ARE SUFIS LIBERAL, ORTHODOX, OR NEITHER? As always, it depends upon context. In this world age, 'Eastern' Sufis – in or from their original countries – use terms and methods based on and interrelated to Islam, and may therefore be considered orthodox. As has been mentioned, many prominent Sufis of the classical era, such as al-Ghazzali and Ibn-al-Arabi, were prominent jurists. However, relative to fundamentalist Muslims, most Sufi orders are considered wildly liberal and unconventional.

MUST SUFIS BE MUSLIMS? The traditionalist, if that term may be applied to Sufism within Islam, answer is "yes." The following, fairly representative 'traditionalist' statement comes from Dr. Javad Nurbakhsh, Murshid of the Nimatullahi Order of Sufis in Tehran, Iran (Shia):

> *The term 'sufism' has meaning only in the context of Islam. That is to say, outside Islam, Sufism does not*

exist — for it is the fruit of the tree of Islam. Although one might find traces of Sufism in other religions and philosophical schools, these cannot be taken to be Sufism as a whole. The name 'sufi' is synonymous with a follower of Ali, himself the disciple (and spiritual successor) of the Prophet of Islam, Muhammad.

Since a sufi must be a Moslem, to be a sufi while not fulfilling the duties and obligations of Islam is an impossibility. With this in mind, one can distinguish those self-centered and ambitious individuals who detach Sufism from Islam and set themselves up as 'sufi masters.'

One should Realize that removing Sufism from Islam will result only in a psuedo-Sufism, devoid of Sufism's true essence. Such a graft onto the tree of other philosophical schools or religions can result only in a dead branch. The living fruit of Sufism, however, grows only on the tree of Islam, and only a true Moslem can receive the fragrance of its blossoms. Thus, whatever is not of Islam is not Sufism; and whoever is not a Moslem is not a sufi.

Rumi seems to disagree, in this quatrain:

Two hands, two feet, two eyes, good,
As it should be, but no separation of the Friend and your loving.
Any dividing there makes other untrue distinctions
Like "Jew," and "Christian," and "Muslim."

The irony regarding this question is that, within the Muslim world, as discussed, there are fundamentalist groups who see all Sufi orders as saint worshippers, using saints as intermediaries to God, & presenting undesirable innovations, bid'aa – to Islam.

THEN WHO MAY BE CONSIDERED A SUFI? Suhrawardi, in his *A Sufi Rule For Novices* (muridin), discusses the people described as 'mutashabbihun,' or 'people who try to resemble Sufis.' Suhrawardi makes a convincing case that these people are truly associated with Sufism, and quotes two supporting *Hadith*: "Whoever makes an effort to resemble a group of people is one of them," and "Man is associated with those whom he loves."

Suhrawardi stresses that even though they don't take on all the obligations incumbent upon initiates into an order, it is by their aspiration (iradah) that these people are one with the Sufis, similar to a regular novice, whose title 'murid' means 'aspirant.'

One could properly say that the effectiveness of the teaching and transmission in any order, anywhere, will reflect in the inner qualities developed in its murids. Are the results permanent, and do they result in detachment, or attachment? Only very long observation, or a developed Sufi, can tell if the changes are real, or simply acting or wishful thinking.

Answers to questions about Sufism vary according to the state of the questioner. The murid (aspirant) will be concerned with the external aspect of Sufism, mutual relations or ethics. This is the exact place which the "Muslim vs. non-Muslim" Sufi question occupies. A Sufi of middle rank, 'mutawassit,' will be interested in the inner states, or 'ahwal,' available to his abilities. The 'arif,' (knower) will be conveyed a touch of 'haqiqa' (Reality).

The beginning of Sufism is learning, the middle is practice, and the end is nothing less than Grace.

Sufism Without Islam

Because a thorough understanding and practice of the Shariat of Islam is seen as an inextricable aspect of and prerequisite for correctly practicing Sufism, those in the Eastern, traditional orders often have a problem with the legitimacy of Sufi orders mostly stripped of Islamic practices. There are many Westernized Sufi orders, most notably various offshoots from the Indian Chishti Hazrat Inayat Khan, who brought Sufism to Europe and the United States in the early years of the twentieth century. While the teaching methods are similar, working with the names of God, employing Zikr in the original Arabic, etc., it is nonetheless true that Inayat Khan's teachings, in the hands of the various offshoot orders, American and European, do not make traditional Islamic practices mandatory.

In an email interview for this chapter, a Khalifa in the Silsila Siraajiya 'Haqqaaniya (a Chishti offshoot) in Lahore, Pakistan, stated:

> *As far as Inayat Khan sahib is concerned, we have serious doubts that the Sufis dislike him because they do not give their opinion on the basis of incomplete information and there is not enough information available about him. We do not think that he stripped strict Islamic practice (prayer, fasting, etc.) from his teachings. The Sufis have always believed that a non-Muslim Mureed will convert due to the Suhba (Murshid's speech at gatherings) as the Murshid is the role model for him/her. They prefer conversion out of love instead of forcing the conversion. In case someone does not accept Islam, we believe that he/she will not be able to go beyond a certain level.*

Take Nizam-ud-Deen Awliya (RA) (a later Chishti,
d. 1325) for example, we know that a lot of Hindus
used to attend his gatherings, both the sermons and
the Zhikr, and he never turned them away because
a Sufi believes that others will automatically start
following him out of love.

Inayat Sahib has his roots in Silsila Chishtiya from
the subcontinent and we respect that.

Private correspondence with several followers of Inayat Khan
indicate that he did in fact prescribe the Muslim life for those
wishing to make the most progress, but, not wishing to alien-
ate most Western followers, has not publicized this nor made
it mandatory.

The symbol for Hazrat Inayat Khan's Sufi organization in the
West is a winged red heart with the Islamic star and crescent moon
in the middle of the heart. Since Islam literally means 'submission,' the esoteric meaning of this beautiful design is, "The surrendered heart grows wings." However, the present day Inayati
organization in Europe, the Sufi Movement (www.sufimovement.
org*) describes this very same symbol in the following manner:
"The Sufi emblem is an illustration of several esoteric concepts
related to the Religion of the Heart. The main symbol in the
emblem suggests a mystical attunement to the heart as a divine
temple within. The two wings illustrate the flight of the heart
ascending toward higher spheres, where human love and divine
love meet across the threshold of self-denial. The crescent moon,
in its waxing and waning play with light, presents an inspiring
picture of the heart's artful ability to offer unconditionally as well
as to receive in humility and appreciation. The five pointed star,
among the oldest symbols of guidance, is seen in the emblem as

---

*Note the absence of any mention of Islam. Indeed, a detailed search of this website
fails to mention either Islam or the Chishti Order.

a reminder of the bright light within, which guides the longing heart, all along the journey toward its divine destination."

In recent years, perhaps due to sectarian and religious conflict in the Mideast, or in response to anti-Sufi sentiments, several prominent Sufi orders have made efforts to expand in the Western world.

The Shia Nimatullahi Order has 13 or more centers in North America, nearly that many in Europe, Australia and Africa. The Shadhili Order has several Western branches, each with multiple centers. This Sunni order, while their websites and literature pay due homage to the order's Islamic roots, does not in fact require conversion to Islam (shahada) when accepting an initiate murid (bayat).

There are some Muslim orders with Shaikhs who reportedly do not require a conversion to Islam: Sherif Chatalkaya ar-Rifa'I (Rifai Order); Khalid Bentounes al-Alawi (al-Alawi Order); Farihah al-Jerrahi (Halveti Jerrahi Order).

Idries Shah (1924-1996) was a tireless writer and promoter of Sufism. His writings provide some of the most accessible information on the historical Sufi world. He also proved to be a most controversial character. Claims were made that he was the Mashaikh, the living head of the Naqshbandi Order in Afghanistan and the world. Counterclaims posited that he learned most of his Sufism from libraries, and that he started writing about Sufism only after a series of trips to the Mideast in the 1950s.

Shah peppers his writings with quotations from many famous Sufis and was especially fond of relating stories about Mullah Nasruddin. When his publisher and estate were queried regarding using short, attributed quotations from various Shah books for this chapter, they threatened legal action. I pointed out in vain that Shah had built his own writing career quoting long dead Sufi personages, people without the advantages of international copyright laws and aggressive solicitors.

Georges Gurdjieff (1866/77?-1949) was a Greek Armenian with a vast curiosity for the mystic. He formed a small group of likeminded travellers, and in the years prior to WWI, combed the Middle East for traces of real spirituality. The only history of his early life comes from his own writing. He attracted intellectuals as followers from Russia, Europe, and the U.K. He established working centers in France, Britain, and the USA.

A book, *Teachers Of Gurdjieff*, by one Rafael LeFort, published 1966, purported to follow clues around the Middle East found in various Gurdjieff writings. These clues seemed to indicate G. had been, among other things, a murid in various Sufi orders including the Naqshbandi. However, this book is considered by many to have been written by Idries Shah and his brother Omar Ali-Shah in an effort to draw Gurdjieff followers to their own organization.

Present Day Muslim Sufi Orders

MEVLEVI ORDER: One Sufi organization very visible to the world is the Whirling Dervishes of Turkey. 'Dervish' is another word for Sufi. These Dervishes belong to the Mevlevi Order, begun in Konya in the 13TH century A.D. by one of the most famous of Sufis, a writer and poet named Mevlana* (Maulana) Jellaludin Rumi. His most famous work is the Mathnavi, a book of intense spiritual insight. Rumi himself had a teacher, Shams of Tabriz (the 'sun' of Tabriz, in Iran), who was one of the Qutubs, or spiritual pillars, of his time. The divine knowledge, or gnosis, that Shams possessed was evidently greater than all of Rumi's formal study; Rumi gave up his books and became Sham's favorite disciple. Rumi subsequently poured forth an ocean of poetry, including one of the most magnificent works in the Persian language, the 44,000 verse *Divan of Shams Tabriz.*[†]

---

*Mevlana means, "Our Master." –LW
†Note that Rumi named his poetic collection after his Master. –LW

Shams, it is said, had begged Allah for higher consciousness.
"What will you give?" Allah said. Shams replied, "My head."
Shams is quoted as saying, "It needs cycles after cycles for just
one advanced soul to realize God."

This statement seems to support the concept of reincarnation,
'hulul,' in discussing how long personal evolution can take. Or, it
may be referring to making thousands of 'rakats,' prostrations,
while praying. Rumi seems to agree with reincarnation in this
quatrain (or he may be talking about something else entirely) :

> *Life is ending? God gives another.*
> *Admit the finite. Praise the infinite.*
> *Love is a spring. Submerge.*
> *Every separate drop, a new life.*

Islam does not recognize reincarnation. Here is a situation where
people with spiritual insight may be speaking in code, because
reincarnation goes beyond the world of the *Qur'an* and *Hadith*
of the Prophet.

After some years with Rumi, Shams disappeared. It is ru-
mored he was killed and beheaded by a jealous faction of Rumi's
disciples. After Shams' death, Rumi introduced a new teaching
method. The Dervish Dancing used by the Mevlevi Order is called
'Sama,' or audition, and is a moving meditation in which the
music, each dancer's energy and movement, and the guidance
of the Murshid combine into a vehicle for transcending ordinary
consciousness.

Much classical Turkish music was developed over the centuries as part of the Dervish dancing ritual. During Rumi's lifetime
he hosted gatherings including his own mystical poetry, Zikr,
music, and ecstatic movement and turning. His son, Sultan
Veled, and grandson, Arif Chelebi, contributed poetry and fur-

ther development and dissemination of the Mevlevi ritual in the form of Dervish dancing.

Qadiri Order

The Qadiri Sufi Order, branches of which are found throughout the Muslim world, was named after 'Abd al-Qadir Gilani, who died in Baghdad in the year 1166. Found from Morocco to India, the Qadiri Order is quite active in the modern era. Abd al-Qadir Gilani is known as Ghaus Pak, or Ghaus-i-Azam, the Greatest Ghaus. The word 'ghaus' has several meanings. Literally, it means one to whom we can cry for help. It also is one of the types of Qutub, or spiritual axis. Lastly, a ghaus type of mystic is one who dismembers his body's arms and legs. The body literally falls apart in praise of Allah, only to be miraculously reunited, in a process related to the Christian stigmata. As a sober jurist, it is unlikely that Gilani was this last type of mystic.

As a young man, 'Abd al-Qadir became an eminent Islamic jurist of the Hanbali school, and had connections to other respected Islamic scholars including Imam Abu Hanifa. But instead of continuing as an scholar, he wandered Iraq's deserts for 25 years as a disciple of various saints. He settled in Baghdad after the age of 50, following a reported encounter and encouragement from the Green Saint, al-Khidr.

His clarity of thought, impressive oratory and many reputed miracles brought an enormous following, which soon coalesced into the Qadiri Order. He became known as the Rose of Baghdad. He is quoted as making this remarkable statement: "I have placed my foot upon the necks of all the saints."

He wrote some of the most influential books on Sufi mysticism, including *The Book of the Secret of Secrets and the Manifestation of Lights*, and *Revelations of the Unseen*, as well as the especially revered on the subcontinent, *Sufficient Provision for*

Seekers of the Path of the Truth. His murids included Shihabud-din Suhrawardi and Moinuddin Chishti.

Hazrat (the Presence) 'Abd al-Qadir Gilani is honored by Sufis worldwide as the greatest Ghaus and Qutub, the center of the hierarchy of Saints around whom the world revolves, behind only the Prophet Muhammad and Caliph Ali.

Chishti Order

The Chishti Order is prevalent in Pakistan and India. The founder of the order was Shaykh Abu Ishaq Shami Chishti. In the modern era, the most famous Chishti is Hazrat (the Presence) Khwaja (the Master) Moinuddin Chishti. As a young man, Moinuddin Chishti met Qutub Abd al-Qadir Gilani in Baghdad in 1156. While formalist Islam discouraged music because of its ability to rouse the carnal soul, it is said that Ghaus-i-Azam told Moinuddin Chishti, "For you, music is permitted."

After travelling extensively, contacting the main Sufi masters of his age, and performing two Hajj, or pilgrimages to Mecca, his master Hazrat Khwaja Usman Harooni sent Moinuddin to India to determine its suitability for the Sufi Work. He reached Ajmer, India, in 1191. A characteristic that has come down to us was Khwaja (master) Moinuddin Chishti's sweet, approachable and forgiving nature. An interesting anomaly among Muslim saints, women are allowed full access to Chishti's dargah (tomb-shrine) in Ajmer.

Like the Mevlevis, the Chishti Order utilizes Sama sessions, with the addition of vocal and instrumental music called Qawwali; the performers are called Qawwal. During the Sama sessions, the Murshid may choose to assist the dancing participants to achieve the 'Hal' state, losing normal consciousness, later reporting seeing angels, saints, or the Prophet Muhammad, and drinking from Tasnim, the Well of Paradise. The

Murshid instructs the Qawwali performers to keep playing the single phrase they were on when the dancers achieved Hal; at that time the music is the soul's only link to this life. There are stories of Sama sessions where the Qawwali singers were exhausted, and stopped singing and playing, and those in the Hal state died.

While there are few or none authenticated statements direct from Khwaja, his successors have created a body of work they call, *Hazrat Khwaja's Message*. The Message includes these statements, which seem to imply that the Dervish or renunciate state is prefatory to that of the mystic, or advanced Sufi:

> *There are ten things necessary for a Dervish, namely, search of God, search of spiritual teacher, respect, surrender, love, piety; constancy and perseverance; to eat less, to sleep less, seclusion; and last of all, prayers and fasting.*

> *For the mystic, also, there are likewise, ten things necessary: to be perfect in Divine knowledge; to be neither sorry and sad himself nor to make others sorry and sad, and not to think evil of anybody; to point the way towards God, and to lead and guide the people towards the Ultimate Good; to be hospitable; to prefer seclusion; to pay respect and regard to everyone, and to count himself as the humblest and the lowest; to surrender his will to the Will of God; to be patient and persevering in every grief and woe; to be humble and meek; to be contented; to repose his trust in God.*

Suhrawardi Order

Diya ad-din Abu 'n-Najib as-Suhrawardi (d.1168) left Suhraward in Persia as a young man and became an initiate of al-Ghazzali in Baghdad. He later built a center on a ruined site along the river Tigris. He wrote Kitab Adab al-Muridin, *A Sufi Rule for Novices*, which describes the proper adab (manner) and attitudes for murids joining a Sufi khanqah, or center. This book has been used for centuries as part of the teaching in many orders. Abu 'n-Najib attracted many murids who later became prominent Sufis. Chief among them was his nephew Shihabuddin Abu Hafs Umar (d.1234), who is regarded as the founder of the Suhrawardiyya.

Shihabuddin maintained a careful Muslim orthodoxy, wrote an influential book, *Awarif al-ma'arif* (Knowledge for Encountering God), and was known as a great teaching-shaikh. Because of his habit of granting the Khalifa's khirqa to many aspirants, the Suhrawardi Order spread far & wide, with a great number of Sufis throughout the centuries claiming to belong to the silsila.

Uwaisi Order

The Uwaisi Order of Sufis is unique. Like a river in the desert which may go underground for long stretches, the Uwaisi Order appears in history for a period, then disappears and reappears. Its founder, a Yemeni named Uwais al-Qarani, was a contemporary of Prophet Muhammad, yet they never met. Merely hearing of the Prophet was enough to create a strong connection – tawaj, rab'ta, tassawur-I-Rasul – between the two men. Once Uwais heard that Muhammad had lost two teeth in a battle, he broke his own in response. According to tradition Uwais was visited by the Prophet in a vision and was granted a Darood, a phrase to be meditated upon and recited, much like Zikr. Uwais was unable to ever meet the Prophet. His followers consider that they are rightly guided by Uwais, similar to the occasional reports of those without a teacher being contacted by al-Khidr. As Uwais was totally absorbed into the Light of the Prophet (nur-I-Muhammad), his followers consider the Prophet to be the loving and living link to Allah.

Malamatis and Qalandaris

There are loose organizations of spiritual seekers in the East called the Malamati, or 'blameworthy ones.' These people conceal their spiritual aspirations, and if they do have a murshid, that person is likely to be hidden – 'mastur'.

Tradition states there have only been two and a half real Qalandars that walked the earth: the original Qalandar Bu-Ali Shah Qalandar, Lal Shahbazz Qalandar, and the already mentioned Rabia al-Adawiyya/al-Basri, who was "half Qalandar." Qalandars closely resemble Malamatis in their disregard for Islamic sensibilities. The word Qalandar may be from the Persian for 'coarse one.' These people have few possessions and travel incessantly. They act as if they are outside the Sharia, in order to be condemned by the Muslim society around them. The Qalandar believes that they earn spiritual benefits from voluntarily attracting condemnation and attendant exclusion from Muslim society.

There is even an order in Pakistan, the Qalandariyya, who consider their Silsila to include Bu-Ali Shah & Lal Shahbazz Qalandar, and Rabia. This is considered a very intense 'Jelalli' Order.

Naqshbandi Order

Naqshbandi Dervishes can be found from Morocco to Indonesia. Oddly, the order existed long before it gained its current name. The Khwajagan ('Masters') were well known for their exercise 'habs-i-dam,' or restraint of breath, and by their use of silent Zikr, Wazifa. The order received its later name from Muhammad Bahauddin who died in 1390. Bahauddin, originally of Bokhara, spent seven years as a courtier, seven looking after animals, and seven in road building, before he became a teaching master.

Someone said to Bahauddin Naqshband, "It must have caused you pain to dismiss a certain student." He said, "The best of all ways to test and help a disciple, it if is possible, may be to dismiss him. If he then turns against you, he has a chance of observing his own shallowness and the defects which led to the dismissal. If he forgives you, he has an opportunity of seeing whether in that there is any sanctimoniousness. If he regains his balance, he will be able to benefit the Teaching, and especially to benefit himself."

What made Bahauddin assume the surname Naqshband? The word Naqsh means a seal, or a symbol, or sign. Another meaning of Naqsh is print or impression, and band is to bind, or fasten. Naqshbandis practice the silent Zikr, wazifa, which is therefore imprinted upon the heart. The Naqshbandis are also known as the builders or designers.

Other Prominent Orders
Rifai, Khalwati, Kubravi, Hanafi, Bektashi, Hamadani, Yasavi, Jalali, Badawi.

SCI-FI SUFIS: In the 20TH century, several well regarded authors wrote science fiction novels examining the concept of perfectibility of man. Robert Heinlein wrote several books examining this concept, the best of which was *Stranger in a Strange Land*. The protagonist was one Valentine Michael Smith, the son of the first scientists to crash on Mars. The next Mars mission was 20 years later, and Smith was discovered, alive, speaking no English, having been raised by Martians. Brought back to Earth, the ultimate innocent, he was a pawn in a political game, because, according to international law, he owned Mars. However, the people with whom he stayed discovered that he could commit miracles at will, by simply thinking in Martian.

Smith began teaching Martian to his close companions, wanting to help mankind to rise, but finding that most applicants had little aptitude for learning Martian. He continued gaining power and influence, spreading his knowledge, and his companions learned to perform minor miracles. This came to the attention of the political and religious authorities, who repeatedly tried to close down various offshoots of his organization.

The novel ends with him voluntarily presenting himself for martyrdom, blessing those who kill him, and ultimately transcending death. By any standard, *Stranger in a Strange Land* is a remarkable book, even more so if looked at as a metaphor for Sufi development; speaking a new language with new concepts, which only a few are prepared to handle, bringing new perceptual abilities and empathy to man.

Time, Place, and People
There is a Sufi phrase, 'Zaman, Makan, Ikhwan,' which is a shorthand recognition that in order for transformation to take place, a certain confluence of conditions must exist – enough of the right kind of time (zaman), the right place(s) (makan), and especially the right, and rightly guided, people (ikhwan).

In Conclusion
According to Shaqiq of Balkh, among the characteristics of a genuine Sufi are: "First, freedom from anxiety for one's daily sustenance; second, sincerity of action and a pure heart." Shaqiq's own resolve to enter the path was triggered during a great famine in Balkh, when he observed a slave who went about without the least worry. Shaqiq asked him, "Aren't you worried about the famine?" "My master has a lot of grain," the slave replied.

☼ ⌇ ▣

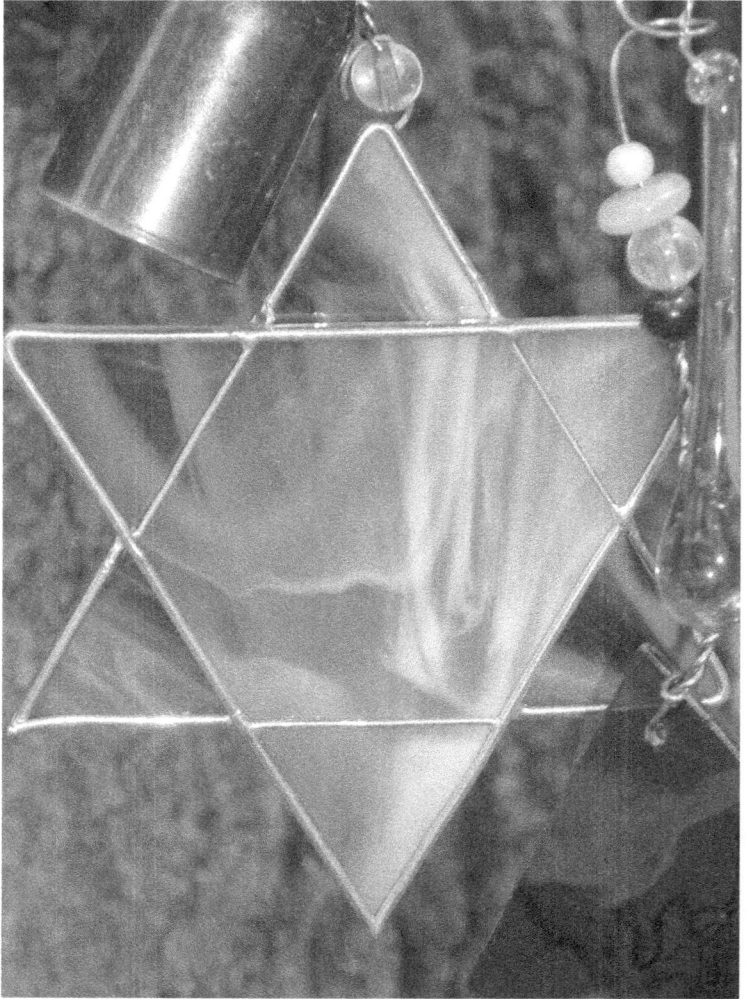

The Star of David, religious symbol of the Jewish faith,
as it appears hanging on a special blue glass wind chime in
Laurent's back yard.

CHAPTER FOUR

Judaism
Yaakov Weintraub

I AM EXTREMELY GRATEFUL for this opportunity to offer you my thoughts on Judaism and being Jewish. This is my deeply felt heritage and the roots of my spiritual journey. The Jewish people are my tribe, the community of my ancestors and my immediate family, and the birthplace of my "chevra" – my dear friends in the Jewish community.

I offer you, humbly, my personal thoughts on what Judaism means to me. I hope that anyone who read these thoughts can accept them in the spirit that they are given, and realize that this chapter is only one person's reflection of what Judaism was, is, and can be, but it is by no means any sort of absolute statement.

I also would not attempt to cover all the many aspects of Judaism, or say what aspect is more important than another. This bead of Judaism is so multifaceted, and has so many sparkling reflections, that it could take many lifetimes to look at them all. What I present to you here are, simply, the aspects that have touched me most profoundly, the ones that have imbued my soul with the unique flavor of my beloved tribe.

Shabbat – The Sabbath

And God rested (ceased) on the seventh day ... and blessed it and made it holy. –Genesis II; 2-3 *

---

*This quote and all other quotes in this chapter are taken from the *Pentateuch*, the first five books of the Hebrew Scriptures. In the Christian *Bible*, these are the first five books of the Old Testament.

Shabbat, for me, is one of the most precious jewels of the Jewish tradition. Every seventh day, on Friday evening as the sun sets, time begins to slow and peace settles within me. This is Erev Shabbat, the evening of Shabbat, and I can rest. I can lay down my work, my cell phone and daily chores, and open myself to the Infinite.

Shabbat is many things, but to me it is most importantly a time to renew our connection to Spirit and community. It is a time when we can put aside our daily lives and reach for the holiness that pervades all of Creation. We can join God in ceasing, open ourselves to the sweetness of that universal peace reverberating from the beginning of time, and add our own voice in harmony to that chord of holiness.

We are commanded to observe Shabbat in the fourth of the Ten Utterings (Commandments):

> *Remember the Sabbath day and keep it holy ... for in six days the Lord made heaven and earth, the sea, and all that is in them, and rested on the seventh day: therefore the Lord blessed the Sabbath day and hallowed it.*
> —Exodus xx; 7-11

This is compelling to me – that the holiness of Shabbat is so core that it is inscribed on the tablets of testimony. As my relationship to Judaism has evolved, this has become more and more important to me – not as a commandment to "obey," but rather as a guidepost to Spirit. When I remember Shabbat, when I join my holiness to the holiness of Shabbat, I feel the blessings of Spirit flowing through me.

There are many rituals and traditions surrounding Shabbat that I love; it is a beautiful time of prayer, of contemplation, and of community. Traditionally, the beginning of Shabbat is marked with the lighting of Shabbat candles in ones home – bringing the light of holiness into our house, marking the beginning of this interval that is dedicated to the sacred. We then gather as a community to welcome Shabbat with the Kabbalat Shabbat prayer service. Kabbalat Shabbat means "receiving Shabbat," and within this beautiful service we greet Shabbat as a bride with song, and prayer, and for me, dance. "Come, my beloved, to greet the bride, let us receive the presence of the Shabbat..." It is an amazing feeling – to stand with a community of people you respect and love, singing with your whole being, and welcoming the Shekhina – the transformational, female, receptive presence of God, the Shabbat Bride – into your midst.

There so many other rich traditions and rituals infusing Shabbat with its special texture; the Kiddush (sanctification) over wine, the blessing at the start of the Shabbat dinner over two loaves of bread (HaMotzei) signifying the two portions of Manna we received on Friday night while wandering in the desert of Sinai, the communal meal, the additional soul* that tradition says we receive from heaven on Shabbat to help focus our inner being on the divine, and so much more.

It is a blessing – this Shabbat – this rest, if we are willing to open and receive it. It seems to me, that with every day that passes, the world moves faster and faster. When Shabbat comes, we are commanded to stop – to cease from our daily labors, to withdraw from the ceaseless bombardment of media and lightening fast communication. We are commanded to reflect, to dwell on the presence of Spirit in our lives, and to make it holy. What a precious gift to us.

The Torah – The Hebrew Bible
We are sometimes called "The People of the Book," and I feel

---

*There is a tradition that on Shabbat you are blessed with a second soul – the better to have the spiritual space to enjoy the Shabbat. –YW

that is such a fitting name for us. The words that have been our guide and companion for thousands of years still vibrate within us. They bring to life the thoughts and taste of those beginning days when the Spirit of God made itself known to us, when Spirit spoke to us and we opened to Spirit.

Those words live in us. Every week we read a small portion from the *Chumash* – the Five Core Books of the *Bible* – in a cycle that has been going on for centuries. We read out loud, in community, from handwritten *Torah* Scrolls that our ancestors two thousand years ago would recognize and be comfortable with. We hear these ancient words and they lodge deep within us, and like seeds of Spirit, they begin a new life, growing on the sustenance of our own inner being.

> *In the beginning, God created the heaven and the earth. And the earth was unformed and void, and darkness lay upon the face of the deep, and the Spirit of God hovered over the face of the waters. And God said 'Let there be light,' and there was light. And God saw the light; that it was good."*
> –Genesis 1; 1-4

I know that when I hear these words, they reverberate deep inside me: "and darkness lay upon the face of the deep." What is my darkness, where is my deep? How does the Spirit of God move over me, my inner waters? And Spirit said, "Let there be light," and I open myself to that light, I open myself to that ancient wisdom and let it nourish the seeds of my own light as they sprout and grow within me.

We read these portions, these "parshot," in a yearly cycle. Every week is another portion, another opportunity to learn from that ancient wisdom and transform with it.

In the last portion of the *Torah*, we read how Moshe (Moses) ascends to the mountaintop and sees the Promised Land. "Let me go over, and let me see the good land that is beyond this Jordan," Moshe implores. Spirit answers, "Get thee to the top [of the mountain] Pisgah … and see with your eyes, for you shall not go over this [river] Jordan." And where is our own Promised Land? And when we implore Spirit, and Spirit answers us, how do we receive those words, how do we surrender to the answer?

Each year, we complete a cycle of reading the entire five books, and on the day that we finish the cycle, we dance. On that day, the holiday of Simchat Torah – Rejoicing with the *Torah* – we take up the scrolls, and we dance with them, we sing with them, we rejoice with them. We rejoice that these holy words are still with us, that they can grow in us, combining ancient and new, and in so doing they are renewed, and we are renewed.

And the moment we have finished the cycle, we start it again. We dance, we sing, and we listen to the cycle begin anew, "In the beginning God created …" And it is my fervent wish that we be renewed again, and again, and again, for many more ages, and that these precious words, the holy books of Spirit, continue to grow and thrive within us.

Eretz Yisrael – The land of Israel
Our homeland for over 3000 years, promised to us in the *Torah*, & our inspiration for over 2000 years of almost complete exile. In prayer, in song, in thought, we would sing "L'Shana Ha-Ba-ah B'Yerushalayim" (Next Year in Jerusalem). And suddenly, miraculously, a few short decades ago, we were home again.

In conversation, we call it Ha'aretz which means, "the land." It is the land that Moshe gazed on with longing, it is the land that nourishes and harbors our roots without which we would be cut off from the nourishment of our deepest parts. It is a land whose soil, whose rocks, whose rivers vibrate with our history, and whose dust is the dust of ages that our ancestors trod upon.

I can still remember the first time I arrived in Israel. I was 13 years old – and this trip was my gift upon becoming a Bar Mitzvah – upon my coming of age according to Jewish law and tradition. I remember stepping off the airplane, and feeling the heat of the sun as a tangible force beating down on me. I felt a vibration deep in my stomach; a resonance; a visceral, poignant recognition that spoke to me on all levels. Home, it said.

I love this land, and I love our people as they are in this land. The desert heat speaks to me, grabbing my attention with its enveloping intensity, and it is reflected in the restless intensity of the people who live here. The walls of Yerushalayim (Jerusalem) press on me with the weight of years, and their ancient stories rise in me like echoes from some inner cavern when I walk the narrow, cobblestone streets. I do not claim this land as mine, or my people's. The land lays claim to us – in some deep, archetypical place that allows no denying. There is a mutual recognition that rings deeply and truly.

The Holocaust

My parents are survivors of the Holocaust, the murder of six million Jews by the Nazis and their willing partners. They were born in Poland, and had not been there for 45 years, but in November of 1989 they had decided to return there once more, and I had decided to go there with them. I had looked forward to the trip with both anticipation and trepidation, but when it finally arrived the reality was far more powerful than I had ever imagined it could be.

I can still remember the shiver that went up my spine as I boarded the Lufthansa plane that would take me to Warsaw. It seemed unreal, flying on a German airline, being served glatt kosher meals by German stewardesses traveling to the place where my family had been born. Where the family I had never known was killed. When I arrived in Poland it was even more unreal, more surreal. I drifted among echoes and memories of people and places I had never really known, but that I somehow knew. I felt that I had entered another world, one where I was cut off from the safe anchor of everything that I had previously known.

We were to stay for one week, and as the time passed I listened to the stories and the memories of my parents, went to the places where they had lived, and where most had died, and all the while I felt as if I was drifting – drifting in strange waters.

And then we visited Auschwitz and Birkenau, its associated extermination camp. I'll never forget that day. I was struck to my very center. Being there possessed me and took me to another place, one of total darkness where I was totally cut off from this world, lost, adrift, and for the only time I can ever remember, cut off from my faith in God which has always sustained me and been the wellspring of my life.

I cannot find words now to describe this descent into eternal night, but on that day I could. I couldn't resist them. They poured out from me – with my tears on the ride back home and in the hotel room that night while my parents slept. I don't know how they slept, but I lay awake crying & writing, possessed by these images of another night that went on and on and on. I share these words with you now – exactly as they came to me that night.

Lost
by Yaakov Weintraub

Row upon row upon row
of beds, of bones, of unseen souls.
Their unfinished lives tear at my heart,

Their unsung songs whisper to me through the mists
as tears stream down my face.

I hear songs of such sweetness, such beauty.
They say the entire world is contained in the
beauty of one such song,
But my heart cannot contain the sadness
as I gaze at row upon row upon row.

Everywhere I go I hear the sound of Nazi boots,
And the people I see aren't really there,
They're just echoes amidst the marching boots.
But the ghosts of my people are real,
And their whispering wind tugs at me,
Until I turn and turn, again and again
Looking for my people in the echoes and the wind.

Yes, I look.
I look in the ovens at Auschwitz,
And I can't believe they're real,
And I put my hands in the ovens at Auschwitz,
But draw them out whole,
And I look at the endless rows of barracks at
Birkenau,
The endless pallets among the cold darkened stones,
And somehow they too don't seem real.

And finally, I see the ghosts of my people.
Four million taken at Birkenau,
Four million cold, lonely, drifting, dead,
And they are real,
And then my flesh is seared,

And my heart is ripped apart,
And I cry out, I cry out to god.
I walk in hell on earth, and cry out to god,
But he didn't listen then, so why would he listen now.

Why would he listen now?
Even though I can still sense the ashes of my people
drifting down to cover the earth,
Even though I can still sense the smell or their
burning,
that fills the air,
Even though I can hear their unheard cries echoing among the
stones,
Crying me into their world of always night.
God couldn't have let this happen,
But it happened.

So now I am lost.
Lost like my people were lost,
Lost like six million worlds were lost,
Lost among the stones, the cries, the unsung songs.

I know this poem is raw and filled with pain. I have rarely
shared this poem publicly before; the pain was too much. In fact,
I didn't look at it for two years after I wrote it, and I have only
shown it before to my family and a few close friends. I share it
now because I find that I don't want to hold it alone any longer. I
need to open that darkness to the light, and I need to share that
pain with others, so that they can know it with me.

And I share this also with the survivors, the elders of my tribe,
so that they can be certain that we who come after know what

you went through, can feel that darkness you lived through. And I share it as a promise to you that we will never forget. And I share it as an affirmation, an affirmation that the darkness will never overcome the light. Because today my faith is whole; though I couldn't feel God for a single moment in that blackness, and though I still don't understand it, my faith remains, and it is stronger than ever.

I will share one last thing. At Birkenau, where most of the actual ovens in the Auschwitz concentration camp were, there are still two ovens that are preserved almost perfectly inside a building. My family and I were viewing them along with other visitors, when, moved by some inner impulse, I snuck over the rope encircling them, by the back of the ovens where no one else had gone. In the brick on the back of the oven, there was a small metal door – I don't know if it was for fuel, to empty ashes, or what. Still moved by this impulse, I opened the door, it was rusted and hard to move, and reached up inside, feeling the brick, the soot that still remained. Suddenly, the impulse strengthened, and I reached into my wallet for a picture of Meher Baba that I had had with me for years – which I had received when I had first heard of Meher Baba. For me, Meher Baba was, and is, one of the beautiful, bright lights of Spirit that have shone on our world, and I have always felt a deep love for and spiritual connection with him. I took this photo, and reached up deep, to my shoulder, in the chute that rose vertically in the brick behind the door, searched until I found a crevice, and wedged Meher Baba's photo into the crevice.

I carry this memory with me still. In the deepest dark that I have known in this life, deep in the ovens where my ancestors burned, the light of Meher Baba's great spirit and love is shining. May it reach, cleanse, and purify all who have been or will ever be there.

Chagim (Festivals) — The Cycle of Ceremony & Celebration
As I write this chapter, it is only two weeks before Rosh Hashana
– the Jewish New Year (literally, the Head of the Year). I love this
holiday; its observance is deeply spiritual and totally unlike the
New Year's observances of most modern cultures. Tradition has
it that on Rosh Hashana we pass before the Creator for judgment
and our fate for the year is recorded in the heavenly book of life.
During the ten days following Rosh Hashana (until Yom Kippur
– the Day of Atonement) we have the opportunity to repent for
any wrongs we have done, and thus be sealed in the book of life
for good. On Yom Kippur, our fate for the year is sealed.

In the days leading up to Rosh Hashana, we also have a beautiful process of asking forgiveness for wrongs we have done others.
Our tradition says that the Creator cannot forgive us for wrongs
committed against another person, until we have received
forgiveness from the person wronged. It is a powerful thought
– one that always draws me into a period of deep introspection
and humility. We all make mistakes, we have all wronged somebody, at some time, and to face those mistakes consciously, to
admit them to ourselves, and to ask for forgiveness is uplifting,
humbling, and powerfully cleansing all at the same time. And
challenging – there are still things that I do not want to face, that
I am still working on in my life, and this season brings them to
the forefront of my consciousness. Again I am reminded that I
always have the opportunity to purify, to cleanse, to seek forgiveness for wrongs I have done.

After Rosh Hashana comes Yom Kippur where we delve deeply
into ourselves, where tradition has it that our fate hangs in the
balance. It is an amazing day; there is a deepness and solemnity
to it, as well as a feeling of joy. In one of the core parts of the
Yom Kippur service, we publicly confess our sins and ask God
for forgiveness. We admit to imperfection, we admit to error,

we admit to weakness, we acknowledge our humanness and our fallibility. And even within that fallibility, Spirit can forgive us, we can still be worthwhile. I love this – I love that it is okay to be fallible, it is okay to frail, to err, to mess up, and that it doesn't mar us forever. We can heal, we can mend, and just as we can forgive, we can be forgiven; we can be renewed in the eyes of God and our community.

Rosh Hashana marks the beginning of a torrent of holidays that come rushing in one after the other. Shortly after Yom Kippur is Sukkot – the Festival of Booths – where we eat our meals in the sukkah, a temporary structure under the open sky, roofed with natural materials, providing shade for us, but still allowing us to see the stars and sky. The sukkah commemorates the protection given to us by the Spirit of God while we wandered in the desert for 40 years. I remember as a child, how delightful it was to have our school lunches in the sukkah, the sense of expansion from being outside, the break in routine, the recognition of the part that nature plays in our lives – living in the city, this was always powerful for me. It is still powerful, and I love gathering with my community to sit in the sukkah, to acknowledge the shelter of Spirit, and the gifts of nature.

On the heels of Sukkot, comes Simchat Torah – a holiday that is very special to me, because I met my beloved life partner, Jessica, on this holiday. Literally, Simchat Torah means "rejoicing with the *Torah*," and it marks the finish of the annual cycle of reading the *Torah*. Every week, we move through the *Torah*, reading the portions in order, and on Simchat Torah, we complete the cycle, reaching the final verse where Moshe tells us of Spirit's command – to love Spirit, to listen to Spirit's voice, and to hold fast to Spirit.

And while we read the verses of this final portion, we dance. We literally dance with the scrolls, the same scrolls that have been guiding us for thousands of years, holding them in our arms and singing songs of rejoicing and thanks to Spirit for guiding us, for remaining with us. It is an amazing feeling, to dance with hundreds of people in joy while carrying the holy words of Spirit. We dance for hours, sometimes into the next dawn, feeling the holy words, opening our hearts to allow the holy words to enter deeply. And when the last words are read, we immediately start the cycle again, "B'Reishit Barah Elohim ..." In the beginning God created heaven and Earth. And the cycle is renewed, and the seeds continue to grow, and we continue to dance with joy with the holy words of Spirit.

There are many more "chagim," some of them holidays of rejoicing, some of mourning. They weave in and out of the year, bringing splashes of color and feeling, rich with their own special flavor and history. To me they are doorways to Spirit, openings that evoke in me, in the immediacy of the present moment, an ancient cycle of teachings, feelings, ritual and guidance.

Halakha - The Law

I have always had a mixed relationship with Jewish law. It is a core part of an observant Jew's daily life, every moment of the day, in everything that they do. Halakha means more literally, "The path to walk" or, the way to walk in the path of Spirit, the way to obey God.

There is much that I love about Halakha. For me, the core, the crux, is as the great Sage Hillel said when challenged to teach the whole *Torah* on one foot. "What is hateful unto you, do not do to another. This is the whole *Torah*. All the rest is commentary." This reflects a core ethos in Judaism, that caring for and respecting others means you are loving and serving Spirit, and this has always struck a deep cord of respect and rightness in me.

But Halakha is deep and complex. The core source of Halakha is the *Torah*, and there are traditionally 613 Mitzvot (commandments) in the *Torah*. Some of these are beautiful:

> *You shall leave a corner of your field uncut for the poor.*
> -Leviticus 19:9

> *Not to destroy fruit trees, even during a siege.*
> -Deuteronomy 20:19

These laws ring in me: to care for those in need & the bounty of the earth, even in times of war. Some of these laws push me away. The following commandment is beyond my comprehension:

> *The man [who has gathered sticks on the day of Shabbat] shall surely be put to death; all the congregation shall stone him with stones from outside the camp.*
> -Numbers 15:32-35

There is much, much more to Halakha – in addition to law from the *Torah*, there are immense bodies of work such as the Talmud – which consists of the Mishnah (which codifies Jewish oral law) and the Gemara (which contains rabbinic commentary on the Mishnah). I am in awe of the devotion and scholarship with which these works have been created. I also deeply respect the choice of deeply observant Jews who navigate their lives with these laws always present in their minds, whose every action is moderated by this Halakha. I love how it can turn every daily act – be it eating, washing, or sleeping, into an act of worship, with an associated blessing that directs our thoughts to Spirit.

Yet still, I am conflicted. I am conflicted by the thread of patriarchy, which to me is visible as a thread woven deeply into the cloth of traditional Jewish law. I am conflicted by the rigidity that I see in traditional observance of Halakah, and of the attitude that I perceive of knowing the right, and only, way for me to walk in the way of Spirit. I am conflicted by the divisiveness and separateness that I sense in how Halakha is interpreted and lived by many.

I am not an observant Jew – meaning that I do not follow Halakha strictly in my daily life. Yet I am familiar with it; I was raised in a traditional home and attended a religious Jewish day school. My life is informed and enriched by Halakha – by this complex weave of commandments, blessings, and observances. I view it as a reflection of Spirit, a human code that reflects divinity and attempts to provide a way of life that is aligned with it. And I respect it, and respect the people who have devoted their lives to it, and sometimes in our long history, given their lives for it.

Reflections

I am writing this final section shortly after Yom Kippur. I have had an amazing, intense 24 hours. I stayed for half the holiday with my family, at the conservative synagogue where I spent a good part of my childhood, and the other half at a "renewal" congregation with many of my dearest friends. Both touch me deeply, yet in very different ways.

The conservative synagogue, Temple Beth El (which means House of God), worships in a very traditional way. I have known many of the members there for decades, and some of them are well into their eighties. I love these people. I love their stories, the richness of their lives, their struggles, their triumphs. Some of them are immigrants whose wanderings have taken them through five or six countries before settling here, whose roots lie in a way of life that has been almost erased from the world.

I love to see these elders of my people still drawing sustenance from those deep roots, praying as their parents prayed, and their parents before them, for generations back in time. I feel them very deeply, and feel privileged to be able to spend time with them, to know them on a human level as we pray together or deal with the day to day challenges of running a synagogue where changing demographics and values have caused the congregation to dwindle. Some of them are in their late 80s, yet they still come every Shabbat and every holiday, and it is inspiring to me to see their devotion and deep commitment.

My beloved parents are very much like this – immigrants from Poland, who came here in the 1950s and started a new life. I have always been amazed at their wholeness, their ability to love even after their lives were so shattered. From them, I absorbed into my being a love of being Jewish, a sense of tradition, and a sense of belonging to a community that stretches back thousands of years. And from them also, I absorbed a generosity of spirit that, to me, represents the essence of truly loving God. When there was need, I have never seen them refuse to give – whether it was to us in the family, to their friends, to their community, or even to strangers.

I have learned much from my parents, and am humbled by their example in life. My father passed away ten years ago, but he is still my guide and my teacher. I often think of his wisdom when faced with a challenge, and I often feel his guiding presence in my life, and am grateful for it and comforted by it. He grew up in an orthodox and observant Jewish family, and over the years I absorbed his deep love for Jewish tradition and ritual. I can still hear him in my inner ear, singing the rich songs of Passover, or saying the Kiddush – the blessing over wine. I miss him greatly, and I am so thankful that I carry this flavor of him, embedded in my own being.

I am fortunate to still have my mother in my life, and even at the age of 86 she never fails in nurturing our family, helping us, loving us unconditionally. There is a teaching in Judaism that says, "On three things the world is sustained: on the *Torah*, on service (to God) and acts of loving-kindness." I have learned so much from my mother about loving-kindness – and I strive to follow her example. She is a shining light in all our lives, and I feel blessed to be her son.

My parents and all the other elders of my tribe that I have been so lucky to meet are a living connection to my deepest roots in Judaism. I feel blessed to have had such a rich and deep sharing with them, and it has shaped me in many ways. I am also saddened to see them slowly, but steadily, departing this plane. They are a touchstone to a way of life that no longer exists – either shattered by the Holocaust, or dissipated by changing values and modern society. I treasure their flavors, their particular, unique way of living and of loving God. I love them for their humanness, their stories, their generosity and their immensity of spirit. I will miss them when, as they must, they finally travel on to the world to come.

The other congregation where I spent this Yom Kippur, called Romemu ("roh-meh-moo" which means to raise up, to exalt) is a renewal congregation. For me, renewal breathes a new life into Judaism, adding to the traditional elements of Judaism a wonderful aliveness and openness in expressing one's devotion to Spirit. While true to the roots of Judaism, and adhering to the core beliefs and rituals, in renewal we allow the branches of our worship to grow freely, and practices such as meditation, music, movement, and others, which may not seem part of Jewish worship to some, are all welcome.

In my spirituality and way of worship, I have traveled a long and winding road rooted in Judaism but also exploring along many other paths: meditation, Meher Baba, and Aikido, to name a few. It has been so wonderful for me to find the Romemu community where I feel that all of my spirit is welcomed, where it is all held valid, and not judged just because it is *other*. It is so wonderful to find this spring of sparkling, fresh water, which reflects my own deep and eclectic spirituality, within my own home of Judaism.

I have been drinking deeply from this wellspring for a number of years, and I have been constantly surprised by new discoveries, constantly amazed by new currents of spirituality arising within me. It is an incredible experience for me, to listen to the ancient wisdom and teachings of my tribe, and at the same time to open my heart, mind, and body and dance with joy as I feel love for the universal Spirit of God coursing through me.

The beautiful and loving friends that I have found in this community touch and enfold me so deeply. They are truly my tribe – my wonderful, loving, unruly and individualistic community. I pray with them, I play with them, and I share my life with them. They have been here for me in so many ways, supporting me with their caring in times of deep pain, ready to drop what they are doing and be present for me in times of need. We share much together: laughter, music, and our dreams for the future, our struggles and challenges, our delight in each other. This for me is a core part of being Jewish.

So I sit here, this night after Yom Kippur, and I reflect. I am amazingly renewed – I have opened myself to forgiveness, and I have let go and forgiven. Our tradition has it that as we act on earth, so are our actions reflected in the heavenly realms, and so as I forgive, myself and others, I open myself to forgiveness from Spirit, to the compassionate grace of the Holy One.

And I marvel how this Yom Kippur has been such a wonderful reflection on my path within Judaism, the intertwining of the old and new. The deep roots and the growing branches are both present, both quickening in me my love for Spirit. I marvel at this ancient way of being, going back thousands of years, and its ability to still inspire in me a deep love for God. And I marvel at the new ways that are unfolding within our tradition to reawaken and quicken that deep love within me. I feel blessed.

I have barely scratched the surface of this bead of Judaism. I do not mean this writing to be a scholarly one, nor is it an exhaustive treatise, so there are many areas that are left unexplored – fruit for another day. What it is, simply, are words from my heart that describe my journey of growth and love in worshipping the Spirit of God as a Jew, a Hebrew, a member of an ancient tribe whose ways permeate my being. I hope that it gives you some idea of what I feel, some idea of the ways of my tribe.

This Yom Kippur was also the first (English) anniversary of my commitment ceremony with my beloved life partner, Jessica. Our journey together has been deeply interwoven with our journey within Judaism and our relationships in the Jewish community. We first met four years ago on Simchat Torah, where we celebrate the closing of one cycle of reading the *Torah* and start the next cycle. That seems so fitting to me, because it marked the start of a new cycle in our own lives where we have knit those lives together into a larger whole. It also seems fitting that our first anniversary falls on Yom Kippur where we make ourselves so vulnerable, admit our frailties and errors, and are forgiven & renewed.

This Yom Kippur has been so deepened and sweetened by sharing it with Jessica, as we reflected upon and celebrated our year together, as we each forgave and was forgiven by the other. I cried many times, touched to my core, and reflected on how blessed we both are.

Many of the people with us this holiday were also with us when we were under the chuppah (the Jewish wedding canopy*), and I was so touched as they embraced us on this holy day and remembered our joining with gladness and blessings. I find it deeply moving to grow within this community, to see how the growth in our relationship is reflected in other relationships, to have our cycles tied to the cycles of the community.

I am blessed in having a partner of deep spiritual beauty and insight to share this journey with, and I am challenged by it also. I am blessed in that our partnership continuously raises us and brings us closer to Spirit, and challenged in having to make my own life a better reflection of Spirit in order to rise to the level of how we want to live together. For me, a true marriage is a joining of spirits in service of humanity, and the last of the vows we made at our ceremony one year ago was this one:

> *As my heart is open to you, I will open my heart to all the world, to multiply the blessings of our love, and to share them in the service of Tikkun Olam.*

Tikkun Olam, the perfecting or healing of the world, is the service that we have dedicated our love to, and this too is part of the core values of my wonderful tribe, where our home becomes a shelter to nurture love for all humanity.

My friends, I am so grateful to have shared my thoughts and feelings here. My journey with Spirit is core in my life, and that journey has been deeply shaped and imbued with the spirit and flavor of my beloved Jewish people. In the words of an ancient Hebrew blessing:

> *Yevarechecha Adonai veyishmerecha*
> *May Adonai (God) bless you and protect you*

---

*The photo of Yaakov and Jessica under the chuppah is in the photos and images section of this book. – LW

Ya'er Adonai panav eleicha vichunnecha
May Adonai shine his face upon you
and be gracious to you

Yisa Adonai panav eleicha veyasem lecha shalom
May Adonai lift her face to you and grant you peace

May this be God's will.

Remains of guru pooja.

THOM KNOLES

CHAPTER FIVE

Exploring the Ancient Veda
and Its Relevance for
Living in Today's World

Thomas M. Knoles

T HE FOLLOWING IS AN EXAMPLE OF THE WAY I like best to teach what I know. I'd had a few ideas, so I brought along some slides, and showed one or two, but immediately before my talk I had no idea specifically of what I would say. I just put my simplest form of awareness in contact with the audience, and let the interaction create the flow. For this reason, what you will read here was structured more by the need of time than by any plan. Enjoy the wisdom, and radiate life for all to enjoy.

Thom Knoles · Flagstaff, Arizona
May 10, 2007

This is a transcript of Thom's presentation at the Eastern Heritage Symposium: Beads on One String (Northern Arizona University, February, 2002). Behind Thom, as he begins to speak, is projected a photo of Guru Dev: *

This is a picture of my master, Guru Dev. Guru means "teacher." It literally means "a remover of darkness." "Dev" is short

---

*It is this photo which is shown on facing page.

for "Deva,"* which means, "Divine," which is of course where
we get our English word Divine. And his real name was "Swami
Brahmananda Saraswati." Swami Brahmananda Saraswati was
the Shankaracharya – the Acharya of the Shankara tradition
– which was started more than 2500 years ago by Adi Shankara,
whose name has been mentioned a few times today (at the Beads
on One String, Eastern Heritage Symposium). From the Veda,
which will be explained below, there's a beautiful Sloka in Sanskrit, is where we get our English word "slogan" – about how we
are to share knowledge and enjoy the knowledge together.

> *Saha nav avatu, (Let us be together.)*
> *Saha nau bhunaktu, (Let us eat together.)*
> *Saha viryam karavavahai, (Let us enjoy the radiance of life*
> *and Truth. Let us be vital together.)*
> *Tejasvi nav adhitam astu, ma vidvishavahai. (Never shall we*
> *denounce anyone. Never shall we entertain negativity.)*

Defining of Terms
First of all, "v d(a)," as it's pronounced in Hindi; in the Sanskrit,
"v 'd ." The distinction between Veda & what we say in the West:
"The Vedas." Another word being used today is "Vedanta." Veda,
or Ved(a), is, on its own, a body of knowledge which is Apaurasheya (pronounced ah-POUR-uh-SHAY-uh). Apaurasheya
means "uncreated by anyone" or, not created by anyone. "A"
for 'negation', "paurasheya" for 'authored' or 'created'= "not
authored" or 'un-created,' i.e. cognized. It's not attributed to
anybody. Ved(a) or Veda is known to be knowledge which is
embedded in the field of consciousness itself.

> *Knowledge is embedded in the fabric of conscious-*
> *ness itself, where all the laws of nature reside.*

---

*Note on Sanskrit pronunciation. Many words ending with "a" are pronounced
almost, but not quite, as if the "a" is not there; The swallowed "a" is indicated
by parenthesis. Also, the "S" of Sloka is that particular "s" that is pronounced
somewhere between the "s" and the "sh" of English.

VEDANTA: EXPLORING THE ANCIENT VEDA   147

In its own description, *Veda* says: "Richo ak-kshare parame vyoman yasmin devah adhi vishve nishedooh." This means "the knowledge of all the laws of nature is embedded in the fabric of consciousness itself." Not just any consciousness but the least excited state of any individual consciousness. In the Vedic world view, individual consciousness is conceived of as a wave on an ocean of pure consciousness. Pure, absolute consciousness. Every individual and all forms are seen as waves on this field.

I have a son who studied physics a few years ago at Sydney University. I went along to one of the introductory talks by the emeritus professor of high-energy nuclear physics, a redoubtable Scotsman by the name of Professor Brian McCusker. Professor McCusker opened up his honors degree program in physics with the following statement: "I'm sure all of you would love to know what it is that physics has discovered. What is the ultimate finding of physics, the hardest of the sciences?" Hardest not in terms of laborious; rather, hardest in terms of most rigorous. He continued, "I'm going to tell you. By the end of this three (or four) year course, you will have to agree with me, because the evidence for this is overwhelming. The truth of this has been proven in the laboratory in study after study. What science has discovered through physics is that the universe is one indivisible whole" – and this was the kicker – " and conscious."

One, indivisible, whole conscious thing. There are not two things. There's one thing. One indivisible, whole conscious thing. And he went on to explain his argument for that over the next three hours. The crux of it was that everything that we think is a particle is, actually, if you examine it very closely, a wave. Everything that seems to be a particle is a wave.

At the end of this presentation, one of the students said to Professor McCusker: "Congratulations. That was a great description. I was really able to follow it." Professor McCusker said: "I got about three-quarters of it from the *Veda*."

This is in fact where modern physicists are going for their very best descriptions of the one, indivisible whole – what they might call the Unified Field, depending on which camp they're in – but they're all describing the same thing. Modern science today is in complete agreement with the ancient rishis, or "seers," of the *Veda*. There is only one thing – indivisible, whole and conscious.

So if the *Veda* wasn't written by anybody, if it wasn't created by anybody, and it's not attributed to anyone, then how do we know anything about it? The way that this is explained by the *Veda* itself, is that the *Veda* is "cognized." It is knowledge that is cognizable through the process of de-exciting one's state of consciousness.

> *Knowledge is embedded in the fabric of consciousness itself, where all the laws of nature reside.*

That is to say, if we can take our individual wave-function, our individual consciousness, and de-excite it, systematically, bringing that wave-function to the point of least excitation, the state of zero excitation has in it oneness with the underlying field which contains all the knowledge of how the universe works. All of the knowledge. And who is the knower? Who is the Knower in this case? The individual who began the process of de-exciting the wave. When that individuality becomes one with that underlying absolute field, that all-pervasive consciousness, then the individual has become the Knower; and the *Veda* states that no individual can experience the Totality; rather, the individual becomes the Totality.

The techniques for doing this, which we've been hearing from all of the different religions, and many of the different religions that have sprung forth from the East, are expressed in all of the various yoga techniques, meditation techniques, the various schools and traditions of knowledge. One common thing which I've spotted in all of them so far today is that they all advocate the process whereby, with eyes closed, one seeks to take one's individuality and allow it to merge with something bigger than oneself through some methodology, whatever that methodology may be. *Veda* describes itself through the process of cognition. The *Veda* seeks out those who are awake to it. The *Veda* states about itself: "He who is awake, my hymns – my riches – seek him out." ("Him" means him or her, by the way.) Whoever is awake, the knowledge of all the laws of nature seeks him out. And so the fundamental precept of the *Veda* is to become awake – to increase consciousness, to increase the quantity of that thing which does the knowing.

> *Knowledge is different in different states of consciousness. Truth is different in different states of consciousness. Reality is different in different states of consciousness.*

Your truth, with a half gallon of Jim Beam in your belly, would be totally different (I hope) to the truth that most of you are experiencing right now. In an altered state of consciousness where the wave amplitude has been lowered but not spread – the individual has lost that substance that we call consciousness – this room, for that person, goes through a change. The knowledge of this room is different in that state of consciousness.

In the dreaming state of consciousness, I could be asleep in that chair and this could be a jungle, there could be a tiger about to pounce on me, and my body would be behaving exactly as if that was happening. Fortunately, we're paralyzed when we're dreaming so we can't get up and act out, but our heart would be beating and the adrenaline would be flowing and at the moment of the pounce the body would jump, and we might wake up. Knowledge of the room in the sleep state of consciousness? Zero consciousness, zero room, zero reality.

So there are different degrees to which one can become conscious, from the consciousness that would be represented by the repertoire of behaviors, say, of a house dust mite. To a house dust mite, this is a completely different environment to what we're seeing it as. To a chameleon, this is a completely different environment again. So there's not one reality because there's not one state of consciousness. However, we can say that there is an ultimate reality which is the reality that belongs to the ultimate state of consciousness.

> *Information is only knowledge to the extent that*
> *there is a knower of it.*

This is another thing that comes out of this previous concept. Information fails to inform us unless we are broadly conscious. Information cannot inform you. Information sitting in a book stays in that book. You could say that's information, but it's not information unless there's consciousness that comes into contact with it. And it only informs you to the extent that you are conscious. The more consciousness you have, the more that becomes information. So this is just another way of saying the same thing. The *Veda* talks about the necessity to expand the Knower, not the known. The Knower. The known will take care of itself by virtue of the Knower broadening and expanding his own/her own capacity to the absolute point. That's another beautiful concept that comes from the *Veda*.

*The state of least excited consciousness is awake to
the richest knowledge base.*

When the wave settles down and becomes the ocean, now it's
the ocean knowing itself. The totality of the knowledge of all
the laws of nature is knowable, cognizable, in that least excited
state. Now I want to spend a few moments on some practical
points and talk about how we can make all of this pass the "so
what?" test. So what? So what if the mind can settle down and
experience its least excited state? So what if you can touch on the
home of all the laws of nature and become that for a moment?
What does it do for me?

What it does for us, basically, is it addresses the issue of suffering. When we suffer, we suffer because somehow we have
mistaken what was needed at a given moment. We were not
conscious enough about how the laws of nature were structuring the evolutionary process at a given moment. We can call it
Nature's Intelligence; we can call it God; we can call it Brahman; we can call it anything that we fancy calling it. But there
is a totality of intelligence which is structuring a sequential
unfoldment – which we call evolution – from lesser to greater
awareness. And when we have misread the need of the moment
– we've mistaken the need of the moment – then we accidentally
violate a law of nature. And we can accidentally violate a law of
nature through omission of action, or we can accidentally violate
a law of nature through action. Either way, there's some kind of
correction process that occurs to get us back on track. And that
correction process is not punitive, it's simply corrective. That's
all. But whatever is needed to cause that correction to occur, that
will occur. If you have to move a long way from the track you took
to the correct track in a very short period of time, then it might
be a little rugged. And so we have words for these things. We

call that "suffering." Suffering is a way of phrasing the process of experiencing a kind of correction which we should not have had really to experience. If we had had the broadest possible awareness we would have been able to avert dangers which had not yet come, and we would have been able to be with the flow of natural laws as they were manifesting themselves at that time, in that place, in that particular geographic setting, under those climatic conditions, etc. *Veda* does not have anything like the equivalent of commandments. It doesn't do any forbidding. It doesn't do any prohibiting. It doesn't say "No" to anything. What it says is "Know." In other words, know what the effect is. Know what the effect is. You need to be able to know what the effect is of everything. What's the effect going to be if I omit action now? What's the effect going to be if I commit myself to an action now? So it's all about knowledge.

The Vedas

Now there's another term – *the Vedas* – and this applies to the attempts by relatively recent scribes to write down to the best of their ability in Sanskrit (which is the ancient language that the *Veda* was often sung in by the seers) what they heard the seers singing. So these writings are referred to as the *Vedas*. The most famous proponent of the *Vedas* was a man by the name of Veda Vyasa. He was also known as Krishna Dvaipayana Vyasa. If you ever want to know more about Vyasa, he was the man who wrote the *Mahabharata*. "Maha" means great, "Bharata" means India. The history of great India at its height, and the history of the Bharata family, which was also the name of the royal family of India 5000 years ago. If you'd like to know a lot more about Vyasa, I would strongly encourage you to pick up Professor Bruce Sullivan's book called, *The Seer of the Fifth Veda*. He is the preeminent authority on this particular man in the world. Veda Vyasa, Krishna Dvaipayana Vyasa, who lived about 5000 years ago, and who himself was a great rishi. Vyasa described the Vedas and categorized them into different groups:

- *Rig Veda:* Cognitions that had to do with general knowledge.
- *Sama Veda:* Cognitions that had to do with the impact of sounds that could be made by the human voice.
- *Yajur Veda:* Cognitions that had to do with ceremony and how to cause the laws of nature to become sympathetic.
- *Atharva Veda:* [which is the completion of the other Vedas and deals with natural law and the form of attention that must be placed on the functions of natural law].

Subordinate Vedas
- *Ayurveda:* the Indian system of self-health care; is the subordinate Veda of Rig Veda.
- *Sthapatya Veda (architecture Veda):* architecture & building
- *Dhanur Veda:* archery, warfare, human interactions, etc.

So the *Veda* is a vast body of knowledge which was divided into groups by Vyasa, which is why he was called "Veda" Vyasa. And Veda Vyasa also made sure that everyone knew, who read any of his writings (he also wrote 18 books called the *Puranas* – he was the most prolific of all of the ancient Indian writers) he also made sure that anyone who read him knew that ultimately it all boiled down to one or two simple things: [1] that you had to learn how to de-excite your awareness and become one with the underlying unified field; [2] then you had to take that experience and plunge into action with it – to become active and come into contact with the demands of the world and enjoy those demands successfully, interactively.

Vedanta

Veda Aanta becomes Vedanta. "Aant" gives us our English word "end" in that word's meaning as the final destination of logic, the result, the conclusion. The end in this case means the final conclusion. The final conclusion. What are the ultimate conclusions of the *Veda*? Veda Vyasa also had a lot to say about that. He wrote a book, another book, called the *Brahma Sutras*, *"The Aphorisms of Totality,"* which is the textbook of Vedanta. You might want to look that up one day too, although be prepared for a very detailed read. It's one of those books where you read a page and then think about it for three weeks, then read another page – and it's a big, fat book, too.

> *Consciousness – meaning consciousness of any kind – conceives, constructs, governs, and becomes the cells and behavior of the body.*

This is moving into the practical. This is one of the tenets of Ayurveda. If you don't think that your consciousness has anything to do with your body, think again. Consciousness has conceived your body, consciousness has constructed your body, consciousness governs your body. Consciousness becomes the cells and behavior of the body. As is the mind, so is the body. You want to know what your body's going to be like tomorrow? Look at your mind today. You want to know what your mind was like yesterday? Have a look at your body today. Today's body, yesterday's mind. Tomorrow's body is today's mind. Consciousness is manifesting itself as your body constantly. People who practice regularly techniques of meditation – my own favorite is Vedic Meditation – but people who practice regularly techniques of meditation have been shown unequivocally to live a higher-grade quality of life.

They've been shown unequivocally by modern medical science to live longer and to improve in every conceivable area of mind/body performance. There have been hundreds of scientific research studies to date published by independent and leading journals on the impact of Indian meditation techniques on daily Western living in terms of all the things you would hope for yourself, including everyone's favorite, which is postponing death. One of the most fascinating studies[1] showed that, on average, people who practice meditation, at the end of a five-year period of practice daily, had a body age which had reversed its biological age by up to 15 years. So stress causes aging, and meditation reverses the impact of stress, which then reverses the impact of aging.

I put that in there as a quick kind of tickler. There's a lot more in all these different areas. I'd now like to open the floor to questions and wait for Laurent's signal to finish that off.

Are there any questions you'd like to ask me?

MALE PARTICIPANT: I graduated from MIU (Maharishi International University, now MUM – Maharishi University of Management) – in 1981.

THOM: You did?

MALE PARTICIPANT: Interesting experience. Are you also a practitioner of the T.M. siddhis program?

THOM: A one-time practitioner, yes.

PARTICIPANT: So what do you think: can people fly or not?

THOM: I don't think people can fly in the way that we think of flying. What I think is that there's a value in practicing techniques which aspire to that, in terms of showing a mind/body connection. And I'm not particularly convinced that the technique that Maharishi taught to people is actually the flying technique. I think it was a technique designed to cause the body to move a lot and hop a bit ... This has been very well publicized.

But I think that any desire to get yogic teachings to revolutionize transport, or to help us out with passing out pamphlets from the air without having to stumble on the chairs and things, is actually probably fruitless. But it was an interesting experiment. And it was labeled properly, by the way.

Maharishi Mahesh Yogi, by the way, is the most illustrious and most famous student of Guru Dev, worldwide. And for a period of time he did what he called "research into consciousness" to see if people's nervous systems would be able to sustain the ability to actually levitate when they practiced a technique that was designed to do so. Now Esther would tell us that San Francisco, St. Francis of Assisi, was a well-documented flyer[2]. And there are other well-documented flyers. I'm not convinced that the world right now needs any flyers. And I think that because of that lack of need, the laws of nature won't support it. Maybe once upon a time it was something that accomplished something. I don't think that that is actually a useful something to accomplish these days, otherwise it would have happened. There have been so many people so intent on it, it would have happened by now if it was useful. Yes, Ma'am?

FEMALE PARTICIPANT: I was just wondering how you became involved in the study [of the *Vedas*], and at about what age?

THOM: There's a long story and a short story. My father was a general in the Air Force. He was stationed at the Pentagon. (Sorry, I haven't told you if I'm giving you the long or the short – this will be the short.) My father, who was the son of Senator Tommy Knoles – many of you knew my grandfather – was stationed at the Pentagon when he was a general in the 1960s. I had attempted to start university and went to Georgetown University and ended up actually in a lecture that was given by Maharishi Mahesh Yogi, the man I mentioned before, who was the student of

Guru Dev. I learned to meditate there, and then a year later I took off on a trip which took me all around the world with Maharishi. I ended up in Australia after having been trained as a teacher in India. And I was based in Australia for about 30 years. And about two years ago my father died and I inherited the Knoles family properties over in East Flagstaff.

These days I'm teaching meditation here and in Los Angeles. I have clients who visit me from all over the world.

But the long and short of it is, the slightly longer version is that my initial time spent was 18 months in the Himalayas in a little town called Rishikesh in north India, training with Maharishi. Also during that time we took a longer trip up to Jyotir Math to the place where Guru Dev spent his 13 years as the King of the Yogis. The position of Shankaracharya, by the way, is tantamount to being the King of the Yogis. This is a person who is elected to that position by unanimous consent of a body of people that can number up to 20 million. This is quite amazing. There is a festival some of you may have heard of – I was at it a year ago – called the Kumbha Mela. It's held every 12 years at the confluence of three rivers in India. And it's attended every year by 10 to 30 million people who come there to check out all of the different masters of meditation, all of the gurus and swamis and what not. And in 1949 they decided unanimously – that means, you know, you want to get a unanimous vote from 20 million people, that's something we're not used to in the West – they unanimously by acclaim wished for Guru Dev to become the King of the Yogis. And he humbly accepted that position and broke his silence, which till that time had lasted 40 years. He'd lived in silence for 40 years in a jungle in central India. So in 1968, I went up there to Jyotir Math to where Guru Dev's successors were, and spent some time there, too. And over the years, I've spent about eight

years in India altogether if you patched together all the little bits.
And that's pretty much my credentials and pedigree. Any other
questions? I think it might be time for me to wind up anyway.

LAURENT: I have a question, Thom. I heard a rumor that there
was a famous Flagstaff person who lived here recently who was
into Vedanta. Is it true?

THOM: As a matter of fact, we've reprinted an article that was
written by Platt Cline.[3] Many of you know Platt. I remember Platt
and Barbara very well. They used to come to eat at our family
house over on Fourth Street with my grandfather. Platt Cline,
perhaps unbeknownst to many of you, was in fact an entrenched
Vedantist, who considered that to be his personal religion and his
personal belief system. And in support of that, we've published
and reprinted by permission today an article that Platt wrote as
far back as 1968, though there are others. That's his best article
on the subject, in my opinion, entitled <u>What Vedanta Means to
Me</u>. And it was published in a journal which is the organ of the
Vedanta Society called Vedanta and the West. We have that free
of charge available for you to read. It's a six-page article by Platt
and it's extremely well written in our opinion.

I have one last thing to say. In the context of the war-like
atmosphere of the world today, I'd like you to know what it is
that the *Veda* says about that. And what it says has been already
said in various ways by other speakers today, but I'll perhaps put
that in our own way, my own way. It's not possible for us to have
a peaceful world that is filled with people who are unpeaceful.
It's not possible for us to seek a peaceful world in any diligent
fashion, if we ourselves, at the end of any given day, are not net
givers of peace to the atmosphere. Each one of us has to begin the
phenomenon of world peace in our self, rather than by running
out in the streets and shouting about how other people are so

unpeaceful and how terrible that is, or running out in the streets and shouting about how somebody's gone to war and how terrible that is. The *Veda* says that this won't do any good. By the time a war comes, it says, the saturation of violence in the atmosphere has become so great already that there probably is no alternative but for a war to occur. But, it goes on to say, if you wish to ameliorate this, and indeed if you wish to prevent future occurrences of it, then the onus is on you. The onus is on you as an individual to examine each day what you can personally do to be a net giver of peace and harmony into the atmosphere. Every one of us, every day, is radiating something into the atmosphere. Are we a net radiator of stress, unhappiness and violent thoughts, or are we a net radiator of peace, happiness and harmony? The onus is on us. No one can do it for us. And no government is ever going to save you from a war. No government is capable of doing that. What's going to happen will be that governments will continue to reflect the average level of stress and unhappiness that the individuals generate. So if we wish to create a more peaceful environment, whether a war happens in a full-blown fashion or whether we have to ameliorate that, or we're simply wanting to prevent the next one, we need to look, first of all, at ourselves, because it's our individual expression of anger, violence and lack of peace – stress – that saturates the world atmosphere and causes that breaking point to be reached. And that's what we call war.

So this is another gift to you from the *Veda*. Thank you very much for your attention. I hope you've enjoyed all of the symposium, and that you'll enjoy the rest of it today. *Jai Guru Dev.*

The Hindu goddess Mother Durga, as she appears at the Temple of the Divine Mother, in Flagstaff.

CHAPTER SIX

Hindu Spirituality
Kelly William McCabe

I T WAS NEVER MY INTENT while growing up along the banks of the Mississippi River in an incredibly loving Lutheran family in Clinton, Iowa, to leave the church and become a Hindu. I loved Jesus and I don't recall a moment in my life, then or now, when I questioned his divinity. Yet, here I am many years later and I find looking back that it is in the Hindu tradition that I feel most at home. It is the tradition that has nurtured my spirituality all of my adult life and lets me celebrate with joy the infinite ways in which countless others have been able to make their own connection with the Sacred. I will try to show in this chapter what it is about this tradition that has been so important to me.

Before I begin I wish to address one issue. On so many occasions over the years when I mention Hinduism I am confronted with a list of all the negative things that one can find in present day Hindu society in India. The implication is that the religion must be inherently misguided (if not fundamentally evil) for these societal imperfections to flourish. I submit that just as it is ridiculous to blame Jesus or St. Francis and the core teachings of Christ for the misguided actions of predominantly Christian societies it is ridiculous to blame the core teachings of Hinduism for the problems that they have. That mankind all over the world (and I include in this assessment many religious institutions) has the proclivity to find infinitely creative ways to cloak their negative tendencies in the garb of religion is certainly worthy of study and attention. But if one is serious about the study of religion itself, as a path to the Sacred, one must look at the core teachings of the religion. What did the saints, the true exemplars of that religion teach? What were their lives like? What were the methods they taught for coming close to God? What were their highest ideals?

It was in high school that I first seriously thought about religion. The divinity of Jesus and his infinite love was self-evident to me from early on. Perhaps I brought that faith with me into this life. Perhaps it was because I was blessed to see it reflected so clearly in the lives of my parents. My questioning took the form: Yes, Jesus is Divine, but what is divinity? What is the nature of God? How serious I was. My teachers say that if one takes a step towards God, God will take ten steps toward you. That proved so true for me. I was not getting any answers at first that I felt were helpful, but reading a book of Mahatma Gandhi's I got my first real hint; God is Love, God is Truth. Soon after, I was to have one of the most transformative experiences of my life.

I was browsing through a bookstore when I saw the beautiful picture of Buddha in deep meditation on the cover of the book, *Siddhartha*, by Hermann Hesse. Can anyone look at the peaceful countenance of Buddha and not be absolutely convinced that he knows what it's all about? I took the book home and immediately devoured it. In the course of the story the young man, Siddhartha, hears that the man who ran the local ferry was a great holy man. He went to him for guidance and the ferry man told him to sit by the river, as the river had taught him everything he knew. I no sooner read that than I jumped on my bike and headed straight for the Mississippi. I sat on a bench and waited for the Mississippi to teach me. I watched the river flow by. I recall that I felt more than a little ridiculous and I recall that I had no idea what I expected it to teach me, let alone how I expected it to teach me. At the same time I wanted so badly for it to do so. I watched the river flow by. There was no way that I could even begin to express what I wanted to know. I watched the river flow by. After some time, I have no idea how long, all of my little high school boy problems floated down the river and I knew, as clear as one can know anything in this world, that Infinite Joy resided in my own heart. I remember getting up from that bench in silent awe at this wondrous universe we live in and knowing that nothing would be more important in my life than learning how to access that Infinite Sacred Joy of my heart on a permanent basis.

It wasn't long after this that it occurred to me that what I wanted to learn wasn't going to be taught at the University of Wisconsin, Madison where I was planning to attend. Momentum got me there anyway and it wasn't until a month after classes had started that I remembered this. I needed to find a holy man, not a university, to study with. Of course I thought I had no idea where to look for one of those. But I did have a better idea than I then knew. I knew I was to stay in Madison and continue going to the absolutely beautiful Quaker meeting every Sunday morning. Such beautiful, simple, loving people sitting in silence connecting with the Sacred within their own hearts. The silence was only broken occasionally with a few words that served to make that connection deeper and stronger. Sure enough, after attending Quaker meetings for six or seven months I met one of the Quakers who was not really a Quaker at all, but a Quaker/Hindu with a Catholic background. It was this man who gave me the books by Swami Vivekananda and Sri Ramakrishna and introduced me to my Hindu teachers.

As I mentioned above, I was raised a Christian and even at that time had no inkling that as much as I was open to Hindu and especially Buddhist ideas I would ever be anything but a Christian. But when I read Karma Yoga by Swami Vivekananda I knew that this was the teacher I had been waiting for. He answered so powerfully the questions I had never heard anyone else even ask. I soon visited their temple and monastery, the Vedanta Society of Chicago. With great eloquence on meeting the resident monk there I asked, "Uh, what's a guy supposed to do?" He knew what I meant to ask and suggested that I visit their monastery in rural Michigan. There I could read and meditate and learn the tradition from the other monks, as well as help out with the farm chores.

Later that summer I did just that. I remember sitting on the bus thinking how incredibly strange it was for me to be joining a Hindu monastery. I also remember thinking that this was exactly the situation I had prayed for and that I had left the university for. The universe had given me what I needed. Now it was up to me. I did pray to Jesus, though. I told him that as strange as it seemed to me to be joining a Hindu monastery this seemed to be the right path for me and that if he had any objections, he should let me know.

As in every major religion there are in Hinduism many different sects or denominations, each with its own take on the tradition as a whole. The current manifestation of my lineage began with Sri Ramakrishna (1836-1886), a saint who lived in Calcutta, India who was one of the first great teachers who emphasized that all religions were true paths to God. His chief disciple, Swami Vivekananda, was the first Swami to come to this country (1893) to have a real impact on our culture. These saints, together with their disciples, played a prominent role in both explaining the Hindu tradition to western audiences as well as revitalizing the best of that tradition within India. Mahatma Gandhi had this to say about Sri Ramakrishna: "The story of Ramakrishna Paramahamsa's life is a story of religion in practice.

His life enables us to see God face to face." And about Swami Vivekananda he said, "I have gone through Swami Vivekananda's works very thoroughly, and after having gone through them, the love that I had for my country became a thousand-fold ... His writings need no introduction from anybody. They make their own irresistible appeal." While this lineage is just one of many within Hinduism, I believe that it's teachings for the most part would be considered widely acceptable to the Hindu community at large. In this country and Europe the centers for this lineage are usually called Vedanta Societies.

God is infinite, beyond words, beyond all mental conceptions. Anything we can say about God, even to use that term 'God' is a limitation. The word, 'Brahman' is used in Hinduism to refer to this. Often the scriptures will use the term Sat-Chid-Ananda, Infinite Existence, Consciousness, Bliss as a name or description of Brahman, but it is understood that that term also is more of a hint than an accurate description of the truth. One can never reach or express that which is infinite with a finite mind. However, the great saints of India tell us that it is possible to experience the infinite.

We can experience the infinite because our real nature is infinite as well. The real nature of all that we see in this world is infinite. Our real nature is beyond words, beyond all mental conceptions. The word, 'Atman' is used to refer to this "self" of ours that is infinite and beyond all thought. Atman is non-different from Brahman.

Our real nature is infinite and not different from the real infinite nature of God. At the same time we experience ourselves to be very finite indeed, "I am so tall (or short), I am so fat (or skinny), I am really good at this, I am really bad at that, I really love this, I really hate that ..." On and on we find infinite ways to put limitations on our infinite self. We view ourselves to be separate from each other, separate from the rest of the world and separate from God.

Why that should be the case can't be explained, but the fact remains that's the situation we find ourselves in. We, who are infinite and unlimited by nature are experiencing ourselves to be so very limited, so alone in a vast universe filled to the brim with beings and things that are separate from us and maybe even out to 'get us.'

The Hindu saints tell us that they have actually experienced the infinite nature of their soul, their 'oneness with God', their 'oneness with the universe' and that experience brings infinite joy, infinite peace, and infinite love into their lives. My teachers never asked me to accept their conclusions on these matters. They merely encouraged me to experiment with their ideas and find out for myself. I was so blessed to meet some of these saints in my life who were so filled with sacred joy. I met one of our old Swamis three or four times over the course of 15 years. According to some of the monks who lived in his monastery he had all sorts of difficult physical problems and his living conditions were extremely austere. He had absolutely nothing external in his life, not even a healthy pain-free body, which would bring him joy. Yet, every time I saw him his eyes were the eyes of a young man in love, radiating inexpressible happiness. All he could talk about was God in the form of the Mother of the Universe. For me personally it did not take much convincing to take the words of people like that seriously. Who else are we going to take seriously in this world if not the ones who have clearly manifested a great deal of light and love and goodness and truth in their lives? I remember reading when I was young some famous western philosopher (don't remember who it was) and finding out what a mess he had made of his life and thinking, Why in the world would anybody pay attention to the ideas – however intellectually brilliant they might be – of someone who was so obviously screwed up? I believe that Hinduism, Buddhism and other Eastern traditions have gained so much popularity in recent years primarily because people can see the clear-sighted goodness, the innate kindness and joy radiating in the lives of the Dalai Lama and other monks and teachers our culture has recently been blessed to come in contact with.

The philosophical framework of Hinduism that I just very briefly described is called Advaita Vedanta or non-dualistic Vedanta. But there are other types of Vedanta. Not all Hindus believe that their real nature is one with the real nature of God. In Vishishtadvaita Vedanta they believe there is only one consciousness, but the individual is just one part of that larger consciousness. In Dvaita Vedanta they believe that the individual is very much a separate creation of God. There are also other philosophical systems within Hinduism that have a completely different perspective.

This leads us back to the beginning of this discussion. God is infinite, beyond words, beyond all mental conceptions. Absolutely no philosophical framework is going to give us a completely accurate description of the totality of God and the nature of this world we live in. That does not make them useless. Swami Vivekananda used to compare them to the scaffolding used to construct a building. Some sort of philosophical structure is useful for 'constructing' our spiritual life. Although our thoughts are within the realm of time, space and causation that cannot begin to touch the infinite, we can use them to develop spiritual practices that will enable us to experience the divine directly. But the scaffolding is just that, a useful tool to build up our spiritual life. Once a building is constructed its usefulness is finished. The scaffolding is not the building and the philosophical framework is not the real experience of the divine.

Sri Ramakrishna and Swami Vivekananda emphasized so much that it is the spiritual experience of the divine that is the important thing, not the particular philosophical system or religious system that we happen to believe in. Some philosophies might seem more sophisticated than others but that is only relevant if it is actually helping you to experience God directly. I have known individuals who could articulate so eloquently the Advaita Vedanta philosophy and yet couldn't translate that into becoming nice, let alone spiritual people. Sri Ramakrishna used to call that "unripe knowledge." I have known others who knew next to nothing at all about religion or philosophy of any sort who manifested such a beautiful, simple, joyous unconditional love. However important our belief system may be in helping us to nurture our spiritual life it can also at a certain stage of development inhibit our experience of the Sacred. At some point the scaffolding has to come down for us to get a clear view of the Magnificent beyond.

Hinduism does not teach tolerance for other religions so much as they celebrate the fact that the Sacred can be approached in so many beautiful ways around the world. During my years as a monk I was able to attend on many occasions the Christmas celebrations held in the temple at our main monastery in Calcutta. A huge altar was set up in the temple, beautifully decorated with a painting of the Madonna and Child as the centerpiece. Those who have experienced Hindu worship know how simple and sweet it can be. The deity being worshipped is treated as an honored guest and offered incense and flowers, delicious food and beautiful music. The monks went to a great deal of time and trouble to offer food they thought a "Western God" would like. I remember especially the little cakes they would bring in from English bakeries in the city, the grape juice (substituting for the wine) and even imported cigarettes and cigars that they imagined he must like. None of this was done for show. Usually just the monks (maybe 100 to 150 monks) who lived at the monastery and maybe a few lay members were in attendance. It was always done with a great deal of love and respect for the life and teachings of Jesus.

After writing the above paragraph I received an email from a good friend who is still a monk in the Order. He was in Calcutta this past Christmas (2007) and was in our Temple for this Christmas Eve worship. Back in the mid 1970s when we were both living in that monastery, Belur Math, the headquarters of our Order, we and some other Americans who were there all sang Christmas carols at this worship. I had forgotten about this, but one of our friends taught these carols to some of the Indian monks who were studying with us at our training center. It turns out that these Indian monks passed these carols down year after year and now over 30 years later they still sing those carols at this worship. While the worship was going on one of our very old, senior monks who can barely walk made his way up the stairs and into the temple with great difficulty to bow before Jesus all the while muttering to himself with great spiritual power, 'Thy will be done, Thy will be done, Thy will be done.'

The most important thing in beginning a spiritual path, my teachers would say, is to just begin. It is not necessary to have your path all mapped out in advance. You could, I suppose, try to *Google* for directions if you really need to. Maybe they have that all mapped out, too. The important thing, however, is to just take that first step with a clear intention that you want to know God or the Truth or whatever you want to call it and that you want to live a good life in the best possible way. You may not consciously know where to start, but there is a part of you that knows just what to do. That part of you is just waiting for you to really begin. Sri Ramakrishna tells the story of a young man who wanted to go on pilgrimage to the famous holy city of Puri which is south of Calcutta. He had no idea exactly where it was but with great enthusiasm he packed his rucksack and headed on down the road. Like many of us he initially headed north instead of south. But his enthusiasm for the journey caused him to tell the first person he met that he was on his way to Puri and he was quickly turned around and pointed in the right direction.

In the case of spiritual life, the Hindu view is that there is no one way that is going to be the best way for everyone. The fundamental needs and emotions of people all over the world are pretty much the same, but look how different the various cultures have tried to meet those needs and express those emotions. In India everything seems to be done with joyful exuberance; everywhere the richest of colors, the sweetest of sweets, the spiciest of spices, the total abandon of "Bollywood" songs. In Japan on the other hand, the aesthetic is totally different. The temples, the gardens, the music and art, the cuisine are all so exquisitely simple and elegant. The same Mahayana Buddhism that one has in Japan is expressed so differently in Tibet. Does that make one culture better than the other? Absolutely not. Does one style appeal to you more than the other? Very likely. Religions are not all the same. Some of their ideas and ways of looking at things are fundamentally different from each other and those fundamental differences can have very real consequences in how we relate to God, each other, our world and our own selves. But however different their outlook may be, each religion is a valid way of approaching the

Sacred and each religion has the power to bring us closer to God and make us better, more loving individuals, if that is our focus. Years ago I used to watch Martin Yan's Chinese cooking show on Saturday mornings. "Yan can cook, so can you", was his motto. One day he was explaining how to cook yard-long beans. "You first cut them into two inch pieces ... or you can cut them up into one inch pieces ... or you can cut them up into half inch pieces ... nobody really cares." When it comes to religion, also, no one really cares how you cook it – just cook it already any old way you like. How lucky we are to live in these days when the cuisine of India, China, Japan, Korea, Mexico, Italy, Louisiana, Brazil and other places are so easily available. All so very different, all so very delicious.

The "goal" of religion, to describe it in a Hindu, non-dualistic philosophical way is to actually experience yourself to be one with the Universal Self or God. One's sense of self expands to include the whole universe. It was described to me once like this. When one identifies oneself completely with the individual mind-body complex, one quite naturally is focused on the needs and wants of that mind-body. Pretty much all of one's energy is centered around getting what one needs and wants and avoiding the things one doesn't want. When an individual falls in love and gets married in a very real sense the sense of self expands to include the spouse and, if kids are involved, to include them as well. People will do all sorts of things for the welfare of their family that they never would have considered before; not because of self-sacrifice, but because their sense of self has expanded.

I had a friend in California years ago whose whole life revolved around his Camaro. It had gold-plated engine parts, it was so fast, he loved it so very much. Then he fell in love with and married a beautiful woman and it wasn't so long after that that he sold his Camaro to get a down-payment for their new house. I was a little worried about how that would affect him until I went over to visit. "Man, you've got to check out all the closet space we have in this house," were his first words to me as I walked through their front door. There wasn't one word of remorse for having to sell his Camaro, just an obvious pride that he was able to provide a nice home for his new family. In the same way, some individual's sense of self expands way beyond their family to include their city, or country or the rest of humanity. When you look at the lives of Mahatma Gandhi or the Dalai Lama you can see how clearly they embody the ideals and the aspirations of their respective cultures. We are amazed at their sacrifice and their sense of purpose but I am sure that they would consider it a natural expression of who they are. To the Hindu sages much of what we call spiritual life is really just discovering who we really are. As we advance along the path our idea of our self can change dramatically and even when we take our first conscious steps on the path we can sometimes get a strong indication that we are by nature something far greater than we ever imagined. It should go without saying that the more conscious we are of making decisions that will expand our sense of self, the more we take responsibility for our own growth, the more direct and straightforward our path will be.

The expansion of our idea of our self can seem very abstract, but I think all of us have seen in our lives that the more we embrace others, the more that we care for others, whether it be family, animal companions, the earth or humanity as a whole, the more fulfilling our lives are, the more love and caring we receive right back. The mother of one of my brother monks was one of the clearest examples that I can think of. She was a wonderful old Texan woman. Actually, she was born in Oklahoma and lived most of her life in California but she was born to Texans and she was Texan through and through her whole life. When I knew her she had lost her husband, the oldest boy had moved to Alaska and never visited and her other son joined the monastery in Michigan (and later India). Many people in that situation would withdraw into their own loneliness. Mrs. Jennings instead adopted the whole monastery, all of her neighborhood kids and pretty much anyone else who for whatever reason came into her life. When I finally actually met her after years of enjoying the care packages that she sent to all of us in the monastery the intensity of her love was overwhelming. I was in a very real sense to her, "her son" and I could tell after a few days that everyone in her neighborhood were "her children." Her sense of her self expanded vastly beyond her own family. She had made the whole world her own, as some of my teachers would say. Not in an abstract impersonal way, but in a way that showered so much love on others and certainly was reflected clearly and intensely right back to her.

In Hinduism, the idea of salvation or enlightenment is not an all or nothing proposition. Wherever we start in spiritual life there is more likely than not a mixture of truth and un-truth in our perception of things. It is a matter of going or "growing" into a clearer and clearer perception of who we really are. Each step we take has its own rewards. Everyone, whether they know it or not, is on a spiritual journey. I have always found it helpful to look at it this way. We all intuit on some level that infinite joy is rightfully ours and we are all seeking that unlimited happiness. Most of us look for that infinite joy outside of ourselves and get into so much trouble in the process. As we progress we get a clearer idea of what brings us true joy.

More than anything else, what has always impressed me about the Hindu tradition is its emphasis, not on form or dogma, but on direct personal experience of the divine. The real strength of the tradition lies in the fact that over thousands of years they have developed such incredible methods for experiencing the divine directly. They know without a doubt that such experience is a very real possibility as they continue to this day to produce people who have had that experience. Sri Ramakrishna who did so much to reinvigorate modern day Hinduism was a simple village boy with almost no formal education, yet the great religious leaders of his day flocked to him recognizing that authority which rested solely in the fact of his spiritual experiences.

When Swami Vivekananda came to this country in 1893 for the Parliament of Religions which was held in conjunction with the Chicago World's Fair he was just a young wandering monk. One of India's many Rajas at that time was impressed with him and told him that he should represent Hinduism. When he arrived he had no credentials, no degrees and did not formally represent any particular religious organization. Yet upon meeting him there was no real question whether he should be allowed to attend.

One Harvard professor involved at the event remarked that asking Vivekananda for his credentials was like asking the sun who gave it its authority to shine. Spirituality is very palpable, it is very real. Looking back at my years in the monastery I was blessed in so many ways, but I think that the most important blessing I take with me to this day was coming into such close contact with men who were so close to God.

If we don't see the reality of the Sacred manifested so beautifully in the lives of people like that how are we to know that such a holy existence is even possible? How are we to know that such a life of unconditional love is worth aspiring to? I am writing this while knowing full well that unless one has come into contact with such a life it is very difficult to have any idea at all what I'm writing about.

I told a friend of mine years ago about the monk I mentioned earlier in this chapter who was so full of love and joy in spite of his external situation. I was shocked at her comment, "I don't believe in that." If she had met the man herself there would be no question of believing or disbelieving. Those who have met genuine holy men or women will know what I mean. I hope that others will at least be open to the idea of exploring the possibility that some men and women have reached a degree of spirituality that their everyday state of consciousness bears little resemblance to our own.

It is not by accident that these men and women have achieved what they have. There are well thought out methods used to develop spiritually just as there are methods to develop any other aspect of our life. All the Eastern traditions, not just Hinduism, have kept these techniques alive and viable to this day. These methods have the power to transform and enhance your life and the lives of those around you from the moment you begin. They can take you all the way to enlightenment if that's what you want. You don't need to accept that on faith. An openness to the possibility that they might be helpful to you and a genuine willingness to experiment with these methods are all that you really need.

Swami Vivekananda tells us in his book, *Karma Yoga*, that every thought we think, every word we speak, our every action is creating an impression on our mind-stuff and that our character is the sum-total of all those impressions. Who we really are as a human being is just the sum-total of all those little impressions we have been putting into our mind, moment to moment all through our life. When I read this, as a boy of 19, I was overwhelmed. At first I was horrified at the thought of all the little mindless hours I had spent in front of the TV while growing up. The next moment, however, came the liberating thought that it was not nearly as important what I decided to do with my life, as it was what I wanted to be in my life, who I wanted to be in the inner silence at the core of my heart and soul. In the stillness of my own mind, where no one else can see, which are the thoughts that I want to cultivate in my life.

In the 60s there were so many of us who longed to know what to do faced with a war that our government was asking us to fight. Back then with the draft these were not idle concerns. Everyone had an opinion. Some were revolutionaries, violent or nonviolent. Some felt the answer was to go back to the land and live a simple life. Many were intensely involved in one political movement or another and, of course, others just smoked a lot of dope. When I read these words of Vivekananda I realized for the first time that all the answers were lying there in my own heart.

Did I wish to end the violence of the war and in our society? Did I wish to calm the irrational fears that led us to war? If I did, I realized that it was never going to happen through political action or escape to the land or escape to a dreamland of drugs but it was going to happen when I took responsibility for my own thoughts and cleared the irrational fears and violence and all the other muck that was cluttering up my own heart and mind. This was a humbling realization as I knew from my first attempts at stilling the mind in meditation that there was plenty of muck in there to be cleared. At the same time it was liberating.

There was no need for some heroic external action that was going to somehow save the day, no need for going to that next big protest rally that was going to somehow make everyone else "see the error of their ways." The most important thing I could do was to take responsibility for my own mind and heart. I might not be able to change one thing in the external world, but I could work to change my own heart. In most religions, including Hinduism, there is much discussion of the grace of God, which of course can be so miraculous at times. But there is also such a thing as the grace of one's own mind. The mind, understanding the power of thought, chooses to think good thoughts, noble thoughts, thought for the welfare of those around us and the whole world, chooses to listen or play uplifting music, read (or write) uplifting books, watch (or make) uplifting movies, associate with uplifting people; chooses to smile and remain joyful and kind in the face of adversity. We have the power to choose each and every moment to fill our hearts with love and kindness and truth and goodness. What an incredible gift that is to the world. What an incredible gift that is to yourself.

The power of thought is certainly much more widely accepted now than it was when I was growing up and certainly much more widely accepted now than it was when Swami Vivekananda was lecturing on it to audiences in the 1890s. But I think we still take our thoughts for granted and don't truly understand their importance and their power. "Oh, it's just psychological," we might say totally writing off someone's very real pain. Thoughts are very real. When we look honestly at our own lives and the lives of those around us don't we see so clearly the consequences of our habits of thought? In my freshman registration at the University of Wisconsin I went up to a fellow student who was wearing an SDS (a radical group popular back then) button to introduce myself. I remember that I had my hand out to shake his when I came up against a field of bitterness that literally made me turn in my tracks. I have never forgotten that face and the intensity of that bitterness even though it is almost 40 years later. I have no idea what caused that bitterness of his; perhaps he had lost someone close to him in the war. I have no idea, but clearly his mind had been steeping in a toxic brew for quite some time. The next time I saw his face was in an article in *Time* magazine on radicals who were on the FBI most wanted list. He and his friends had killed someone when they bombed the Math Research building on campus later that year.

On the other side of the equation I can never forget the face of Swami Shantananda. They say, in the Hindu scriptures, that if one chants the name of God long enough one sometimes reaches a state where the name of God will come up continually within the heart of its own accord without conscious effort. When I knew Swami Shantananda (I was able to see him pretty much every day for two years) he was in his 90s and the mantra, "Om" had been bubbling up from within his heart ever since he was a young man. The spiritual presence in his room was indescribable.

I have over the years gone to see various groups of Tibetan monks who have come to Flagstaff to share their chanting. It is always so moving and everyone can feel the love and peace that is generated. What isn't always so well known is the fact that much of the love and peace was generated not just that evening, but in countless hours of prayer and chanting in their monasteries, far from the gaze of the public. I was taking a stroll in Darjeeling some years back and happened upon a Tibetan Buddhist monastery. One of the monks noticed me and invited me in and said that if I liked I could join the monks during their prayers. When I entered their small shrine there were maybe twenty monks who had clearly been chanting for quite a while already. I sat there enjoying their chanting for maybe two hours when I realized I should be moving along. I had the distinct impression that they would be going on for quite some time after I left.

There was a beautiful article by Sharon Begley in the January, 2007 edition of *Time* magazine called, "How the Brain Rewires Itself." In this article she tells about the work of the neuroscientist, Richard Davidson of the University of Wisconsin at Madison. She writes, "Earlier in Davidson's career, he had found that activity greater in the left prefrontal cortex than in the right correlates with a higher baseline level of contentment. The relative left/right activity came to be seen as a marker for the happiness set point, since people tend to return to this level no matter whether they win the lottery or lose their spouse ... might meditation or other forms of mental training, Davidson wondered, produce changes that underlie enduring happiness and other positive emotions? 'That's the hypothesis,' he says, 'that we can think of emotions, moods and states such as compassion as trainable mental skills.'"

She goes on to describe how he recruited Buddhist monks and a control group of students who were given a short course in meditation techniques. He had them meditate inside his fMRI (or functional magnetic resonance imaging) tube so he could measure their brain activity in various mental states. She continues, "During the generation of pure compassion, a standard Buddhist meditation technique, brain regions that keep track of what is self and what is other became quieter, the fMRI showed, as if the subjects – experienced meditators as well as novices-opened their minds and hearts to others. More interesting were the differences between the so-called adepts and the novices. In the former, there was significantly greater activation in a brain network linked to empathy and maternal love. Connections from the frontal regions, so active during compassion meditation, to the brain's emotional regions seemed to become stronger with more years of meditation practice, as if the brain had forged more robust connections between thinking and feeling.

But perhaps the most striking difference was in an area in the left prefrontal cortex – the site of activity that marks happiness. While the monks were generating feelings of compassion, activity in the left prefrontal swamped activity in the right prefrontal (associated with negative moods) to a degree never before seen from purely mental activity. By contrast, the undergraduate controls showed no such differences between the left and right prefrontal cortex. This suggests, says Davidson, that the positive state is a skill that can be trained."

The most important experiments, though, can be done ourselves in the quiet of our own hearts and minds. No fMRIs are required. Studies like the one mentioned above are so incredibly valuable, but it is when we try these mediation practices and pay attention to our moods and we see for ourselves how our feelings of love and compassion grow that we will have real conviction in the efficacy of these practices.

Before discussing specific methods of spiritual practice used in the Hindu tradition to come close to God I need to bring up an important point. I mentioned in the beginning of this chapter that God is infinite and beyond all mental conceptions. While that may be true in an ultimate sense, to the Hindu that does not mean that it is useless to try to think of God with form. On the contrary, they believe that the Sacred reveals itself in an infinite variety of beautiful ways. Perhaps most important of these ways is through the Gods and Goddesses and through the Avatars or incarnations of God.

In reference to the incarnations of God Hindus believe very much like Christianity does that it is possible for God to reveal himself in the form of a real live human being. And very much like Christianity they usually describe this process of the fullness of God coming as a real person as a mystery. Where Hinduism differs dramatically is the belief that this has happened more than once. What better way for humans to get some idea of the unconditional love of God than seeing it embodied in a form to which they can relate. Vivekananda said once that if God were trying to reveal himself to the fish of this world he would probably come in the form of a really big, unimaginably beautiful fish. Hindus believe that God comes down periodically to this world in the form of a man to help reestablish righteousness in this world. Many modern Hindus, including many of our monks, believe that Jesus Christ and Buddha were both incarnations of God, right along with Rama and Krishna and others within their tradition.

Worshipping such an incarnation, contemplating the life of such an incarnation, developing a real love for such an incarnation provides us with a mystical gateway into the heart of God. How do we know an incarnation when we come across one? To me the answer lies in witnessing their power to transform lives. Jesus lived 2000 years ago and people today still have their lives transformed through his life and his love. Buddha lived 2500 years ago and his compassionate presence reverberates to this day in the loving hearts of so many.

To me the Gods and Goddesses of Hinduism are even more of a mystery and contemplating them makes me stop in silence and sit in awe of this wondrous, magical, beautiful universe that we live in. Like everything in India these Gods and Goddesses seem over the top. So beautiful, colorful, playful, so many arms and heads. And so very real. I believe in them and yet I totally understand why many looking at Hinduism from outside the tradition would try to anthropologize or psychoanalyze them right out of existence. But there is a power with the Gods and Goddesses to effect our day to day lives and transform our lives right up to enlightenment whether that can be explained or not.

I have a shop in Flagstaff, Arizona, called Sacred Rites where I sell sacred art and music and healing instruments from around the world. One of the great benefits for me in having this shop for the last 15 years is being able to meet all sorts of people and listen to their stories and get their perspective on religion or witness what does or does not resonate with them spiritually. In the past few years, especially, I have heard some amazing stories about Ganesh. He is the God with an elephant's head whose chief role is the remover of obstacles.

A young man came in one day and told me this story. He had lost his best friend in a car accident. He fell into a deep depression for months and wasn't able to get beyond his grief. Then one night he dreamed of a little boy with an elephant's head who removed all of his sorrow. He woke up feeling good about his life for the first time in months and totally able to get on with his life. He was a regular American boy who had never heard of Ganesh nor had any contact with anything Hindu in his life, yet Ganesh came to him in dream and released him from his pain.

Another day a young woman told me this story. She was walking along with a friend one day towards Wheeler Park in Flagstaff. They both noticed a cloud that was shifting rapidly and quickly turned into a very detailed image of Ganesh. She made a point of saying that this wasn't just a vague elephant form that could, if you exercised your imagination, become Ganesh. She said it was as detailed as some of the Ganesh T-shirts that you see around. There was no mistaking him and as they both stared at it in awe, it quickly shifted into a man holding a child which made her immediately want to call her father who had, much prior to this incident, told her and her brothers and sisters that they were never to contact him again and that he wanted nothing to do with them. She called anyway and said, "Dad, I know you told us to never call, but I simply had to." He was overjoyed and their family was soon able to reconcile and get past whatever had split them up in the first place. Months later, she said, a friend told her that Ganesh is the remover of obstacles.

In India there is a mountain that the Goddess Durga resides in. During the British Raj the British decided that they wanted a tunnel built through this mountain so they gave the job to one of their best engineers. Before the tunnel could be completed it caved in and they had to start all over again. Once more they began and before it could be completed it caved in again. Needless to say this engineer's superiors were not at all happy and they told him that if he could not get it right they were going to demote him and transfer him to the end of the earth. Then he had a dream. Mother Durga came to him and told him that she would allow him to build the tunnel, but that he must honor Her with a temple to be built on each side of the tunnel. He agreed and the tunnel and the two temples to Durga exist to this day.

All of these stories are true. None of these people had any reason to lie about them. They weren't Hindus before these experiences and they weren't Hindus after them as far as I know. Do these stories make any sense to my rational mind? Not at all. Why in the world would an elephant-headed Hindu god appear to an American boy in a dream and remove his sorrow? Why in the world would he take the form of a cloud to heal a suffering young woman and her family? It doesn't make any sense at all. It doesn't seem reasonable. It doesn't seem rational.

Yet these irrational experiences had profoundly real consequences in the lives of these people. Is it then rational to believe that these experiences weren't real? Is it rational to believe that we can expect our finite minds to have even the faintest idea how this infinitely vast universe works?

Whether we believe in these Gods or not my experience has been that this universe is vastly more mysterious and magical than we can begin to imagine. We don't need to believe or understand everything told to us about such things, but the more we can open our hearts and minds to the limitless possibilities in this universe the better off we are. It's always a dicey game to limit the limitless.

When I use the words mysterious and magical I don't mean to suggest that spiritual truths don't conform to the laws of nature. I mean that however sophisticated we might feel our current state of scientific understanding of the universe to be, it is still very limited. Wouldn't our computers, iPods, TVs and radios seem totally unbelievable, totally magical even to the best scientific minds of just 100-150 years ago? Just because something doesn't conform to our current understanding of the laws of nature doesn't mean that it doesn't conform to the laws of nature.

Reason and intellectual discernment are important aspects of spiritual life. One of our Swamis was fond of reminding us that while it is good to be open-minded we should be careful that our brains don't fall out. To live a spiritual life it is not necessarily important to believe in the gods, angels, miracles, ETs, any of this stuff. But when one declares that none of this can possibly be true one is not limiting the Limitless so much as limiting oneself. Rather than denying all of this outright, to my mind it is healthier to just put those concepts in your pocket and save them for that day when you have a dream or a vision or a "thought" that comes out of nowhere making everything clear.

The whole key to understanding Hindu spiritual practice is this one idea of the importance of each thought. Each and every thought is creating an impression on our mind. All the disciplines, all the modes of meditation are geared simply to making it possible for us to integrate all aspects of our personality and our life and direct them to the Sacred. The principles behind these spiritual practices are universal and really could be used, I would think, by most anyone interested in growing spiritually. Discipline. Spiritual practice. That sounds like hard work.

Does anyone else remember Maynard G. Krebs on the Dobie Gillis show years ago? And his intense reaction to any suggestion that he get a job? Work! The Hindu teachers would respond that you don't have to do anything you don't want to do. If you are totally happy with your life the way it is and happy with the world the way it is that is great. You don't need to do anything. In my case, the idyllic life I had as a boy growing up in a loving, stable family on the banks of the Mississippi ran head on into the realization that the world as a whole did not seem right at all. It was clear to me that nothing would be more important to me than trying to help the world regain its balance and that I would have to start right in my own heart. Once I started and realized the joy that comes with bringing the Sacred into one's life the words, 'discipline' and 'spiritual practice' hardly seem appropriate. But there is a certain amount of 'effort' involved in beginning to be conscious of our every moment.

Swami Vivekananda categorized the different types of spiritual practice into four main groups:

1. Raja Yoga, the path of mental control;
2. Jnana Yoga, the path of knowledge;
3. Bhakti Yoga, the path of devotion, and
4. Karma Yoga, the path of work.

Each of these paths is a distinct approach to God but for most of us these paths are blended and balanced so we can bring all aspects of ourselves on board for the spiritual journey.

Raja Yoga

Raja Yoga is the path of mental control. Patanjali in the Yoga Sutras writes that yoga or union is the state which comes when all the movements of the mind have been stilled. Hindu teachers often compare our mind to a lake. If the water in a lake is rough we cannot see down into it even if the water itself is clean and pure. However, if the lake is still we can see deeply into it. When our mind is in turmoil and constantly moving from one thought to the next it is impossible to see deeply into ourselves.

I believe this practice of stilling the mind is the foundation of spiritual life. Stilling the mind, turning our mind inwards away from infinite distractions trying to catch our attention ... silence ... listening with a patient heart for our deepest self to speak.

Carl Jung wrote that people would always complain to him that God doesn't speak to us anymore like he did to the prophets in the Old Testament. His reply was that God does still speak to us. We just stopped listening. We have found so many ways to keep from listening.

Being born in 1951, I was part of the first generation to grow up with television as a major force in my life. Even that, with the limitation of three channels to choose from, was distracting. It seems to get crazier every minute in this regard, doesn't it? We can now carry 40,000 songs in our shirt pocket with a broadband connection, any number of games and TV shows to boot.

And every year at MacWorld, Steve Jobs will promise us even more ways we can be connected. How cool is that? The only problem is the more connected we are the less connected we get. When our mind has infinite ways to distract itself it makes it just that much harder to sit still and be quiet and let the mind rest in itself. But that is exactly what we need to do. My friend and coworker, Lisa, put a sign up in my shop next to our meditation cushions, "Don't just do something, sit there." It's the most important thing we can do ... sitting in silence ... patiently ... giving ourselves a chance to listen to the deepest part of ourselves ... getting to know the deepest part of ourselves.

Infinite joy is right there in my heart. When I sat by the Mississippi as a young man I had absolutely no idea what I was doing and I am amazed to this day that I just stumbled across this idea of sitting and listening. I am amazed to this day what a profound impact that afternoon had on my life.

There are many meditation techniques available and it is not my intention in this chapter to discuss them in detail. Here are some suggestions, though:

- Sit with your back straight but relaxed, breathe slowly and deeply, close or half-close your eyes. Focus your attention in your heart or between your eyebrows.
- Be still, be open ... just witness the comings and goings of the mind ... no judgment.
- The mind wanders, gently bring it back.
- There is nothing to be attained.
- You are simply enjoying the company of your highest self ...
- Start with even a few minutes in the morning and in the evening. If you like you can start your meditation with a gong or Tibetan singing bowl and follow the sound of that into silence. Blessed silence.

The mind can be so restless. I remember so well my earliest attempts at stilling my mind in the Quaker meetings I attended in Madison in 1969. My mind was all over the place, jumping from one thought to the next. It was really quite alarming to me how little control I had. But there are things you can do to help. How we live our life moment to moment greatly impacts our ability to still our chitta-vrittis (mind-waves).

The Yoga Sutras lay a great deal of emphasis on character and ethical conduct. For one thing, a controlled mind is a powerful mind and teachers really only wanted to teach people of good character who would not misuse their power. Equally important, it is next to impossible to have a clear, focused mind if our lives are muddled up with all the usual things we associate with bad or unethical behavior; drugs and alcohol, addictions of any kind, greed, violence, anger, fear, lying and other forms of dishonesty, inappropriate sexual desire, overeating, lack of exercise etc. On the other hand, if we keep our life clean, if our dealings with others and ourselves are respectful, kind and helpful, if we choose to fill our minds with good, positive thoughts, it will be much, much easier to sit quietly and dive deep into our self. I have one further suggestion that Patanjali never mentioned for some reason. Do not, I repeat do not, listen to the *Calypso* CD put out by Putumayo a few years ago. You absolutely cannot get those Calypso melodies and rhythms out of your head.

When the mind becomes still to some degree it is not unusual to have profound experiences such as visions or deep insights. My teachers say that to the extent these experiences have a lasting positive effect on our life they are real and useful. Sometimes, however, they are just interesting fluctuations of the mind that are of no real importance. If we pay attention to our dreams we can see this as well. I have had dreams that have deeply affected me in a positive way all my life, but most nights my dreams seem to be just dreams – with the mind floating aimlessly. I mention this because there is a tendency for many to believe that these unusual experiences are the goal of meditation and that if they aren't having visions or unusual experiences in their meditation they are somehow failing or at least not progressing. That is so far from the truth.

The goal of spirituality has nothing to do with having exciting, far-out "experiences", but coming into close, intimate contact with our own true, infinitely beautiful self in the silence of our heart. The goal of spirituality is expanding our heart, expanding our conception of our 'self' to include the whole universe. My teachers emphasized that this is best accomplished in a gentle, natural way through regular practice of stilling the mind. In a genuine and sincere desire for real spiritual growth it may be tempting to think that psychedelic drugs or extreme breathing exercises may provide a shortcut to spiritual experience. In this matter, as in most matters relating to spiritual life, I personally think that it is wise to look to the lives of genuine holy men and women who clearly are manifesting the sacred joy and love in their lives that we all seek. These are the people who really know and understand the ins and outs of the inner spiritual journey.

In the opinion of all the great Hindu (and Buddhist) teachers I know of, drugs are totally unnecessary and can cause genuine harm. They can open up (read break down) doorways of perception that really should be kept closed until they open in the natural order of things. It is much, much healthier to let these experiences come in a natural organic way. Trust your higher self. You will know what you need to know when you need to know it ... What's the big hurry? There is no hurry. Controlling the mind is a process that requires practice, moderation, gentleness with oneself and patience. There really is nothing but the present moment anyway.

I will mention it once more. Spirituality, according to my Hindu teachers, is about truth, love, kindness, developing genuine compassion and wisdom. It is not about the attainment of unusual, exciting "experiences" and it is also not about the attainment of psychic powers. When I first moved to Flagstaff, I was asked to give a talk to a group of people who had heard that I was a Hindu monk for 15 years & was interested in hearing of my experiences in India. It became clear that they were primarily interested in knowing if I had come across the really great yogis of India who could do amazing things with their psychic powers.

I tried to explain that my teacher, Sri Ramakrishna, while acknowledging that psychic powers are occasionally attained by someone on the spiritual path, taught that they had absolutely no value or purpose for one seeking true spirituality. Rather, they were only a big stumbling block and should be avoided. The people in attendance at my talk assured me that they knew that, however they really, really wanted to hear all about the magical powers of the yogis. They were disappointed that evening.

Sri Ramakrishna tells the story of two brothers. One renounced the world as a young man and became a monk. For years he practiced intense spiritual disciplines. After many years he visited his family. His brother was so excited to see him and asked him what great things he had been able to achieve after leading such an austere life. By way of an answer the monk led his brother down to the riverbank and proceeded to walk across the water to the other side. The brother then crossed over on the ferry. Totally unimpressed he told his monk brother, "I can't believe you sacrificed so much just to be able to cross this river. It only cost me ten cents to do the very same thing."

Jnana Yoga

Jnana Yoga is the path of knowledge. In this path the intellect is used to discriminate and look deeply into the nature of reality and our own self. Two great saints of the 20TH century, Sri Ramana Maharshi and Sri Nisarga Datta, are good examples of people reaching illumination primarily through this path.

Sri Ramana Maharshi taught the path of self-inquiry or atma-vichara in which one meditates deeply on the 'I-thought' to find its source. Who am I?

Sri Nisarga Datta wrote an incredible book called, *I Am That,* which should be read by anyone seriously interested in Jnana Yoga. The title, *I Am That* is taken from a quotation in the Am-ritabindu Upanishad, "That in whom reside all beings and who resides in all beings, who is the giver of grace to all, the Supreme Soul of the universe, the limitless being, I am That."

He describes with great simplicity his journey on this path, "When I met my Guru, he told me: 'You are not what you take yourself to be. Find out what you are. Watch the sense, 'I am,' find your real Self.' I obeyed him, because I trusted him. I did as he told me. All my spare time I would spend looking at myself in silence. And what a difference it made, and how soon. My teacher told me to hold on to the sense 'I am' tenaciously and not to swerve from it even for a moment. I did my best to follow his advice and in a comparatively short time I realized within myself the truth of his teaching. All I did was to remember his teaching, his face, his words constantly. This brought an end to the mind; in the stillness of the mind I saw myself as I am, unbound. I simply fol-lowed my teacher's instruction which was to focus the mind on pure being 'I am' and stay in it. I used to sit for hours together, with nothing but the 'I am' in my mind and soon peace and joy and a deep all-embracing love became my normal state. In it, all disappeared – myself, my Guru, the life I lived, the world around me. Only peace remained and unfathomable silence."

I love the simplicity of his life. He found a teacher he could trust who was grounded in enlightenment and pure character, he listened to him, trusted him and then did as best he could to follow his teaching.

Another meditation often used in Jnana Yoga that I really find useful is from the Chandogya Upanishad, 'sarvam khalvidam brahma,' 'All this is verily Brahman.'

As you go about your day try to be aware of that. Everything we see, hear, taste, smell, and touch is Brahman; Infinite Existence, Consciousness, Bliss. The scriptures say it is so, the great teachers say it is so. I believe them, even if I am not yet perceiving that truth. The practice of Jnana Yoga is hearing this truth, believing it, meditating on it and developing a strong desire to actually experience that to be true.

Every now and then, even without being anywhere close to a full realization of it, at least a glimmer of that truth comes peeping from behind the veil we put over our eyes. My shop used to look out on a brick wall which was the side of what is now Arizona Music Pro in Flagstaff. As far as brick walls go, this wall is really pretty ordinary; nothing special about it at all.

Years ago, when I was new to Flagstaff, I spent a great deal of time at my shop. Many evenings I would sit out in front of the shop, not really meditating but sitting quietly enjoying the evening air. My view was this wall on the other side of our parking lot. At some point during this period this wall actually began to feel conscious to me. There was a certain glow to it, almost like my attention to it had awakened it. Soon after this my brother came to visit. When he returned home to Wisconsin he sent me a poem he had written about his visit in which he mentioned the consciousness of this wall, although I had not mentioned to him anything about my own experience of that.

Another exercise that I like to practice which falls into the Jnana Yoga category is looking at our experiences in this world as if it were a dream. If you pay attention there is definitely a dream-like quality to much of what we experience and much of what is written about dreams can be applied to our everyday experiences. Paying attention to our nightly dreams and our waking dreams can provide us with incredible insights. Also, if this is all my dream, I can choose exactly what I want to be in my dream. We can decide to fill our dreams with all that is good and noble and holy. If terrifying things intrude on our dream, whether it be communists or terrorists or presidents who fight terrorists we can choose to face those fears with strong, determined love and prayers for the happiness of all beings.

While going through a difficulty that was consuming my attention and was a little overwhelming I had a dream (at night) in which I was in a classroom. A holy man made it clear to me that what I was going through in my waking life was not all that real and that I could choose to wallow in it or I could step into the beautiful golden cube of pure consciousness that was at the front of the classroom. It was that easy. It was my choice.

The study of sacred geometry and sacred sound are also paths within Jnana Yoga that help us understand our higher self and our connectedness with all things in this universe.

Again, I love the simplicity and beauty of Sri Nisarga Datta's approach. Someone once asked him, "How do I go about finding who am I?" He replied, "How do you find anything you have mislaid or forgotten? You keep it in your mind until you recall it."

Bhakti Yoga
Bhakti Yoga is the path of devotion. Sri Ramakrishna believed that of all the yogas for most people it is the easiest path. That is because love is such a powerful emotion. One can theoretically meditate on anything at all and find truth, as described in the Yoga Sutras of Patanjali, but if one has a real love for the object of one's meditation it is easy for the mind to stay focused. Is it

difficult for a young man or woman to think of their lover? In fact, is it possible for them to think of anything else?

So if one can develop a close, loving relationship for a form of God it makes it easy to meditate. Meditation ceases to be a spiritual discipline at all when one finds real joy in the thought of the beloved. I spoke once at a conservative theological seminary in Holland, Michigan about the Hindu tradition. The students there made a point of telling me that in their tradition they had no need for meditation. I understand that from their theological perspective they did not feel that meditation was required, but I found it curious that they would not want to spend time thinking of Jesus.

It is common to believe that this path of Bhakti Yoga is fundamentally a dualistic path and has nothing to do at all with non-dualism and is diametrically opposed to the path of Jnana Yoga, or at best is something for simpler, less evolved souls who are not yet ready for the pure truth. I don't believe that is the case at all. As I mentioned in the last section on Jnana Yoga the focus is meditating on the real nature of your self: Who am I? With deep and prolonged meditation on that question you may at some point have the realization that Sri Nisarga Datta had, 'I am That.' In Bhakti Yoga, the 'That' is merely given a form. The Gods and Goddesses and the incarnations of God like Buddha, Jesus and Krishna are not presented in Hinduism as tests of faith. Do you or do you not believe? They are presented as beautiful, mysteriously god-given forms that give us a glimpse – a portal, if you will – into that which is Sacred and beyond all mental conceptions. Why that should be so and how that is possible is a mystery.

In the Eastern Orthodox Christian tradition they call their icons, "windows into Heaven." These forms can give us a beautiful glimpse of the Sacred that our mind can hold onto and as our meditation deepens have the power to propel us to an experience beyond the mind where we realize the divinity of our own soul. The goal of Bhakti Yoga is not to simply have a vision of a particular form of God that might appeal to us but to understand who we really are, just as it is in the path of Jnana or Raja Yoga. We are made in the image of God. We are not old men with long, grey beards (some of us, anyway). We don't have blue skin and multiple arms. But we are infinite. Infinite compassion, infinite joy, infinite love, infinite consciousness is our birthright. When we meditate on Jesus or Buddha or Tara in our heart the love and compassion and wisdom they so clearly exemplify becomes very real to us and begins to reveal to us that love and compassion and joy is who we are. The boundaries that we thought existed between us and everything else begin to dissolve.

The common meditation technique in Bhakti Yoga is to choose, often with the help of a teacher, a particular form of God that appeals to you, place a shining, living image of that form of God in your heart (which is the seat of consciousness) and silently recite the mantra of that form of God. The mantra always includes the name of that form of God.

For example, "Om Buddhaya Namaha" (Om Salutations to the Buddha). "Om namah Shivaya" (Om Salutations to Shiva). The name of God is said to be non-different from God. When we chant his name, God is really there. This is such a powerful technique and is very common in Hinduism, Buddhism and Eastern Orthodox Christianity. The millions of people in these traditions can't all be wrong. Well, of course they can. But in this case they are so right.

I mentioned earlier that a fundamental idea behind all Hindu spiritual practice is that each and every thought we think is creating an impression on our mind. We are the sum total of all the little impressions we have been putting into our mind. This is true for all thoughts, but the impression made is much more powerful when our mind is very relaxed and the thought is very focused. By choosing a form of God that appeals to you and reciting the appropriate simple prayer or mantra while visualizing that beautiful form in your heart you are creating a connection that liberates you from your mind and allows you to dive deep into your heart and the core of your being. Long eloquent prayers may have their place in certain contexts, but in the context of spiritual practice they just keep the mind revolving around inside itself while the real action is found in the heart.

Simplicity. When we quietly or silently chant our mantra we are choosing that moment to dwell in the Sacred Presence. Like all the practices I have been discussing one cannot have a real idea of the power and beauty of this unless you try it and work with it.

The habit of saying the mantra, either out loud or silently, can be developed so that every moment can be "sacramentalized" with the Sacred Name of God. Yes, the mind will wander and yes, often the mind will need to be more focused on whatever task may be at hand, but the undercurrent of prayer will make every moment a blessed one. My teachers believed that while it is important to say the mantra as much as we can during the course of the day, it is also important to set aside some time in the morning and evening specially for this purpose.

This quiet time, even if it is only for a few minutes, will give us a chance to go deeper into our heart and listen to the stillness. We had two smokers in our monastery. One of them asked the Swami if it would be alright if he smoked while he meditated. The monk replied that really he should not. Couldn't he get by without that for a little bit each morning and evening to fully concentrate on his meditation? Really. The other monk asked the Swami if it was alright if he meditated while he smoked. He replied, "Of course! You should try to have a meditative consciousness in all of your activities."

I first came upon this practice of saying the mantra when I joined the monastery when I was nineteen, but it wasn't a Hindu text that drew me to love it so much, but an Eastern Orthodox Christian one called, *The Way of a Pilgrim*, translated by R. M. French. This book continues to be an inspiration to me even now. The pilgrim is a simple Russian peasant. When his very devout wife passed away he decided to go on a pilgrimage on foot to various holy places to find a teacher who could explain to him a passage in the *Bible* (first Epistle of St. Paul to the Thessalonians) which tells us to pray without ceasing. He went from teacher to teacher only to get advice which his heart told him didn't adequately explain this biblical verse. Then one evening after a long day of walking he met up with a monk who invited him to supper and to take rest that night at his monastery. He replied that he had plenty of dried bread in his knapsack and that he wasn't concerned about where he would spend the night. All he really wanted was for someone to explain to him how to pray without ceasing.

As it turned out, this monk was a holy man who taught him to say what is commonly called the Jesus Prayer, "Lord Jesus Christ, Son of God, have mercy upon me." He taught him how to make a habit of saying this prayer at all times and how by saying this prayer continually all of our thoughts are filtered through the sweet name of God. Every moment is sacramentalized.

The book goes on to relate his experiences with this inward prayer of the heart: " ... what does come from the grace of God

in the case of the prayer of the heart, is so full of sweetness and
delight that no tongue can tell of it, nor can it be likened to
anything material, it is beyond compare. Every feeling is base,
compared with the sweet knowledge of grace in the heart ... The
Prayer of my heart gave me such consolation that I felt there was
no happier person on earth than I, and I doubted if there could
be greater and fuller happiness in the kingdom of Heaven. Not
only did I feel this in my own soul, but the whole outside world
also seemed to me full of charm and delight. Everything drew
me to love and thank God; people, trees, plants, animals. I saw
them all as my kinsfolk. I found on all of them the magic of the
Name of Jesus. Sometimes I felt as light as though I had no body
and was floating happily through the air instead of walking ...
Sometimes I felt as joyful as if I had been made Tsar. And at all
such times of happiness, I wished that God would let death come
to me quickly, and let me pour out my heart in thankfulness at
His feet in the world of spirits."

Clearly the theological foundation for this holy pilgrim's practice on the surface seems light-years away from the philosophical
foundation for the practices of the Hindus but aren't the expressions of his experiences so reminiscent of Sri Nisarga Datta's?

"I used to sit for hours together, with nothing but the 'I Am'
in my mind and soon peace and joy and a deep all-embracing love
became my normal state. In it all disappeared – myself, my Guru,
the life I lived, the world around me. Only peace remained and
unfathomable silence."

There is another aspect of the use of the mantra that I wish
to discuss. All prayers that we may have for ourselves and others
can be folded into a simple mantra or prayer just like you can fold
chocolate into a nice tasty mousse. Let me explain.

There are so many things that happen in this world whether

it be natural or man-made disasters, accidents, illnesses and the like that call out to us for our attention and our help and our prayers. This is a good and natural response to want to help and we should. Prayers do help, but it is really easy also to get caught up in the emotions and the drama of things and that does not help you or anyone else. You do not need to – or want to for that matter – know details in order to offer powerful prayers. Prayers are the most powerful when they are simple and deep. When we come across anything worth praying about we can gently with a movement of the heart fold those prayers into our mantra.

When we genuinely connect with the Sacred in our heart we are connecting with everything else as well. When our own heart is made whole, the world is made whole. When our own heart is brought into balance, the whole world is brought into balance.

A loving, personal relationship with a form of God can be cultivated in other ways besides interior prayer. I doubt if any other culture has been so creative in finding ways to do this as they are in India. I mentioned the worship of Jesus on Christmas Eve in our monastery in Calcutta, and to what great lengths the monks went to please Jesus.

It is common in India for Hindus to have a shrine in the home where a form of God is the permanent guest of honor. They wake God up in the morning with songs, prayers and chants, bathe Him/Her, offer breakfast & other meals, prayers and offerings in the evening and again put God to bed at night. This may seem simple-minded but I believe it is so profound. It is a way of making God a very real and integral part of all aspects of your life.

Expressing love for God in this kind of external way certainly isn't required or needed by God but it enhances the feelings of love and closeness. When I offer flowers or nice things to eat and say, 'I love you' it enhances the relationship as surely as it does in a human relationship. Offering our love opens the heart in a very sweet and special way, that also makes the heart receptive to receiving love. They say that Sri Ramakrishna's father would walk miles to find a particular flower that he wanted to offer in their home shrine. Clearly unnecessary from one point of view, but how beautiful to think of the love he held in his heart and the joy he took in finding that special flower. Elaborate rituals like you find in India aren't required. You can make up your own. It can be as simple as wishing, 'good morning' to the gods, the morning sun, your trees, "I love you." Maybe you could offer them a cup of coffee and a bagel.

In the Bhakti Yoga texts such as the *Narada Bhakti Sutras* it describes a number of personal relationships we might develop with God. In Western religious traditions God is most often thought of as father. In India, especially in Bengal where I lived, God is more often thought of as mother. In the Hindu texts, God can also be thought of as a child or friend or even as a lover.

Sri Ramakrishna had a wonderful woman disciple who came to him one day and told him that she couldn't meditate. She was a widower who took care of her young nephew. She told him that she loved her nephew so much that she could only think of him. Sri Ramakrishna told her to look upon her nephew as a form of God and thereby make all of her service to him and her thoughts of him a form of meditation and worship. She did this, and because of the intensity of her love for the boy quickly attained a high degree of enlightenment.

Karma Yoga
Karma Yoga is the path of action. We all have to "do something" in our lives. Even if we are trustafarians (one who has a trust fund and doesn't need to work for a living), we still have to act.

Karma Yoga gives us an idea of how to act in this world in a way that enhances our spiritual journey, rather than distract us from our spiritual goals.

Sometimes our monks would refer to it as spiritualizing every-day life. Hinduism has an interesting concept called "dharma," or one's calling or path in life. For example, one woman may really feel called to be primarily a mother and home-maker, while another equally fine woman may be called to be a doctor, lawyer, dancer, teacher, or something else entirely. One man may be called to be a scientist while another equally fine man may be called to be a soldier.

Each person has a calling, which may be as simple as working an ordinary job to support one's family. It may be running a large business, or even leading a country. That will be different for each individual and it may be different for the same individual at different times in life. Some actions which are totally appropriate for some, are inappropriate for someone with a different calling.

An example of this is nonviolence, which is totally appropriate for a monk, but not for a soldier defending his country. Every honest calling is a good calling. None are "better" than the others. All of them can be used as a path to the Sacred. All of them can be totally mundane and boring as well if we're not paying attention. The "best" path is the path you feel called to take at the time. Of course, Karma Yoga is not just limited to the work we do for a living, but all of our actions.

I think this concept of "dharma" is important because there is a tendency in the West to believe that there is one ideal way for all, but that is just not the case. Monastic life, for instance, can be a healthy, liberating life-style allowing an individual to be totally free to devote all his energy to spiritual life and serving others. However, if this life-style was forced on someone or they forced it on themselves thinking that somehow it was a better lifestyle, they would surely find it repressive, a tremendous burden and for them it would be definitely unhealthy.

I found it interesting when I was a monk that many people thought we were especially holy; others thought we were totally nuts. The ones who really got to know us knew that we weren't holy and knew that we weren't all that nuts, but were just ordinary guys trying to live good lives, trying to understand true spirituality and apply it in our lives. Just as there are various ways in which we can conceive of the Sacred there are various valid ways in which we can live our lives that will lead us to the Sacred. We don't need to concern ourselves so much with how other people choose to do that. We need to look within our own heart and find a way of life that is suited to ourselves.

The underlying premise of this path is that this whole world is divine. "Sarvam khalvidam brahma," means all this world is verily brahman. For the purposes of my discussion I will use that premise, however a more dualistic understanding could be used as well. All of this world is a creation of God. Either way everything and everyone in this world should be treated with love, kindness and respect.

The beauty of this path of Karma Yoga is that, with only a change of outlook most of what we are already doing can be given a spiritual turn, greatly enhancing our lives. When we cook or do other things for our family we are serving the divine in them. When we interact with people in the course of our day we can see the divine in them and treat them accordingly. When we interact with our environment, our tools, our cars and anything else we can treat them with respect. We can treat our own self with respect and kindness and gentleness and forgiveness.

I had beautiful examples growing up with my parents and

observing how kind they were with everyone who came across their path. My father was a junior high school science teacher. I am sure he was a good teacher but I would not be surprised at all if his biggest impact in life was as someone who treated all of his students with kindness and respect. As simple as this may seem, the importance of this cannot be overstated. When we set up a vibration of loving kindness within our own being, this vibration is transmitted to everyone and everything around us.

If we are in the habit of saying our mantra during the day or letting it flow internally this will help us keep the consciousness of the divinity of our surroundings alive and greatly enhance this practice and its effect on us and those around us. The concept of oneness in Hinduism is not abstract. By honoring the divine in our surroundings we are connecting with others and building relationships with others (other people, other nations, our animal friends, our house, our tools, our vehicles, our environment) in a very deep way.

By nurturing these relationships with attention, love, respect and honesty, we can roam through this world with hearts full of love and nary a care in the world. The whole world becomes our own. I mentioned my father whose whole life was filled with songs and kindness that manifested in a beautiful smile. Later in his life he developed Alzheimer's and he was still smiling. He walked into his bedroom one day and saw someone in the mirror smiling at him. Rather than be afraid he smiled back and the smiles between these new friends just got bigger and bigger. When he went to the nursing home he was still smiling and the nurses who remembered his kindness when they were his students in school reflected that smile and kindness right back to him.

As with all the yogas it is a good idea not to make it overcomplicated. Much of Karma Yoga is really so simple. There are a couple of things however that I wish to mention that will make this path easier. First, I want to reemphasize the importance of leading an ethical life. Some lines of work, however 'legitimate' or 'acceptable' they might be from an ordinary point of view make it really difficult to treat others with the respect they deserve. Second, it is important as much as possible to surround yourself with good and honorable people. One doesn't need to be judgmental to recognize that some people, divine though they may be at their core, bring us down.

Sri Ramakrishna used to say that god is indeed in everyone, but some gods we are better off saluting from a distance. I have had to make much use of that teaching in my life. We should respect all beings as divine and an important element in that is insisting that we ourselves are treated with dignity and respect.

Swami Vivekananda was, I believe, the great teacher of Karma Yoga, at least in the present era. In India at the time of Sri Ramakrishna and Swami Vivekananda (the end of the 19th century) the prevailing religious attitude was that this world is unreal; the good, religious person should have as little to do with it as possible and preferably renounce it altogether and spend his days in the temples or monasteries or forest and strive to realize God. This view, while not necessarily "wrong," was one-sided. Vivekananda declared with a strong voice and vision that if "all this world is verily Brahman," it was time to start seeing the divine in the poor, the sick, the homeless and uneducated and begin worshipping the divine in them.

The Divine is every bit as much in the poor villages and the slums of the cities as it is in the temples and monasteries. The goal of spirituality is to realize the oneness of our own self with the universal self. All feelings of separation are dissolved in that realization. While some people indeed are called to live an exclusively solitary life in pursuit of this most people, and society as a whole, are better served by seeing the divine in this world and developing compassion. By serving or "worshipping" the divine in the poor, the sick and others the focus of our attention is less and less on our own 'little' self and more and more on others. This helps to break down the barriers we have enclosed ourselves in. As I mentioned earlier in this chapter our sense of self expands. Service of others as spiritual practice helps us to see the divine essence in all things and in all beings. Karma Yoga is really quite simple. We are living and breathing in the presence of the Divine.

This world as we are experiencing it is our church and our holy temple. The more we treat it as such, the more our eyes will open and see it as such. This complements and strengthens the experiences attained in the practice of meditation and the other yogas and does so allowing us to live full and balanced lives. Practice of each of the yogas strengthens and enhances the practice of the other yogas.

I have tried in this chapter to give a glimpse of why the Hindu tradition has meant so much to this Iowa boy who grew up on the banks of the Mississippi River. It has given me the tools I continue to use to this day to connect with the Sacred and has given me a world view that allows me to expand way beyond any tradition at all. I give thanks to my teachers and I give thanks to myself for taking them seriously.

Om.

Infinite joy is our birthright. Infinite Existence,
Infinite Consciousness, Infinite Joy is our true nature.
We can run throughout the Universe searching for happiness,

searching for love, but That Joy, That Love resides in our own hearts and the hearts of all beings in this world.

Be still and treasure that Joy within yourself.

Be still and honor the Sacred shining in the sky and the sun and the moon and the stars and the planets, the earth and the rivers and oceans and mountains and trees.

Shining in all the great spiritual traditions of the world, in our teachers, ancestors, parents, children and animal companions.

Shining so brightly within our own hearts.

Be still and follow the sound of a flute, the sound of a holy mantra into the inner recesses of your heart and claim that Joy which has always been yours. With every breath you take, every thought you think, every word you speak and with your every action embrace that Joy and share it with the world. Let that Joy wash over you removing all vestiges of fear and anger and resentment and alienation.

It is time to choose. It is time to choose a world full of goodness and truth and love and light, a world where all beings, all nations and our Earth itself are treated with respect and kindness and love.

☼ ❖ ▣

Chapter Images

1. Don Stevens giving a talk at the Los Angeles Meher Baba group on May 21, 2005.

2. Jane Chin and her son, Jaden, whom Jane views as her youngest spiritual teacher.

3. Beads on One String gathering, Flagstaff, Arizona on November 4, 2006. (L-R) Haring Singh Khalsa, Ameeta Vora, Laurent Weichberger, L. Chandi New, Esther Stewart, Karl Moeller.

4. Laurent, November 4, 2007 in Flagstaff, at the Beads on One String gathering to discuss our process, and work to date, creating this book.

5. We sat in a circle at the Beads on One String gathering, November 4, 2007, in Flagstaff. L to R: Kelly McCabe (Hindu), Ameeta Vora (Jain), Laurent Weichberger (Meher Baba), Thom Knoles (Vedanta), Esther Stewart (Christian), and Haring Singh Khalsa (Sikh). Not shown: Yaakov Weintraub (Jewish), Karl Moeller (Sufi), Lopon Tsultim Wangmo (Buddhist).

6. The compassionate eyes of Maitreya, Buddha of the Future, gazes serenely from the Tikste Monastery, in Ladakh. –JO

8. Ganesh, the divine son of Lady Parvati and Lord Shiva.

7. When we visited Agra, India, November 2007, I met this Muslim husband and wife who allowed me to take their photo. –LW

9. "Avatar," a watercolor painting by Laurent Weichberger.

10. Mohammed (d. 2003), his given name was Tukaram. According to Meher Baba, he was a 5TH plane Majzoob (Mast-Allah) who lived at Meherabad, near Arangaon Village, Maharastra State, India, under Baba's care.*

11. Tomb of Hazrat Khwaja Banda Nawaz, d. 1422 ACE. His real name was Syed Mohammed Hussaini. He was possibly the son of Sayed Yusuf al-Husseini (Shah Raju Qatthal). This dargah is in Gulbarga, Karnataka State, India.

---

*For more about planes of consciousness and masts, see *God Speaks*, by Meher Baba, Chapter 8. See also, *The Wayfarers: Meher Baba with the God-Intoxicated*, by W. Donkin, Chapter 2, Section 1: Mohammed, p.43. (Myrtle Beach: Sheriar Foundation, 2001). For the life story of Mohammed see: *A Tribute to Mohammed the Mast* by Eric Nadel, in <u>Tavern-talk</u>, June 30, 2003.

12. Bismillah, "In the name of Allah."

13. Karl Moeller

14. Keeper of the Sayed Yusuf al-Husseini (Shah Raju Qatthal) dargah, near Khuldabad, Valley of the Saints, India.

15. Yaakov Weintraub and his beloved Jessica receive a blessing while wrapped in a tallit during a traditional aspect of their Jewish commitment ceremony. The tallit, a special shawl worn only during prayer, is wrapped around the couple at this time to symbolize their unity.

16. The Star of David, religious symbol of the Jewish faith, as it appears in the "Welcome to My World" mosaic at Meherabad, India. The mosaic contains tiles made by followers of Avatar Meher Baba from around the world, and all of the symbols from each faith.

17. (Above) Thomas M. Knoles; 18. (below) Kelly McCabe at the Beads on One String gathering, November 4, 2007 in Flagstaff.

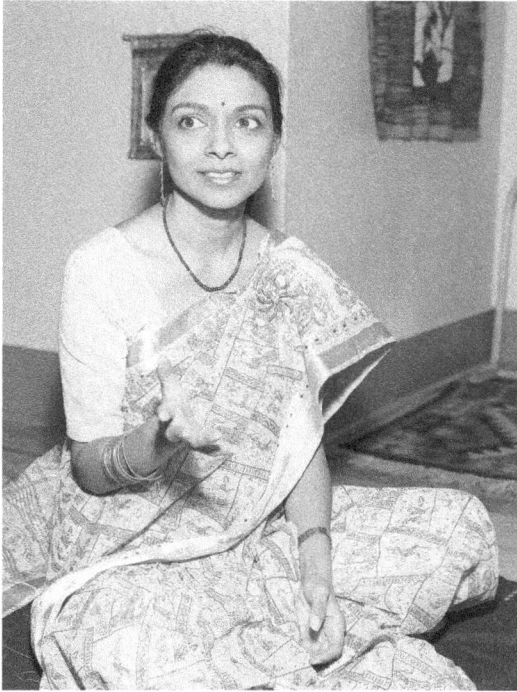

19. Ameeta Vora
at the Beads on
One String gath-
ering, November
4, 2007.

20. This photo looks out through
a window in our ancestral family home, called Hemnivas, in
Jamnagar. In the background,
a Jain temple can be seen. The
window depicts the form of a Jain
Tirthankara who sits beneath the
sacred Om. –AV

21. Mary Esther Stewart at the Beads on One String gathering, November 4, 2007 in Flagstaff.

22. An ancient Roman instrument for torture and execution, the cross is the accepted symbol of Christianity because it is through His death on the cross that our God in the person of Jesus took on the worst of our humanity and gave His all for love of us. The cross tells us that there is nothing in our lives that our God has not experienced with us.

23. Ek Ong Kar: The Creator and the Creation are One.

24. Haring Singh Khalsa at the Beads on One String gathering, November 4, 2007 in Flagstaff.

25. Avatar Meher Baba at his 1965 Poona Darshan.

26. In the Spring of 1986, I was handed this exact copy of Meher Baba's Universal Message in a coffee shop in Manhattan by Doug Stalker. Upon seeing Meher Baba's photograph for the first time, I immediately recognized Him as my Ancient One, my Master. -LW

27. (Above) Islamic Calligraphy, translated by Karl Moeller, reads: "Allah Beauty (or Grace) Power (or Majesty)." *
28. (Left) Laurent walking towards Meher Baba's Samadhi at Meherabad, India in November 2007.

29. One of the most important personages in the Valley of the Saints, Chishti master Zarzari Bakhsh, giver of the essence of gold. His real name was Muntajib al-Din, and he came to this area of the Deccan at the request of his teacher Nizamuddin Awliya of Delhi in the 14TH century. The modern Qutub-e-Irshad Shirdi Sai Baba had a profound spiritual connection to Qutub Zarzari Bakhsh, (see *Lord Meher*, Vol.1, pp. 70-71).

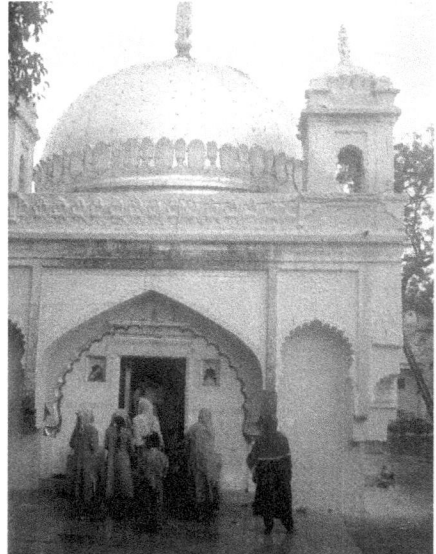

---

*Muslims are not allowed to make representations of God in art, however they are allowed to write about God's attributes. Tile is from the private collection of Laurent Weichberger.

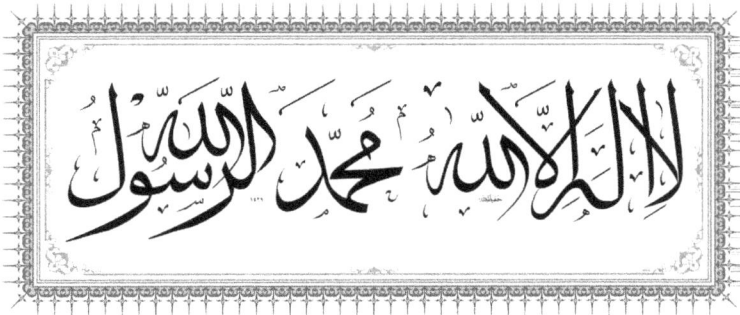

30. The First Kalimah: "There is no God but God, (and) Muhammad is His Prophet." (La ilaha illa Allah wa Muhammad ar-Rasul Lillah)

31. People come from around the world to meditate at the Golden Temple, which is surrounded by a large tank of water and a beautiful marble walkway known as the parkarma. The devotional songs of the Sikh Gurus are being sung continuously, 24 hours a day. This prayerful sound current, known as Shabd Guru, carries throughout the surrounding area. Just sitting on the parkarma, listening, and gazing across the water at the temple, is known to bring peace to one's mind. -HSK

The depiction of Shri Ghantakarna Veer*.

---

*The temple for Ghantakarna Veer is located in the ancient city of Madhumati, today known as Mahudi in Gujarat, India. In our home, this image of Ghantakarna Veer is placed such that his arrow points to the main door. Ghantakarna is worshipped for protection from evil. His symbol is the bell, which creates auspicious sounds in the atmosphere and clears stagnant energies. –AV

CHAPTER SEVEN

Jain: Radical Intent

Ameeta Vora with Geeta Vora

O M NAMO ARIHANTANAM
Obeisance to the Arihantas, I go to the feet
of those who have known
I bow down and offer my namaskar to Arihantas,* perfect,
omniscient souls. These humans have destroyed all of their
karma, which is the enemy of the soul's liberation.

Om Namo Siddhanam
Obeisance to the Siddhas — liberated bodiless souls
I bow in veneration to those who have shed all Karma and have
attained spiritual perfection. They have perfect knowledge
and have achieved liberation of their souls.

Om Namo Ayariyanam
Obeisance to the masters — heads of congregations
I bow down to those who lead the sangha, the Jain community
in the practices of being a perfect Jain.

Namo Uvajjhayanam
Obeisance to the teachers — ascetic teachers
I bow down to spiritual teachers, who teach sadhus and sadhvis.
They continue to learn from the masters and they teach us.

Namo Loe Savva Sahunam
Obeisance to all the ascetic aspirants in the universe

---

* "Ari" means enemy, and "Hanta" means destroyer. –AV

I bow down to those who strictly observe the five great vows of conduct and to all the sadhus and sadhvis (ascetics) in the world regardless of their discrete religious beliefs.

Jains are radicals! A Jain is a follower of Jainism, an ancient religion based on nonviolence. Simply, it can be said that it's based on the principle of respect for all Souls (Jiv) and therefore of absolute non-harm.

Having said that, you may already expect that a Jain is a vegetarian, perhaps even a vegan but can you imagine not ever having eaten any root vegetables such as potatoes, ginger, onions and garlic? Can you imagine not doing so because you believe harvesting the root, kills the mother plant; and disrupting the soil kills numerous microorganisms?

Jainism is a religion based on principles of nonviolence, a practice that is socially responsible, fostering a world that is safe for all living beings and leaving a very low impact on the environment. Jainism is a code of conduct that insists that all Jain practitioners consciously choose their actions with care.

A Jain walks a spiritual tight rope which is stretched over the chasm of "could be," with "must be" keeping them balanced. Although spiritual people in most religions think about how they could live their lives, Jains live their lives with radical intention. Jains show what and how it must be; there is no gray area for them.

Jainism is an ancient religion. Jains are followers of Jina or Tirthankara[1]. The most famous and recent Master is Mahavir[2] who is the 24TH Tirthankara and who was a contemporary of Buddha. Mahavir updated the religion and its philosophy, as there were 23 Jain Masters before him. Jainism as a religion is prehistoric, and monks or ascetics (called Shramana) who followed the precepts of the Jain faith are even referenced in the

Rigveda* and other ancient traditions. Jains do not believe in God as personified in other religions, nor is it a God that is a Creator and Destroyer as perceived by other religions.

There are two sects in Jainism:

1) Digambara (meaning sky clad)

2) Svetambara (meaning white clothed)

Digambara monks, called sadhu, choose to wear no clothes at all. Svetamabara have two sects within them: one that believes in the Supreme Being as one who is Niranjan Nirakar – shapeless and stainless, this sect is known as Sthanakvasi. The other sect is called Deravasi, and it is they who have built magnificent temples, such as the Dilwara Temples on Mount Abu.

Jains live by a code of conduct preached by these Masters (those who have gained victory over the cycle of life and death). A Tirthankara is born human and is a role model for all Jains. In their lifetime, the Tirthankara live an austere life of renunciation and meditation to come to understand the soul's true nature. All souls are perfect, and divine, and immortal – they come from a greater source. We believe in transmigration of soul, which is the same as reincarnation.

Jains define God as Godliness, it comes from right behavior (conduct), right thought and right knowledge. Love for all living beings, respect and honor for all points of view and having disciplined non-attachment, all of these virtues are attained only through self-control which are demonstrated by Tirthankara.

A Tirthankara has destroyed his or her ego and that destroyed anger, greed, and passion (cravings). They have reached God-consciousness, and ended their cycle of suffering which inevitably comes with the privilege of life.†

Mahavir's message is that karma is the cause and effect of our actions (present and past).[3] Jains believe that all life forms have a

---

*Rigveda is one of the first ancient Hindu scriptures, and it has been handed down from generation to generation as an oral (chanted) tradition. –AV

† The 22ND Tirthankara, Shri Aristanemi, was a cousin of Lord Krishna. –AV

soul. Although the soul has no weight, a soul's karma does. The weight of karma attaches itself to the consciousness of the soul and keeps it in the lower realm of consciousness. Karma traps us into superficial thoughts, and actions based on greed, wants, dislikes, and general negativity.

Karma obscures the soul's innate consciousness; therefore every living being suffers bondage due to the accumulation of karma. It confuses the priority for the soul's upliftment and it seeks bliss in wrong places through wrong action. In this process time that cannot be regained slips away. Imagine spending 20 minutes meditating on any aspect of the Divine, rather than watching a celebrity gossip show. Human life is a privilege, we are not merely instinct driven, and we are given a faculty of control over our sense, far greater than other creatures. This control of the senses by a human being is the spiritual path for Jains.

Each day, Jains are dictated to spend a period of 48 minutes (two Ghadi) in Samayik. This time is dedicated to meditation and prayer. Samayik is prepared for by wearing clean clothes on a freshly cleansed body, then after carefully sweeping the designated space with a soft broom (Rajoharan, or Okho), Jains lay down a woolen meditation mat.*

Once ready, Samayik is started with a short prayer that is a declaration not to move from that space for the following 48 minutes and to spend all of the allotted time in spiritual practice only. This is followed by time spent on prayer that narrates the 12 vows (Vrata†) of a Jain practitioner. By performing Samayik everyday Jains recognize and remember their Jain duties to themselves and the society.

At the fulfillment of the Samayik, there are some sutras

---

*Preparing for Samayik is a process of mindfulness, of checking the clothes that it doesn't have bugs that could be killed. –GV

†"Vrata" also means 'restraint.' –AV

(shlokas) we have to chant, and then ask for forgiveness if during that 48 minute period our thoughts have wandered. If we have thought to hurt someone, or spoken any words that hurt someone's feelings before Samayik, or if we have physically hurt someone, for all those things we ask forgiveness. We say Mitchami Dukaddam when we ask for atonement.

Twelve Vows
The Twelve Vows, called Vrata, are divided into three sections of conduct:

SECTION I: FIVE GREAT VOWS   The first five are referred to as Mahavrata, the Great Vows or the Key Codes of Conduct:

1. The First Vow is Nonviolence, Ahimsa. One of the most important ways that Jains demonstrate the code of Ahimsa, and compassion for all life, is through everyday choices in our diet and lifestyle. A natural conclusion for a Jain is vegetarianism. We insist on a diet of grains, legumes, and vegetables. The process of fermentation, such as wine and cheese making, involves the unsustainable rise and inevitable demise of numerous microscopic lives. Therefore the production and ingestion of wine and cheese is unacceptable as well as forbidden.

The consumption of milk, ghee (clarified-butter), and yoghurt is considered healthy and acceptable in Jainism since an animal is not harmed in the process. But many Jains choose to 'go vegan' to relieve the suffering of animals in modern dairy farms. Cruelties suffered by the dairy cattle include unhealthy life, physical injuries through unnatural diet, cramped living space, painful milking machines, overworked mammary glands and eventual slaughter.

Meat is forbidden for Jains because it requires an animal to lose its life. Jains feel that even the most miserable creature clings to life. In our opinion, the innocent animals raised for food are treated worse than prisoners of war. There are no protocols for humane treatment of animals or the emotional trauma that is suffered by the handlers and workers in this industry.

The animal farming industry creates an environment in which humans commit inhumane acts onto the helpless and speechless animals, which degrades the human soul, allows them to deny all kindness and creates unimaginable suffering in those animals. The creature suffers a variety of tortures, such as debeaking, burning, dehorning, castration, painful injuries, infections, unnatural diet and other unnecessary sufferings.

Jains are also actively involved in merciful acts such as endowing and running animal and bird shelters, veterinary hospitals, etc. This act is called Jiva Daya[4] – Mercy for the Soul. This is the most important principle for Jainism.

Clothing and accessories made with silks and leather goods are shunned by Jains. They are considered untouchable products as they are procured by cruelty. The products involve killing of animals for leather, and boiling alive of numerous silkworms for silk thread. These fabrics are unlike humanely harvested wool and cotton. Honey is also forbidden.

2. The second Mahavrata is Satya (truthfulness). The word means truth and the term implies living in truthfulness, and pursuit of truth with correct actions. It means living honestly, and avoiding falsehood. Living the life in the pursuit of truth one becomes the catalyst that insists on equal justice and equal rights for all – dignity for all life forms.

Mahatma Gandhi was deeply affected by the Jains in his life. His Satyagraha, insistence of truth, was a peaceful social movement that was his powerful act of defiance. He demanded from the ruling British government social justice for all native Indians.

Satya also means truth that is universally constant: undeniable, unchangeable, and undistortable.

3. The third Mahavrata is Asteya (not stealing). This vow is to guard against deception, corruption, and the temptation to shirk from social responsibilities. That includes the temptations to resist paying enough in taxes, not sharing with rightful owners, and justifying one's wrongful deeds.

4. The fourth Mahavrata is Brahmacharya (abstinence). The law of brahmacharya is different for monks or laypeople. Monks (sadhu) and nuns (sadhvi) are celibate for life, but all other Jains seek sobriety in their relationships. They avoid pre-marital and extra-marital sex. They are loyal to and respectful of their spouses. They avoid sexual indulgence, excessive infatuation and passion towards others, including the spouse. Sex as a goal towards procreation is promoted.

5. The fifth Mahavrata is Aparigraha (non possessiveness and non-attachment). Moderation is the key to a good Jain life. Possessions are inevitable; however, we seek non-attachment towards those possessions. This is an act of control over the mind and temptation of the soul.

Jains seek to live a simple lifestyle. They own few possessions, and those that have abundance seek to be helpful to others in the community. Jains give generously to Jiva Daya, improving and fortifying the quality of life of humans and animals alike. They are philanthropic leaders in helping the poor, creating better living conditions for the needy, sick, elderly and rescuing and funding sanctuaries.

These first five vows have most impact on the dignity of all souls. The following three vows help minimize the ecological impact – a smaller carbon footprint if you will.

SECTION 2: THREE VOWS OF VIRTUE   The three Gunavrata are Vows of Virtue or a code of social conduct:

1. The first Dishavrata (Dikh) vrata (to cultivate a discipline in one's nature to limit the amount of personal travel – the control of wanderlust). The ambition for unnecessary travel affects the earth by consuming resources needed for others, creating refuse (and pollution), and also causes unnecessary death for many creatures.

When the Jain monks travel, they do so with bare feet. They sweep the ground before them with a soft broom when they see bugs in their path. The monks and nuns do not travel during monsoon season, to spare the insects and creatures which abound in that season. Jains do not wear hard soled shoes. This fact has limited the spread of our religion.

2. The second vow of virtue is called Bhoga-Upbhogvrata (means enjoyment and re-enjoyment). In other words, we limit the excessive use of resources such as food, and forbid the use of drugs and alcohol. This vrata warns against the wants of accessories such as multiple cars, homes of excessive size, innumerable gadgets, costly fashions, and jewelry which inevitably come from disturbing the earth, mining and enslavement.

The attempt to pursue happiness through mere possessions, and indulgence of our senses, is checked through this vow. The soul seeks fulfillment through these things and it has an adverse impact on self-esteem and the environment. Many Jains choose to fast, about four days out of each month, in relation to this vow. Along with not indulging in rich and fatty foods, occasional fasting helps the digestive system to cleanse itself and release toxins. Tha Jain definition of fasting means that one takes an oath of no food intake for 36 hours. Only consumption of boiled-filtered-water is allowed.

3. The third vow is called Anartha Danda (means to abstain from harmful activities that serve no useful purpose). One shouldn't spend one's idle moments in activities that do not directly pertain to uplifting and improving quality of life. Examples of such harmful activities are gossiping, backstabbing, and spreading rumors.

The three preceding Vrata are a code of virtues that forge a Jain in this malleable world of multiple choices and newest offerings. The following four Vrata pertain to the discipline that Jains need to keep us in check with our moral code.

SECTION 3: FOUR SIKSA VRATAS The four Siksa Vratas are training exercises in self-discipline:

1. The first is Samayikvrata (a vow of meditation). Jains carry out this vrata by sitting in meditation to bring about tranquility of mind as we come into balance with our core values and resolve any ethical conflicts.

2. The second Sikshavrata is Desavakasika (the vow of limited duration of activity). Unlike the Dishavrata which speaks more to the area of travel, this vow sets boundaries and seeks to limit one's movement even within the house, to a single room. One vows to limit certain activities to a specific period of time, such as a Prahara (three hours) or a Muhurta (48 minutes).

This vow is an exercise in self-discipline & self-control, by creating boundaries for oneself, by creating small sections of time, you are limiting yourself according to your promise of what you will and won't do during that time. The example of this pertains to food, as Jains do not eat or drink after sunset.[5] They then take a vow called Chauviahar, which they have fulfilled in the morning after. What Chauviahar means literally is that during the four periods of Prahara (12 hours total), we take no food or drink.

3. The third Sikshavrata is Pausadha vrata (the vow of a limited ascetic's life). This encourages a layperson to live for a day strictly as if being a nun or a monk. Most Jains do so as a retreat from householder's (samsaric) life and spend a day every year in reorganizing priority and go to an Upashray or sthanak (an apartment where nuns and monks reside, teach, & counsel lay persons). During this day, the layperson is required to go begging for food, but only from Jain homes, and eat whatever he or she is given, and all of it as sadhu and sadhvi do when they accept alms.[6]

4. The fourth Sikshavrata is Atithi Samvibhaga. This vow is essential in teaching little children to have reverence for and extend help to others, including nuns, monks and members of the community. It basically involves being respectful and being cordial toward those souls that we don't recognize as friends, acquaintances or family. For example, we offer food to a guest before consuming ours in their presence. We teach our children from a very early age to extend kindness towards people in the community that need help. Giving to the ascetics in the community, of all faiths, is very important in the Jain Dharma.

Jain ascetics usually start as laypersons in the community who are drawn to the ascetic life at a very early age. Men and women are both inducted into the monastic order. Any practicing Jain can become a sadhu (monk) or sadhvi (nun), as gender, birth order (oldest son), and caste doesn't factor into this consideration as it may for Hindus. There are some exclusions, since those people who are attempting to escape societal obligations and human conditions such as debt and sickness, or criminals trying to escape sentencing cannot join.

Monastic life in Jainism is especially demanding. One goes through rigorous training before the initiation ceremony. There are many stages to becoming a Jain sadhu, and each stage is a deepening of the resolve and commitment towards a day of renunciation, which is particularly spectacular. After shedding all of one's worldly possessions, usually there is a parade in which all of the monetary wealth is strewn out towards the crowd of well-wishers. The final stage consists of plucking away all of the new sadhu's hair from the head, one by one.

The renunciate sadhu puts on white cotton and wool clothing and takes an Okho and after this the monk is ready for the life of an ascetic. They all wear a white cloth across their mouth (muhapatti), it signifies the straining of words, as well as restraint of passion and thought needed to do no harm. The muhapatti also encourages them in the path of Dharma. It is also worn so that they don't accidently kill any bugs by inhaling them.

The sadhu does not live in any particular shelter for an extended period of time. They live a very austere life. Their only possessions are the clothes on their back, a bowl with a lid (for bhiksha, food offered to them to eat), their Okho, and their religious books. They are not allowed to posses anything else.

They travel from community to community, except during the monsoon season when they are allowed to stay put for a maximum of three and a half months. Their travel is always barefoot, on foot, and only during daylight hours. They do not cook their meals, because they accept only what is given to them. This food cannot be made especially for them, except that the food should be prepared by strict Jain standards: freshly cooked, no leftovers, no animal products, no root vegetables, and it cannot be excessive in taste or ingredients. The monks and nuns must live a celibate life.

Jains believe in a very simple concept that's actually rather difficult to practice – compassion for all forms of life, all souls

(Jiva). This requires being mindful of the divinity of all life forms, human and non human, because they are essentially eternal and perfect. This compassion is an active and radical life style with little room for complacency. All souls have perception. A human birth is a privilege and an opportunity. As a human we have an ability to think about our decisions, how it affects our actions, and how our actions affect others. We must be more than basic instincts.

The greatest gifts we have been given in human birth are the gifts of reason and speech, which liberates our thought for communication of our highest aspirations. We can build our karma with words we use. Even when we have to correct someone harshly, we must think from a place of compassion, use gentle words of compassion, then with compassion we help the other person by compassionate example, thereby informing their consciousness. They may not correct their action immediately, but brushed by something nice, they have picked up some of those niceness-particles, and it has gone along with them. When you come from a place of compassion it keeps you from accumulating negativity, thereby minimizing your own stress, and karma.

Living a conscientious life means to live a life which reflects respect and reverence for all beings, no matter how small the life form. No life is insignificant. Harm done to any life form adds to the burden of the soul's karma. The type of action is what binds subtle matter, called karma, to the soul.*

Karma weighs the soul down, a bondage which makes the soul's liberation (Moksha) difficult. Such karmic activity distracts the soul from one's own true nature, causes unnecessary suffering to the soul and causes inflammation, disease and speeds the deterioration of the body, ushering in untimely death. Our

---

* Karma can be positive or negative, light or dark, if you will. –AV

activity and its karmic payout directly affect our body, mind, family, and society. Jains live a life of actively avoiding negative karma by living a gentle life.

The pursuit of most spiritual people is to find bliss for themselves (for their soul) and peace in the world. We all seek happiness, and we all seek to avoid pain. Religion keeps us from being just carried in the flow of wants and desires; it gives us a place to anchor, and a way to stay strong. There is a Pali word, Anekantavad, which means "multiplicity of views." It is so complex and so simple: everybody is right from their own perspective. Having a different view point doesn't invalidate the other person's experience and perspective.

The nature of Reality is so complex that you can look at it from a physical perspective, you can look at a table even, or the earth that we stand on, and see how firm and solid it is ... but if you look at it from the perspective of particle physics, or from space, you can't even see it, if you look at it as fire, it is destructible, but if you fall against it, it will break your bones. So the reality is ever changing, it has many perspectives, and as history has taught us, revisiting a piece of truth reveals so many different ideas, which were not apparent at the moment it was first presented.

Dr. L.M. Singhvi describes "Syadvad" simply and eloquently by saying, "Anekantavad leads to Syadvad (or relativity) which states that truth is relative to different viewpoints. Absolute truth cannot be grasped from any particular viewpoint alone because it is a sum-total of all the different viewpoints that make up the universe."[7]

Jainism is often misconstrued as a pacifist religion, and to call a Jain a pacifist would be a misnomer. Jains live a life of an absolute insistence on non-injury, hurt, harm, stress and pain towards self and others through physical, verbal, and mental awareness. Such harm can be caused to a living being (intentionally or unintentionally), through negligence, impulsiveness, or emotional stress. Harmful trades and vocations that harness bad karma are avoided by Jains, who choose instead professions that revere and protect life, free of violent livelihood and injuries to another Jiva. A disproportionate number of Jains choose livelihoods of business, finance and trade.

There is a musician who my daughter loves, adores, and admires. He is a man who is a pure vegetarian, to the point where he talks about his soy-milk, and vegan bran muffins. He is socially conscious, so he doesn't eat animal products, he wears "pleather" which is a vegan alternative to leather.

He screams his poetry into the microphone at concerts, thrashes and bashes like any good ol' punk, but he talks about gentle and beautiful things. Ok, the poetry has references to more thorns, blood and salvation than my Jain outlook but it is appropriate for his Catholic upbringing. He is kind and respectful, but when you see him you see a punk-rocker. He has tattooed arms and tattooed wings covering his back. He wears fake eyelashes and painted nails. He doesn't smoke or drink.

There is a movement in the punk-culture, it wasn't started by him, and it won't end there, called straight edge. It was started by a band, in Washington, DC, called Minor Threat, by a group of kids who decided that they were tired of watching kids burn out and die from abusing their bodies, all the while wanting to make a small change in their world.

The straight edge movement followers use no drugs, no alcohol, and do not engage in casual sex. The followers of the straight edge movement wear three Xs on them (in form of jewelry or tattoos), and it represents their movement. It looks like "XXX."

So my daughter thinks she's going to freak me out when she declares at a young age, "I'm going to marry him some day, Mom!" But the way I see it, she's going to bring home a nice Jain boy.

✦ ❖ ◉

Buddha in Sarnath, India *

---

* A golden Buddha displays the Vitarka Mudra, a symbolic hand gesture that illustrates The Turning of the Wheel of Dharma. –JO

CHAPTER EIGHT

Journey Into Tibetan Buddhism

Lopon Tsultim Wangmo

J ANGWANI SECONDARY SCHOOL WAS MY FIRST teaching assign-
ment after I graduated from Nazareth College. I was so excited
to go to a newly independent African country – Tanganyika.
What a beautiful name. The people had a beautiful song for their
country. The chorus was "Tanganyika, Tanganyika na kupenda
Tanganyika ..." (I love you, Tanganyika). The melody was un-
believably sweet. It was so wonderful to travel all the way from
Louisville, Kentucky to far away, far away Tanganyika on the
east coast of Africa. Kenya was to the north, Rhodesia bordered
the south, the Congo was to the west and 26 miles off the coast
was the enchanting little island country of Zanzibar. Oh, was I
such a lucky girl to be in for such a great adventure.

I truly needed this trip. I would be in Africa for two years. That
trip seems like a dream now – it was over 40 years ago. Among
the many reasons that I needed the trip is that I needed time to
think about my future. I needed a place of quiet and beauty in
which to think. I was lucky to be going to Dar-es-Salaam.

The program, Teachers for East Africa, asked the participants
their preference of location – did we want to be in a city or up-
country ... boys' school, girls' school or co-ed. There may have
been other questions regarding preference but I don't remember; I did not have a preference. Without stating a preference,
I got a location that I loved, Jangwani Girls Secondary School.
Someone must have told me what Jangwani means but I have

forgotten. I just love the sound of the word so it must mean
something beautiful.

As an urban school Jangwani did not have housing for teachers and staff on the compound. I lived in the Kinondoni Flats, a
residential compound for Europeans and other expatriates which
was about a five minute drive from the gentle and magnificent
Indian Ocean. After knowing only the rough grey white-capped
waves of the mid-Atlantic, the Indian Ocean was a mesmerizing
magical beauty. The shore was covered with soft tiny, white sand
pebbles which stuck to your feet and legs as you walked along.
Dar-es-Salaam, port of peace, was, indeed a very suitable place
for me to do the thinking about life that I needed to do.

While walking along the seashore I thought that I would
be able think about things at my leisure. But I wasn't that sure
when I returned to the flat with two roommates. The three of us
were assigned to Jangwani but Jangwani did not need three new
teachers. Fortunately, the roommates were transferred, the flat
was quiet and I could reflect on life, or so I thought. Before long
another American woman came to live with me. Even with one
roommate I had a hard time because her boyfriend was often
there. They were both wonderful people and good company, but
that wasn't the issue: I needed the continuous open space and
quietness. And, I had another problem. I had a boyfriend, too.
I did not call him a boyfriend but that is probably what he was.
It was fun having a "boyfriend" especially since this one was so
handsome, so engaging and many other women were attracted
to him. It was fun but it wasn't what I wanted.

So, we had an off-and-on relationship for nearly three years
& two continents. When I left Nazareth College, I was thinking
about entering a convent. I thought that I was trying to decide
whether to enter a service or contemplative order and that the

quiet of an isolated spot in Africa would help. I didn't realize that I really wanted to know whether I wanted to enter an order at all.

Although I was in the capital city, I thought the Kinondoni Flats, being near the ocean and far from downtown night clubs, would provide the quietness needed for reflection. The lure of the clubs and private house parties was too great. I found very little quiet time for reflection. My thoughts of convent life gradually faded. In fact, my enthusiasm for Catholicism also faded. Although I had good enthusiasm for my work as a teacher, I was otherwise unhappy.

In Dar-es-Salaam there was a large modern European bookstore that I enjoyed wandering through. One of the wonderful books that I found was a little paper Penguin Classics, Lao Tzu *Tao Te Ching*. I paid four shilling and fifty cents for it. I don't remember little details like that after more than 40 years, but I still have the little book and the price is in it.

Yes, it is quite worn, the pages are brown, very brown, and fragile. The cover is falling off and the binding has become unglued but not completely gone. I keep this little friend in a plastic bag now. This little book awakened me to the possibility. The possibility of what? The possibility of something else. No, not just something else, perhaps something more. Something more? More of what? No, not something more. The *Tao Te Ching* awakened me to the possibility that I can think about the expanse of being without limitation. The *Tao Te Ching* offered me a way to open my mind and experience the limitless. Times with the *Tao Te Ching* were moments of joy and expansion during years of bleak internal sorrow and suffering. Probably while still in the bookstore I read the first chapter:

The way that can be told
Is not the constant way:
The name that can be named
Is not the constant name.
The nameless was the beginning of heaven & earth;
The named was the mother of the myriad creatures.
Hence always rid yourself of desires in order to
observe its secrets;
But always allow yourself to have desires in order to
observe its manifestations.
These two are the same
But diverge in name as they issue forth.
Being the same they are called mysteries,
Mystery upon mystery —
The gateway of the manifold secrets.[1]

"The way that can be told is not the constant way ..." What on earth is the author talking about? I had no idea but I was fascinated. I wanted to know. The writer seemed to have some knowledge of my questions ... no, no not questions but confusion. I cannot say that I had questions because I did not know what I wanted to ask or find out about. I just knew that my life was confused and I did not know why. I had been told by family and friends and society at large what I ought to aspire to and what I ought to do. I tried to follow that guidance but I was not comfortable and had no idea that there were other possibilities or that my discomfort was legitimate. So, when the author says "The nameless was the beginning of heaven and earth," Is he talking about God? I wondered, If he is talking about God why doesn't he say so. From time to time I would read a segment from the little book and reflect on it. It was so wonderful to read a little then think, What does that mean? I would think and think and think, then conclude, Maybe it is this ... I don't know. The not knowing was encouraging and relaxing to me. I was confident that I would find what I was looking for. In retrospect, I realize that the words of the little book were indicators of possibility. They do not give a final answer, but suggest to the reader how to approach and live in harmony with the infinite. Even today I figuratively bounce up and down with excitement as a fan while watching her favorite sports team score winning points or an opera lover sigh when she hears an aria by Pavarotti. But these worldly comparisons do not come close to the exalted rapture of spiritual upliftment no matter how small it may be.

The *Tao Te Ching* helped me appreciate that Christianity or Catholicism are not exclusive holders of divine knowledge and wisdom. The two short years at Jangwani reinforced this message on a day to day tangible level. Under the old colonial system Jangwani was a school for Indian girls. With the gaining of independence from British colonial rule Tanganyika's schools were desegregated. For Jangwani this meant that European and African girls could attend. The girls of Jangwani represented many different religions. Sometimes I would think about the girls and their religions.

Soon after I arrived at the school with my two roommates, our English headmistress told us that often you could know the religion of a girl by her name. There was cute little Pratiba a Hindu, and Nassim a Muslim and Fatma a Muslim too but a different sect. Then there was the very bright and very attractive Parsi. Some of the African girls were Christian and, of course, some were Muslim. I adored all of them. That sounds like an exaggeration but I cannot remember one unpleasant girl. If there was one who was unpleasant and I have forgotten that she was, then I rejoice

in my faulty memory and may that girl be a good woman now.
When the girls appearing oblivious to my presence had their head
bent over test papers, I looked at them and wondered, How can
it be as I was taught? During my first year of college at Howard
University, I converted to Catholicism. I was taught that only
Catholics were in heaven. Here again I hope that my memory is
faulty or that I misunderstood the priest. I could not understand
why these good hearted young Hindu girls, these good hearted
young Muslim girls, these good hearted young Lutheran girls
... Why none of them would have a place in heaven. Little did I
know, at the time, that most religions are exclusionary. Little did
I know, at the time, that I was gradually developing a universal
and all inclusive view of spirituality.

When I returned to the United States, I was neither a nun nor a
Catholic. This was the spiritual doldrums. Then one day while
working as the secretary to an alternative private school in San
Francisco, a piece of junk mail was wrongly delivered. Since the
postman had already gone, I decided that I would walk it down
to the house where it should have gone. A week went by and the
folded piece of paper was still on my desk. I was curious about
the piece of paper so I carefully took the staple out and read
the notice. There was going to be a talk on *The Tibetan Book of
the Dead*. I had heard of that book but did not know what it was
about. So now was an opportunity to find out what the book was
about without having to read it. I copied down the address and
carefully re-stapled the paper, then walked it up the street to the
proper address.

The next Sunday afternoon, I stood on the porch of a large
and beautiful old brick house on 24TH Street, just off Delores in
San Francisco. The porch looked strange to me because it was

covered with shoes. People went in and left their shoes on the porch. I looked around and found a spot for my shoes, then went in too. A man seated behind a table greeted people and took their donation. Since I did not have any money that week I had called before and asked if I could come and pay later. I told this story to the man behind the table; fortunately he was the man I had spoken with on the phone who told me that I could come. I was then directed in to the front room which probably had been the living room. Now, however, there was no furniture in it. The walls were bright yellow with many pictures on them. There were two high altars with statues, little cups, candles and other things on them. But, the strangest thing in that room was that it was filled with people, quiet people sitting on cushions on the floor. So, I found a spot and sat down, too.

We sat quietly for such a long while that it seemed that this is what we were supposed to do and I gave little thought to our waiting to hear a talk on *The Tibetan Book of the Dead*. Suddenly there was a rapid booming sound of someone running down the stairs. Almost a quickly as that sound started the people jumped to their feet. I scrambled up too and barely had a glimpse of someone in red flash through the center aisle. Then the people quickly fell to their knees and started bowing. "Oh," I said to myself, "I think I will just stand here since I have no idea of what they are bowing to." I was very happy when they sat down then I could sit down too and hide my foreignness in the crowd.

After we sat down I could see that the person in red was seated on a high seat next to one of the altars. He began chanting from some papers. He chanted for at least two hours, I think. At the end of the chanting and the afternoon of teachings on *The Tibetan Book of the Dead*, I had no eagerness to hasten away even though the chanting was in a language that I did not recognize and not a word of English was spoken. In fact, I was looking forward to the next Sunday afternoon of teaching. I found my shoes and walked away from the big beautiful brick house very pleased but mystified. I still did not know the first thing about *The Tibetan Book of the Dead* but I was quite satisfied if not happy.

I still wanted to know what *The Tibetan Book of the Dead* was about. Over the years, I have read different translations of this book beginning with a translation by W.Y. Evans-Wentz. I wanted to know about life after this life. What else is there? In Christianity I had heard only enough to cause me to aspire to be good – to be rewarded by living forever in heaven with God. But, I never read or heard much about that heavenly paradise. I had heard about a place called hell but nobody talked about that place much either. Then there were ghosts, spirits, angels, demons and so forth but what I heard about them only caused me to be afraid or as in the case of angels be in awe. I wanted to know more. Well, I did not gain any empirical data that Sunday afternoon at the big beautiful brick house but I did gain a little happiness, similar to the happiness in reading the *Tao Te Ching* many years before.

From that day forth I went to KDK, the Tibetan Buddhist meditation center on 24TH Street, on a weekly basis. Within a short time I went to meditation on a daily basis. Before long I found a way to attend morning and evening meditation almost every day of the week. I feel very happy that my Buddhist life began in a center that offered twice daily meditations every day of the week, sometimes more on the weekends. This delightful period lasted about a year and then I was on my own. From then on I visited the center once in a while but never again on a regular basis. In fact, I have not attended any center with such enthusiasm on a regular basis for any significant period of time.

I became the supervisor of my own instruction and meditation guide. When the Shakyamuni Buddha walked the earth, he admonished his followers to know for themselves. He said to them, "Do not do this because I said so; know for yourself."

It is so much easier to quote the teacher rather than think for oneself and be the living truth of those words. It is so easy to ignore or forget that words are only indicators, symbols of something. And, our lives are also only indicators and symbols. All are symbols of a truth that we understand or do not understand. As it is said in the first chapter of the *Tao Te Ching*: "The nameless was the beginning of heaven and earth; the named was the mother of the myriad creatures ..."

My frequent, although sporadic, reading of the *Tao Te Ching* prepared the way for the study of the *I Ching*. About 10 years after my tour in East Africa, a psychology professor at San Francisco State College (now San Francisco State University) recommended that I read the *I Ching*. Oh, more riddles of life. I understood this ancient book to be a problem solver ... it could think for me and get me out of trouble or get me to where I wanted to be. As a tool of divination the *I Ching* did not quite work for me. Certainly a great part of the problem was that as soon as I tried to formulate a question, a new question from the original question arose, and I often ran out of time before I had found the final question. Because the *I Ching* is so fascinating it was hard to abandon the ancient text entirely. A few years after meeting the professor at San Francisco State, I was guided to a wonderful spiritual teacher called Ellen.

Through Ellen, I received a good grounding in Western astrology, but more importantly Ellen took me to a deeper and more spiritual level of the *I Ching*. Now my life was really changing. I was beginning to understand change. I was beginning to understand the folly of fighting against change. I was understanding the nature of a turbulent but ordered world and the nature of a tranquil mind. There could be no understanding of turbulence without an understanding of tranquility. This was very slow learning, segment by segment, with no connecting of the segments. There was an understanding of a yin, and of a yang, but no conscious understanding of yin-yang. An understanding of "Wu," the sacred whole, unity, and oneness was yet to come. *

First Noble Truth
Clearly Lord Buddha's, First Noble Truth, the truth of suffering was a new revelation. All beings are aware of the suffering or discomfort in the ordinary course of events of their lives. Most human being suffered the discomfort of wet diapers, but we don't remember those times. Suffering doesn't just mean moaning and groaning or screaming in pain. It is not carrying a heavy load on our shoulders, both figuratively and literally, day in and day out. Suffering can be simply missing a phone call that we wanted to get. It can be answering the phone with a telemarketer on the other end. It can be running to catch a bus, sitting in traffic, standing in line at the grocery store, opening the mail box to a stack of junk mail. Suffering is not getting what you want, and getting what you don't want. Suffering can be very simple – a tossed salad when you order Caesar or very profound – a tsunami when you expected a smooth suffering wave.

Suffering as expressed in religious dogma sometimes seems foreign and mere words of doctrine. When, however, listening to the lyrics of American blues music, one can hear the expression of suffering complete with its primary component parts. Most blues music is an extraordinarily poignant expression of the inseparable intermingling of pain and joy within the same

---

*For a great book on Wu and its relationship to sacred oneness through the medium of physics, read: *The Dancing Wu Li Masters: An Overview of the New Physics*, by Gary Zukav (Harper One, 2001) –LW

experience. One of the best known blues is the "St. Louis Blues" by W.C. Handy. In it a woman is lamenting the loss of her lover, "I hate to see the evening sun go down …" Many of us, particularly children, have enjoyed a late afternoon of fun and play, and then suddenly realize that it is getting dark and the fun of the day must come to an end. As beautiful as the evening sun is, there is often a sigh of, "Oh, no, I have to stop now." Later in the song, the sighing woman sings:

> St. Louis woman wid her diamon' rings,
> Pulls dat man around' by her apron string.
> Twant for powder an' for some store-bough hair,
> De man I love would not gone nowhere.

Oh, yes, it is someone else's fault that the man left. Although the man is gone, the poor woman cannot let go …

> I loves dat man lak a schoolboy loves his pie,
> Lak a Kentucky Colonel loves his mint an' rye.
> I'll love that man till the day I die.

Worldly suffering must contain an aspect of attraction. There must be something wonderful in the person, item or event to which we are attracted. Without that aspect of beauty the attractive would have no power over us. Throughout the song the lamenting woman speaks mainly of the physical beauty of her man. Only once does she speak of any internal quality, and this is not an admirable virtue.

> "Dat man got a heart lak a rock cast in de sea, or else he wouldn't have gone so far from me …"

When we have an off-balanced attraction it is difficult to appreciate the power of other qualities in the attractive to cause unhappiness or, in other words, to cause suffering. This feeling of loss is common in the Blues.

Suffering is the experience or feeling of loss. More significantly, it is a subtle but pervasive feeling of the fear of loss. An often unrecognized feeling underlying the gaining of anything is a concern over the loss of that thing. We lock our homes, our cars, our lockers at school or work And tragically some of us even lock our hearts from fear that we will lose something that belongs to us. When the whole of existence on the earth is examined, the element of loss – whether gross or very subtle – pervades everything in the material world. When I was a little girl of nine years, my father was completing a tour duty in post-World War II. The family was leaving the little town of Kitzigen. Among all the tasks my mother had, she also had the chore of dragging me from the house, trying to comfort me while again dragging me along the platform to the train that was to take us to the port for sailing back to America. I did not want to go; I loved the little town and my life there. All this is suffering. My mother tried to trick me into wanting to go by telling me that I would see my grandmother again and "Don't you want to see her?" Of course I did, but I did not want to leave my beloved Germany forever – suffering. No more tears, but suffering none the less.

The poor woman singing the St. Louis Blues would have had no suffering if she had not been in love with her man, in her words, "... I'm most wild 'bout my jelly roll ..." The obvious cause of her suffering was that she was in love with a man who left her. The obvious cause of my suffering in 1949 was that I was in love with a way of life that I had to leave. Neither the woman nor I understood that great personalized attachment based only on self-interest inevitably leads to suffering. This personal self-interest suffering leads to quarrels between people and wars between nations.

After experiencing the initial hurt of a discomfort, many of us look for a cause. Probably we first learned cause-finding as little kids overhearing adult conversations, If she just hadn't ... then ... would not have happened or, Now, see what you have done! or, Aren't we the lucky ones; Mr. Smith has given us ....

Even little animals know cause and effect. Once I heard a loud crash in a room where my young cats were playing. I went into the room. One cat was standing on a table. One cat was standing on the floor near the table. I don't know where the third cat was. The two little cats appeared frozen, and with wide eyes stared at me as I looked at them. As soon as I looked down and saw the broken lamp on the floor, the two cats ran like greased lightning. They knew that their wild play had knocked over a lamp, broken it, and that the human would probably yell angrily at them. How could they suspect that something went wrong with their play? By observing other living beings we see that without knowing the words, almost every living being has a sense of cause and effect. Even considering that some responses of humans, and other beings, may be instinctual – the natural law of cause and effect functions in beings and phenomena of the universe.

Having recognized and verbalized to himself the universality and inescapable nature of suffering in the world Siddhartha, the great Bodhisattva, wished to know why. Perhaps my little cats wondered why the lamp broke when it touched the floor; why didn't it just bounce around like they do? If the cats had given thought to the matter they would have figured it out. The great Bodhisattva did give thought to the matter of why there is suffering in the world. He realized that there are causes for suffering.

While walking about the town of Rajagha, Shariputra (who at that time in his life was known as Upatissa) saw one of the Shakyamuni Buddha's advanced disciples, Assaji, on his morning alms round. Upatissa was intrigued by the deportment of the monk and, at the appropriate time, inquired about the Buddha (his teacher) and his teaching. Assaji gave a succinct reply. He said,

> *Of those things that arise from a cause, the Tathgata has told the cause ...*[2]

Those are the first words from the historical Buddha which Shariputra ever heard and he understood them clearly.

Second Noble Truth
There is a cause for everything. In the first Noble Truth that the unenlightened experience suffering, the Shakyamuni Buddha stated in fairly simple language that which was already known, and he uses the known as a first premise to lead logically to the next statement of the Four Noble Truths. That is, there is a cause for whatever exists. Things, events, experiences do not come into existence without a cause. The statement of Assaji to Shariputra does not exactly say that nothing exists without a cause. Rather it implies that whatever comes into being comes from a cause. In the second line we understand that the Shakyamuni Buddha knows that cause and is willing to tell others what that cause is. This second Noble Truth that things arise from a cause (or causes), is also not particularly new, but it is not something that people in ancient times or present times often think about. As related to the First Noble Truth of the existence of suffering, the Second Noble Truth tells us that there is a cause for suffering (or any discomfort we may feel). Certainly this is understandable

in the physical sense. I stub my toe on a stone, trip and fall and have pain in my foot and my knees and other places in my body. Immediately I may think that the stone is the cause of my pain. If, however, I examine the situation further I may think that my not seeing the stone is the cause of my pain. If I look even further into the situation I may see that my inattentiveness to my stepping caused the pain. The cause of suffering is not necessarily a linear tracing of events. Maybe more like a geometric pattern or like the movement of a kaleidoscope with one slight movement causing multiple movements.

Third and Fourth Noble Truths

Unlike most of his contemporaries, the Shakyamuni Buddha did not identify God as the First Cause or the Uncaused Cause. Rather he identified the cause and result of things in a view which describes interdependent origination or dependent origination. This seems similar to the concept of the *Tao* in Chinese philosophy. By taking a superficial look at the *Tao* through the *I Ching* we see that the beginning concept is of oneness. In the Third Noble Truth we are told that there is a way to live in peace with a calm and compassionate mind, never again to be confused by the ordinary nature of life. It is the Fourth Noble Truth that contains the sum of the Shakyamuni Buddha's teaching.

Over the centuries, many schools of Buddhism have developed emphasizing particular aspects of Buddha's teaching. The particular schools are also "dressed" in the styles of the cultures in which they arose. Yet, all hold confident faith in the Great Teacher, the Shakyamuni Buddha, his Teachings and in the community of beings that follow (or at least attempt to follow) those great teachings on liberation from suffering. All Buddhist teachings are essentially an expansion of the Fourth Noble Truth.

Liberation
The Shakyamuni Buddha, began his last human life, his last life
as an ordinary sentient being as the Prince Siddhartha probably born in the 6TH century BCE (before the common era). His
father was King Suddhodana and his mother was Queen Maya,
belonging to the Shakya clan.[3] The word "muni" means a sage
or wise person. There are at least four significant places of the
historical Buddha's life which have become places of pilgrimage;
they are his birth place at Kapilavastu (now in Nepal)[4], the place
of his enlightenment (modern Bodhgaya, India)[5], the place of
his first teaching (modern Sarnath, India) and the place of his
parinirvana, the location of his "last death" where he physically
passed away at Kusinara, India.[6]

There are many more holy places but these are principal
milestones in his impressively long life of 80 years. Having begun his life as a child of the privileged class, a prince, he wanted
for nothing and was doted upon well into his twenties when he
married the lovely princess Yasodhara.[7] Sometime before Siddhartha consented to marriage, he appeared to be uncomfortable
with his lifestyle. In fact, according to some reports, he was not
enthusiastic about marriage. In the commonly told story of how
disenchantment with his life and the condition of life in general
arose in the young prince, he was traveling about the town when
he witnessed four extraordinarily disturbing sights: an old person, a sick person, a dead person and lastly, an ascetic.

On each trip after seeing the unusual person, he expressed to
his charioteer, Chanda, his disturbance in seeing that person.
He asked Chanda to explain what had happened to that person.
Chanda's explanation of the first three people – the old person,
the sick person and the dead person, left prince Siddhartha so
disturbed that he cut his pleasure trip short and returned home

to reflect upon the scene. Chanda's explanation of the tranquility of the ascetic was not particularly disturbing, but rather was intriguing. Nevertheless, prince Siddhartha shorted his pleasure trip and went home to ponder all four experiences.

A summary of his ponderings can be put into two questions:

1. Why are the people suffering?
2. Why did the ascetic seem peaceful without any suffering?

It is not clear from the literature that I have seen how long he meandered about his home pondering the questions before he decided that he had to leave home and pursue the course of the ascetic, since it appeared that his lifestyle might have some answers he sought. Certainly, it was clear that the ways of the old man, the sick man and the dead man were not lifestyles that he cared to pursue. Much to the dismay of many (including his parents, and wife, and Chandra the charioteer), the prince Siddhartha left home to follow the path of a wandering ascetic. Because Buddhism currently has many different forms, it is important to understand that the primary focus of the noble quest of Siddhartha was to find a permanent end to suffering which included within it a permanent way of peace.

In his brief stay and study with his first teachers, Alara Kalama, and subsequently Uddaka Ramaputta, two of the leading master teachers of his time, Siddhartha, the Great Bodhisattva, mastered their teachings. The Great Bodhisattva realized that while the teaching he had received brought him great peace, they did not offer him (or any practitioner) a permanent release from suffering. In the Sutta of the Noble Search[8], the Great Bodhisattva describes Alara Kalama's Dharma in this way:

> *This Dhamma does not lead to disenchantment, to dispassion, to cessation, to peace, to direct knowl-*

edge, to enlightenment, to Nibbana, but only to reap-
pearance in thè base of nothingness.[9]

The Bodhisattva thanked Alara Kalama for what he had given him, and then continued his spiritual search.

His study with the teacher, Uddaka Ramaputta, brought a similar result. Through the application of his "faith, energy, mindfulness, concentration, and wisdom" Siddhartha mastered Uddaka Ramaputta's teaching. On this Dharma of Uddaka Ra-maputta, Siddhartha commented:

> *This Dhamma does not lead to disenchantment, to*
> *dispassion, to cessation, to peace, to direct knowl-*
> *edge, to enlightenment, to Nibbana, but only to*
> *reappearance in the base of neither-perception-nor-*
> *non-perception.*[10]

These levels of awareness are profound and difficult to reach, yet the great Bodhisattva knew that there was something more and he intended to find that something more. But, now he had no teacher so for approximately the next six years he became his own teacher. He searched through his mind, simultaneously expanding his consciousness beyond the finite mind. This was a concentrated daily and nightly search. There were no breaks to go to an amusement park or have dinner with friends. After nearly six years of constant meditation, the Buddha-to-Be re-membered a childhood experience while sitting under a tree in a field waiting for his father. By entering that same form of meditation, the Buddha-to-Be transcended all that he had previ-ously experienced and in successive stages blossomed into the ultimate of the unconditioned.

What marvelous persistence. When we look at the stages of development of the Prince Siddhartha, we can benefit from considering our own stages of spiritual development.

Through his Noble Search to find an end to suffering, an end to the suffering of sickness, of old age and of death, the Great Being found the path to enlightenment. Probably for most of us, our first meeting with discussions about enlightenment (and the unconditioned), our unspoken initial response is, What? Being aware of the difficulty for others to understand what he now understood, the Shakyamuni Buddha felt an initial disinclination to teach it to others. However, realizing the value of what he had learned, he found a method for teaching those who would understand and who wanted to understand. The underlying support for his initial teaching was the Buddha's great compassion for the suffering of others. It is good to remember that according to the personal history of the Shakyamuni Buddha (as the Prince Siddhartha) he was shocked to realize that he, too, would grow old like the old man he saw in the street; he too would probably get sick like the pitiful man he saw lying on a pallet; he too would definitely die and lie like the corpse he saw in the street. This is a typical human reaction to the apparently harsher aspects of existence.

I don't know how old I was when I knew that I was going to die – one day. Certainly I was aware before my teenage years. One day, I heard my mother talking with her friend about some person. Her friend said that the person had been his friend for ten years. I think the person had died, but I stopped listening to the conversation when her friend said, "... friends for ten years..." Why, I had not even been alive for ten years.

Part Two: The Heart of Buddhism
The Buddha's teaching is abstracted in the "abidharma" litera-

ture. The Buddha's direct teaching was in story form, parables and metaphors. These are methods of gradual understanding. Direct understanding is often overwhelming or shocking – shocking enough to kill. I recall the story of the two frogs: one from a little pond and one from a big lake:

> *Once there was a little frog who lived in a small pond. A big frog from a big lake came to visit him one day. The big frog commented on how small the pond was compared to his lake. The little frog exclaimed, "That's impossible! There is no water bigger than my pond." Since the big frog could not convince the little frog of the hugeness of his lake by mere talking, he invited the little frog to go with him to his home. The little frog consented and they both traveled out to the big frog's lake. When they arrived at the edge of the lake, the big frog said nothing. The little frog's eyes, big as they were, got even bigger. Before the big frog could say anything to calm his little friend, the little frog slowly blinked his eyes then fell over in a faint. Some say he died because he could not grasp the vastness of the big lake that the big frog lived in, however, I think the big frog patted his head and revived him because the big frog had no intention of killing his little friend.*

What then happened to the little frog was similar to what happened to my little friend, Juma, when I took him on his first trip to the shore of the Indian Ocean in Dar-es-Salaam, Tanzania. Juma was anywhere between five and seven years old, maybe older I don't really know. He was the son of one of the housekeepers at the apartment where I lived. Juma was so cute. He had a smooth round face which was either smiling or looking with curiosity from around a corner of the building when I drove into the garage. One day, with the permission of his mother, I took him to the ocean which was only about a five minute drive away. When we reached the ocean I drove along the road which ran parallel along a high bank about 50 yards from the ocean until I saw a good place for us to walk down to the water.

I got out of the car and started down to the water. I was feeling very happy and cheerful being very sure that Juma would also enjoy the trip to the ocean. Juma didn't move. He was fixed to his seat. He didn't get out of the car. After much anxious cajoling by me, he at last got out, took a few steps then stood as if paralyzed in the sand just staring at the gentle waves of the water. I became more and more anxious fearing that I had done a very bad thing. The little boy looked traumatized. How would I explain this to his mother? My heart began to pound as I thought, He's going to cry. He's going to run away. What shall I do? Suddenly Juma jumped in the air, rolled in the sand, jumped in the air again, then ran down to the water, splashed his feet, laughingly threw himself down and rolled around on the sand. That's what the little frog did after the big frog revived him. He realized that there is so much more to the world than his little pond ... and it is glorious.

The little frog and the big lake, Juma and the Indian Ocean, remind me of the blessing of Great Compassion in Buddhist teachings. I thought I knew what great love is and that I had it until I studied the teachings on compassion and practiced calm abiding meditation. My feelings of love for humankind were based in the teaching of Jesus that I learned in Sunday School. By the time I was nine or ten, I felt an overwhelming sense of love. I felt almost as if I were made of love and that I had too much love for one person to hold. I had no idea of what to do with such a great love. At the same time I felt sad. I felt sad because I knew that I could never marry. A person who had as much love as I had for all people and all things could not be content limiting that love in an ordinary marriage. I thought that the ideal thing for a girl to do was to get married when she grew up; it was a bad thing to not be married. This thought made me very unhappy. In time I resolved the conflict by deciding that I would marry a missionary minister who worked with people on a Caribbean island. I saw myself as a fat little round lady with a sweet smile. All the children loved me and I loved them all. In my fantasy I could hardly walk with all the children hanging about my waist. What a great fantasy.

Probably in thinking of my great love I was not very different from most people. We often think we have great love and good love and good feelings and good wishes for everybody, but usually these feelings of loving-kindness and compassion are extended to others in the shape of our own personal feelings of love and concern for the welfare of others. These good feelings are often limited to those whom we know and to the good people we imagine to be in the world. These feelings, good and kind as they are, are actually limited extensions of the personal ego, just as the little frog's pond was the extent to which he could view life. From wherever he sat on the edge of his little pond he could see all the edges of the water where it met the land. Juma had never seen the ocean before so his sweet mind was shocked by the vast expanse of water. My childhood fantasy as a good minister's wife on an isolated island in the beautiful Caribbean Ocean was limited to the island and the people of the island; I did not think beyond the water's edge. I was like the little frog in my pond. When I learned that there is more to loving than what I knew as a ten year old – real or in my fantasy – the new knowledge was almost ungraspable.

The Loving-kindness and Great Compassion that is met in Buddhist studies initially sounds so wonderful and ungraspable. Sometimes I heard people say, upon hearing that attachment to the ego must be released to experience the beauty and vastness of Loving-kindness, Compassion and Wisdom of the Buddhist teachings, that it sounds wonderful but they cannot give up their ego. Such a release, they say, is too scary. Who then would they be if they had no ego? Perhaps with the gradual release of attachment to the ego they would become Bodhisattvas or Buddhas? Certainly, they would not be lost in a vast expanse of nothingness. Abandoning attachment to the ego is recognition that the personality has limited function; it does not last forever, but it has the important function of relating to oneself and the world in which one lives. The ego (or personality) can be a unique vehicle through which Divine Love and Wisdom is expressed. What is lost by abandoning attachment to the ego is a limited view of life which carries with it a fear of the unknown. What is gained by abandoning attachment to the ego is an endless expression of loving – limitless and vibrant hope for the permanent expression of universal good for all beings.

When it is realized that this kindness and compassion extends beyond family and friends, community and country, this world and universe, this galaxy, this present time, the past time and future, one can faint like the little frog or become paralyzed like Juma. The wish that all beings have true happiness and be free of suffering of every nature is an ever expanding and encompassing view which at the same time reduces egocentricity. Although initially this concept may be difficult to hold in the mind, through the power of meditation and study, the individual is able to fearlessly, gradually, abandon attachment to her or his own being and experience the incredible wonder of Great Compassion.

When Great Compassion and wisdom is experienced even marginally, the individual realizes that she has been living within the invisible shell of the personal ego. Once the shell of the personal ego has been broken, we can see (in an embarrassing way), the smallness and narrowness of our love for others. Becoming aware of that we, as lovers of all that lives, allow our reservoir of Divine Loving-kindness, Compassion, and Wisdom to expand to unimaginable depth, breadth and height. Divine Loving-kindness, Compassion, and Wisdom are three different facets of the same magnificent way of being.

What is Divine Loving-Kindness?
When I was a little kid, I suspect that I thought of myself "a being of love" in a very vague sort of way, but I didn't use those words. I had never heard that particular combination of words. Nevertheless, I felt a self-consciousness in caring about other people and things. I felt hurt and outrage when others were unjustly hurt. On one occasion when I was about eight years old, my friends and I were playing on the streets of Kitzigen, a little farming town in Germany. A man was talking with us and someone must have asked him about the numbers tattooed on his arm. He told us how he had gotten the numbers in a concentration camp during the war (World War II). He was really a very pleasant man and we listened to him with great interest.

In retrospect it is a strange memory. I don't remember the friends I was standing with but I think most of them were little German kids who I played with near my home. I remember the man's smiling face with very kind, soft blue eyes and the patch of skin on his arm with a stream of blue-green numbers on it. I was very sad and I think my friends were, too. I think we were sad about his being in a concentration camp. I was very sad that he could not wash the numbers off. They had been on his arm for years. The man's story gave me another reason to not like war.

I disliked war even before I knew what it was. My mother, sisters and I joined our father who was in the American occupation army in Munich, Germany in January, 1949. Many of the buildings were broken down. I did not know why the buildings were broken down. I saw people looking in garbage cans for food. Later we moved to a little farming town called Kitzigen. In those days, the farmers used ox drawn carts to haul things. Sometimes I saw people scooping up the manure of the oxen from the street. I didn't know why they did that.

One day I saw a old woman scooping up the manure. I was upset because I knew that the German people didn't have enough food and were hungry. I tugged at my mother's skirt and whispered up to her my question, "Is she (the old woman) going to eat that?" I was pleased to hear my mother say no. I do not recall if she told me that the woman was going to use it to fertilize her garden or not; I was just very relieved to know that she was not going eat it. I knew the "war" had caused this terrible situation.

Luwall was the husband of a lady who helped my mother around the house. One day he came to our house wearing his German army uniform. He had just come home from a prison camp in Russia where he had been during the war. Luwall had such a strange look on his face. I had never seen such a look before.

Now, more than 50 years later, I guess that look would be called shock. I saw that look again in 1963 or 1964 after a violent revolutionary upheaval on Zanzibar. A friend who had been living there came to Dar-es-Salaam where I was living. When I saw his face I knew it was the same look that Luwall had when he came home from Russia. Since I knew what had happened in Zanzibar, I immediately had a sense of what Luwall must have experienced in Russia. No, I don't like war, but I knew that in 1948 when I was only eight or nine. War causes too much sorrow and suffering. Prince Siddhartha as a young man was led to seek a way to be free of suffering after witnessing suffering and sorrow in his town.

There are other early memories of sad things. Some of the sad things are sorrows that I caused to others. It is good to remember these events, then clean out the sadness and infuse the memory with kindness and understanding people, event and times. This helps to purify the mind and increase attentiveness in all one's activities and thoughts. This improves one's ability to express love and aspiration to higher good in one's life.

Sometimes a person's own religion is so special to him, that it is easy to neglect the value of other religions. My childhood was based in a Protestant home. I understood the kindness of Jesus. I am sure that in a subtle way, observing the suffering and sorrow of people around me as a child in Germany made it so easy for me to embrace the love of Jesus that I learned in Sunday School. And this, the love of Jesus (strange as it sounds) lead me embrace the teachings of the Shakyamuni Buddha almost 30 years later.

Over the years I have read some teachings on mind training & the development of compassion. I have tried to practice some of the methods of training. No method touches my heart or moves my mind with the shame of not helping or with the desire to totally dissolve into the energy of loving-kindness and service as does the well-known prayer of Saint Francis of Assisi: "Lord, make me an instrument of your peace ..." It may be asked, How can a Buddhist make such devotion to the meaning of this prayer composed by a Roman Catholic? Obviously when the good monk wrote the prayer he did not have the Buddha Shakyamuni in mind. I see the "Lord" and the "Divine Master" as the Buddha Shakyamuni.

Compassion, Wisdom and Emptiness

The ordinary definition of compassion is a feeling of great sympathy for the discomfort, suffering, pain of another to the extent of wanting to relieve that suffering. Sometimes compassion can be so greatly felt that the sympathetic one feels physical pain or mental anguish. We have heard of the sympathetic labor pains of a father-to-be. We have heard of people who feel such pain and suffering for another that the sympathetic ones are unable to eat or sleep. We have also heard of the stigmatics[11], the people who so identify with the suffering of Jesus the Christ, that open and bleeding wounds appear on their hands, feet, forehead and other significant parts of their bodies. In contemporary times, Theresa Neumann of Germany is probably one of the better known stigmatics.

Many of us have had the experience of so strongly identifying with the suffering of another that we wish we could take on the suffering to relieve the one so dear to us. I recall an occasion many years ago when my cat Bella was sick. I did not know what was the matter with her and I felt so terrible that I wished that I was the sick one, because I could tell the doctor what was bothering me. Poor little Bella looked so unhappy and could not say anything.

Within the day I felt quite sick and Bella was well. I had only made a wish; I did not know that the transference could really happen. When seeing the loved one free of pain and happy, the compassionate one is happy despite her own pain. The true compassionate one will endure this suffering again and again to bring happiness to others. I, however, was really glad when I wasn't sick any more. My prayer thenceforth was that neither of us gets sick ever again; I did not enjoy it and didn't want the experience again. It is easy to write about compassion in an idyllic fashion but it is difficult to experience it with a pure heart and mind.

Compassion or its semblance is also difficult to think about, much less experience, when a person feels angry about something. However, once it is realized that compassion is the better feeling, the person suffering from anger must examine the anger. She must ask herself, Why am I angry? What did that person do to me? Why was that situation so upsetting? When the situation or encounter with another is carefully examined, it is seen that the angry person's reaction is the "anger" and not the other person or the situation. The other person (or the situation) is the condition which allowed the anger to arise. Now, it is important to ask, Why did anger arise?

Again, careful examination shows that anger arose because the "angry person" was hurt in some way. The "angry person" was offended in some way. The offense was a wounding of the angry person's self-hood, her sense of well being, her feeling of being whole, her ego. The anger has put us in a scary situation whether or not we consciously recognize it. We've been offended, anger has arisen, and the anger has brought along with it a companion, fear.

Fear tells us that there is no room for compassion in our lives. Anger tells us that the cause of this terrible situation is external to ourselves; the only way to restore a harmonious situation is to destroy the external cause of the anger. If we follow this path of reasoning we do not realize that anger arises from fear, and fear arises from misplaced attachment to the self or ego.

Now, we must ask, What is this self or ego that I am so attached to? Why do anger and its buddy fear so quickly rush to its defense? In American society, we are taught from childhood (or even maybe even infancy) that we must have a strong ego. But we must also realize that this ego we are taught to develop is only a superficial and limited view of the being. The ego (or self) that we become unconsciously attached to is only functionary, it is limited in scope and use.

The greatest limitation of this particular ego is that its primary concern is its own particular welfare. It is only tangentially concerned with the welfare of others. Consequently when threatened, it must defend itself and the almost instinctive defense is anger. It is interesting that people who have cultivated compassion have little anger. How is that? By cultivating concern for the welfare of others, the compassionate one cultivates a view of the world from the suffering one's point of view. The compassionate one also sees how the situation has brought on the suffering. The compassionate one sees how there can be a relief to the suffering which benefits all.

The vision of peace and harmony that the compassionate one has arises from wisdom. It is not enough to feel sympathy for the suffering one. It is not enough to want to relieve the suffering. The compassionate one must also envision a way to bring about the end of suffering and the growth of peace and harmony in the situation; this is wisdom. Wisdom is more than knowledge. Knowledge tends to be factual and wisdom tends to be always blessed with spiritual awareness. Wisdom "knows" something more than the obvious or the logical. Wisdom knows love.

In deepening our understanding of love, we see the emptiness or impermanence of anger. In love fear vanishes. We also see that the small ego, the ego of our worldly existence is impermanent in nature. What then is enduring? The universal (or cosmic) love energy which sustains our being endures. Through it we are able to experience Great Compassion for all other beings – not just animal-type beings, but for plant beings, for spirit beings, for all that exists.

Aspiration Prayer of Self-Healing,
Commitment to the Beings
of the Six Realms
by Lopon Tsultim Wangmo · March 31, 1999

As long as beings suffer from meanness and
hate in the hell realms,
I wash anger from my mind,
and pray for our release.

As long as beings suffer from hunger and thirst
in the hungry ghost realms,
I wash greed from my thoughts,
and pray for our release.

As long as beings suffer from unawareness
in the animal realms,
I apply myself to the study of the Buddha-dharma,
and pray for our release.

As long as beings suffer from desire
in the human realms,
I train myself in contentment,
and pray for our release.

As long as beings suffer from jealousy

in the realms of the titans,
I rejoice in the success and happiness of others,
and pray for our release.

As long as beings suffer from pride
in the god realms,
I live each day in gracious humility,
and pray for our enlightenment.

May all beings be released from their suffering
and enjoy the Great Happiness.

Trinity *

---

*One cannot draw a picture of God; one can only use symbols. The hands represent God the Creator who holds all things in existence. The drawing of the man represents Jesus: God who took on our humanity to walk intimately with us. And the dove represents God as the spirit who hovers over us and dwells within us in love, grace and peace. These symbols have been used throughout Christian art for centuries.

CHAPTER NINE

Christianity
Mary Esther Stewart

Before I describe my life journey through Christianity and how I practice Christianity, I feel that I should address Christianity in general, especially those aspects in which Christianity differs from other religious groups mentioned in this book.

What Christians Hold in Common

We Christians are very diverse in our own relationship to each other, so describing Christianity is not easy. Christians claim a history of 2000 years. In that time we have had many "ups and downs." Wars, politics, economics, visions and revelations, schisms and heresies, saints and sinners, personal interpretations and individual preferences have battered us about through the ages.

Christians are found in every land, every culture and every language. Christians are liberal, conservative, idealist, and fundamentalist. We are Baptist, Methodist, Roman Catholic, Greek Orthodox, Anglican, Presbyterian, Church of Christ, Coptic, Russian Orthodox and Pentecostal to name only a few groups. Christianity and Christians are very diverse.

Faced with this dilemma, I struggled in my attempt to represent Christianity to you in such a way as to describe the basic elements that all Christian groups have in common. Using Meher Baba's image of beads on a string, I want to address three beads on the string of Christianity that I believe all Christian groups agree on and hold in common and, at the same time, set us apart from the other groups represented in this book, God as Trinitarian, the person of Jesus the Christ, and the *Bible*.

GOD AS ONE AND TRINITY We say, with our non-Christian brothers and sisters throughout the world, that God is One. For us Christians there is only one God, but we understand that oneness of God as an expression of three. To us, God is love. Love, of its very nature, involves two: the lover and the beloved. Our own experience demonstrates that love cannot exist without a receiver of love. I love chocolate, my children, my country, my husband, etc. The action of loving is transitive; the verb must take an object. Love involves two, the lover and the person or item loved.

Love between two generates a third. A very weak example is that I love my dog, and she, in her dog way, loves me, so I knitted her a sweater. If I didn't love the dog, and if she didn't respond positively to my love, I probably would not have made the sweater. Of course, a much stronger example of lover and loved generating a third is the relationship of husband and wife when, through their love, a third person is generated, their child. Even social issues reflect an example of love as trinitarian: a social worker serves a community in a poor area. The community accepts the actions of the social worker, and because of their collaboration, programs are initiated that benefit everyone.

For us Christians, God is One, but we say that in God there are three "persons." This sounds like three isolated individuals and, therefore, three gods. But not so. God is Lover, God is Beloved, and God is the Loving. We can communicate this by considering the unique qualities that each person has. We speak of God in terms of generation, filiation, and spiration, i.e., outpouring of love. These personal yet relational aspects of God actually unite the three as one because they are constantly sharing and giving without the limitations of time. Persons in a love relationship are the most real thing we know. God as Trinity is the model of and source for the plurality of persons and the unitive principle of any love relationship. Christians have traditionally used the words "Father," "Son," and "Holy Spirit" to describe the Trinitarian nature of God. We call the God as Lover "God the Father." The one who receives this love and returns it to the Father, we call "God the Son." That love which is generated by the interaction of the two we call "God the Holy Spirit." We assign certain attributes to each of the "persons" of God: creation to the Father, God's identity with and salvation of humankind to the Son, and God's power of love and holiness in the world to the Spirit.

In attempting to explain the Trinity, I am frustrated by the inadequacy of our human words (as folks have been for 2000 years before me). I imagine the Trinity as a single circle, a great single Divine Dance of Love in which the three act so intensely and simultaneously that God is totally one. We Christians don't pretend to understand this, but rather we accept the concept of God as Trinity on faith. Knowing that we carry the image of the God who made us, and understanding the nature of love as a three function process, we say that God as Trinity is a mystery. Our vocabulary limits and compartmentalizes what we understand as the divine – so far above and beyond us, yet so close within us. When I meet my Maker in the next life, should God tell me that my description of the Trinity isn't quite how it is, I believe that I will be pleasantly rewarded to find that God is far more than what we can ever imagine. However, I hope I have represented our Christian image of God in a way that is somewhat understandable by our brothers and sisters of other faiths.

JESUS THE CHRIST   Every religion has a prophet, a leader; Jesus is ours. We understand Jesus as a human, historical person who lived and walked and died in a specific time, country and culture. We also understand Jesus as God, the great love expression (Word) of the Creator of the universe, who took on our humanity to "walk in our skin," to connect us to our God, to make known to us the depth of God's love for creation. For us, Jesus is more than an avatar, a guru, or a prophet. He is not a human infused with divinity. Jesus is the God of the universe in human flesh. We call this "Incarnation." We believe that Jesus did not have a human father in the sense that humans are brought into the world through the sexual activity between man and woman. We believe that Jesus was conceived by the power of God, the Holy Spirit, within the womb of Mary, a simple Jewish peasant girl. We believe that He was born and grew like all the rest of us; that He was like us in all things except sin. Our story tells us that through the person of Jesus, our God bent very low in great humility to walk with us in our ordinariness, our needs, our limitations. Christians understand Christianity as the only world religion whose God actually and fully became one of us.

Jesus came to open our eyes to the Kingdom of God. He taught, cured the infirm (of both body and spirit), and accepted the poor and lowly. Through His teachings, He revealed to us God's (His) great impartial all encompassing love, an understanding of God not always found in pre-Christian societies. His teachings challenge us with a new norm for our lives. Everything that Jesus did was love directed, love demonstrated, love modeled. As Christians we are called to know, love and imitate Him.

Historically, Jesus was a victim of His own mission. He was put to death by His own people because His teachings were too radical, His powers too threatening, His claim to relationship with divinity too frightening. It was too much for humanity for God to walk among us. Christians understand Jesus' death as a sacrificial action to atone for the sins of humankind. We use the word "Christ" to describe Jesus as the "anointed One," our Divine Savior, a bridge between God and humanity. Jesus is God and man, lovingly taking on all that we can do to harm ourselves, saving us from ourselves by the ultimate sacrifice of His own Divine self, a complete outpouring of love for us. We believe ours to be the only world religion whose God, in the person of Jesus Christ, willingly suffered and died a human death to demonstrate solidarity with mankind. For us Christians, Jesus makes God's love intelligible to us. Through Jesus, God bends low to embrace His creation.

THE BIBLE Like our Jewish and Islamic brothers and sisters, we too are "people of the Book." We Christians have incorporated many of the Jewish scriptures into our written tradition. These were the written traditions of Jesus and the first Christians who converted from Judaism. But besides the Jewish writings (the Old Testament), our Christian *Bible* contains our story of Jesus and his teachings as well as letters written by early Christians to the members of early Christian communities (the New Testament). In contrast to the *Koran*, revelations written by one author, Mohammed, in a relatively short period of time, our *Bible* (Jewish and Christian scriptures) is the collected works of many authors over many centuries. There is a general universality to our Biblical content. For example, the Psalms, written thousands of years ago, are applicable to one's prayer life in the 21ST century. The teachings of Jesus, although containing time and place colloquialisms, are relevant to the life of today's Christian. For us, the content of the *Bible* crosses the barriers of time to be a living inspiration for us in the present. For us, the teachings of Jesus give us an insight, a view into the life of God, the life of the Trinity. Within the pages of the New Testament, Jesus tells us of the Father, of Himself as the expression of the Father in our time and space, and of the Spirit which is the love emanating from Father and Son that fills the world. All that Jesus does and teaches demonstrates love that leads to justice and peace. This, we believe, is sacred, divine revelation. We believe that we are called to imitate these teachings by basing our conduct and our life values on the messages contained within the pages of our Sacred Book.

We believe that the *Bible* is the inspired word of God. However, within the Christian community, groups differ on the meaning of "inspiration." Fundamental Christians take every word of the *Bible* as literally from the mouth of God and thereby see revelation as co-terminus with the *Bible*. Mainline Christian groups such as Lutherans, Anglicans, Episcopalians and Roman Catholics consider the *Bible* in light of its historical context, symbolism, poetry and myth as well as fact. For them, the *Bible* is part of revelation. Whatever differences we may have among ourselves, our book, the *Bible*, forms the basis of our Christian values and our distinctive forms of worship.

Roman Catholicism as a Form of Christianity
Catholicism, in all its many forms, is deeply rooted in the very beginnings of Christianity. It can be considered as the oldest form of Christianity, tracing its roots to the first disciples of Jesus. We say that the Catholic Church was born 50 days after Jesus' resurrection, on the feast of Pentecost, when His followers took on the "full time job" of spreading His message and small communities began to form around the disciples of Jesus.[1] The

Apostles, those first and chosen followers of Jesus, are credited with spreading His message and establishing small communities of believers from the Mediterranean region to the East, possibly as far as India. The first name given to this movement was "The Way," but early on the title "Christian," first used in Antioch, took hold. By the end of the 1ST century, St. Ignatius of Antioch (d. 107) used the word "catholic" to describe the universality of Christian practices.[2]

Besides Roman Catholicism, the largest Catholic group, there are Byzantine Catholics, Ukrainian Catholics, Coptic Catholics, Greek Orthodox and Russian Orthodox to name a few. Over the years the groups gravitated toward their own customs and languages. Some groups separated from others based on geographical or political boundaries. Others separated based on very tragic diplomacy. At the present time, not all these groups recognize or accept the Pope as the leader of the Church. Despite differences in cultures, languages, practices and allegiances, we share basic doctrinal and liturgical commonalities as opposed to Protestant Christians whose origins began in European Roman Catholicism in the 16TH century and whose doctrinal beliefs and practices differ significantly from Roman Catholicism or any other Catholic rite.[3]

My own relationship to Christianity is through Roman Catholicism. Several characteristics of Roman Catholicism mark it as unique among other Christian groups.

APOSTOLIC SUCCESSION As we read the Gospels, it appears that Simon Peter, a Galilean fisherman, was singled out by Jesus for leadership among His followers. We know that after Jesus' death, resurrection and ascension, Peter became a true leader of the Christian communities in the Middle East and the Eastern

Mediterranean area. He then went on to Rome where he became the leader of the Christian community there. Community leaders were given the title of "bishop." The subsequent leaders of the Roman Christian community after Peter became known as "popes," the Greek for "father," and by the 5TH century were recognized as having leadership over the Christian community as a whole throughout the Mediterranean world. They succeeded one after another from the original leadership of Peter. Governance of the Roman Catholic Church has been ultimately centered in the Pope of Rome since the time of Peter, the Apostle. It is through Apostolic Succession, a direct succession from Peter, that we trace our roots directly to Jesus and His first followers.

A VERY LONG TRADITION   The Gospel stories of the life, deeds and teachings of Jesus were first conveyed through oral tradition. By the end of the first century the first collection of stories had been written down. There are four sets of Gospel or "good news" stories written between the mid 60s and about the year 110 that give us the teachings of Jesus. These, along with letters from early Christian missionaries and community leaders such as Paul of Tarsus, form the basis of our Catholic/Christian tradition. These constitute what we call the New Testament or Christian Scriptures.

We also have other writings from leaders of the early Christian communities. These leaders expressed the community's understanding of Jesus' teachings. The leaders helped the community to formulate their belief system and left their writings for the community to follow after the leader's death. These letters and writings make up an ancient tradition that tells us how the early Christian message was understood and lived. Some of these early writers were Polycarp (69-155), Ignatius of Antioch

(50-98?/117?), Cyril of Jerusalem (315-386), Cyprian of Carthage (3RD century), Ambrose (340-397), John Chrysostom (347-407), and Augustine (354-430) to name only a few. We read their writings today and base much of our theology on their understanding of scripture and their teachings.

As the Christian message began to spread, there was, from time to time, a lack of uniformity in the way the message was understood and a confusion about the person of Jesus. This is understandable as communication during the first few centuries after Jesus was not what it is today. People questioned the humanity as well as the divinity of Jesus. It became necessary to gather the leaders of the Catholic/Christian churches together and form a creedal statement that would define us as Christians, that would state what we believe about God the Father, the Son, Jesus, the Holy Spirit, and the Church. Councils were called and several hundred leaders gathered in one place to define our beliefs. This group of councils began in 325 and continued through 451, four councils in all. By the time of the final council, the Council of Chalcedon in 451, a creedal statement was agreed upon that we still hold today and which will not be changed in the future. We all recite this creed each Sunday when we pray together in our churches as a Catholic/Christian community.

PUBLIC PRAYER FORMULAS Christianity is rooted in Judaism. Just as our Jewish forefathers celebrated the Passover each year, the deliverance of the Israelites from oppression in Egypt, we celebrate Jesus' Last Supper (the Passover meal) with his followers before His death. We take seriously what happened at the Last Supper. Jesus took bread and wine, the staple food of the people, blessed these, told his disciples to take and eat/drink for, "This is my Body. This is my Blood." Jesus also said that we were to do the same in remembrance of Him. Re*member* in this sense is to make a member again, to make present again. We Catholics believe that our priests are empowered by Christ to change bread and wine into the Body and Blood of Jesus so that He is physically present to us each time we come together at the Mass.

The Mass is the source, summit, and most solemn of our official public prayers. It consists of readings from the Jewish Scriptures (Old Testament), the Christian Scriptures (New Testament), the offering of bread and wine to God (symbolic of our basic staples), the consecration of and changing the bread and wine into the Body and Blood of Jesus, and communion in which the Body and Blood of Christ is consumed by those present. This format for public prayer (Eucharist) was begun immediately as Christian communities formed after the death of Jesus Christ and has not changed in its basic form for over 2000 years. The word "Mass" comes from "misa/misio" meaning to be sent out, the same root as "mission." We are sent out from our public prayer to live the Gospel message of Jesus.

Another of our ancient official public prayers is the Liturgy of the Hours. "Liturgy" is the word given to public prayer meaning "the work of the people." The Liturgy of the Hours is a daily prayer practice built on the Psalms from the Jewish Scriptures and readings from the New Testament and other writings from the early leaders of the Church. The Liturgy of the Hours is designed to be chanted in groups. Monks and other dedicated people have used this method of communal prayer since the early days of the Church.

OUR SEVEN SACRAMENTS Within Roman Catholicism we have seven physical events which we consider sacred and hold in particular reverence. These we call sacraments. Each of these events involves something that can be experienced by the senses and that, within the event of the sacrament, the sensate experience accomplishes what is signifies. Each of the sacraments is a public, communal experience meant for commitment on the part of the participants and meant to bring the participants into unity with each other and the greater Christian community. All seven sacraments call down the power of God upon those who receive/experience the sacrament. And each of the sacraments is rooted in the teachings and the actions of Jesus. These seven sacraments are:

1. *Baptism:* This sacrament is intended to initiate a person into the Christian community through the action of water, the external sign of Baptism, and the invocation of God the Father, Son and Holy Spirit (Trinity). Such an initiation takes place after a person has been instructed in the tenets of Christianity and agrees to acceptance of these by faith & the commitment to live according to the teachings of Jesus. Water is poured on the head of the new Christian and they are immersed into water. Water is symbolic of cleansing from the sins of one's past life and taking on a new way of life. Baptism would be the first sacrament that one would receive in becoming a Catholic Christian. Some Christian denominations prefer to baptize only adults or those who are old enough to make a personal choice for following the teachings of Jesus; other Christian churches, Roman Catholic included, baptize infants because of the belief that Jesus acts for their benefit based on the request of others, in most cases, their parents.

2. *Confirmation:* This sacrament follows the sacrament of Baptism. In ancient times people were anointed with oil to symbolize moving to a new level of existence and strengthening. In the sacrament of Confirmation, the bishop anoints the new Christian with oil demonstrating to the community that

the person is strengthened by faith through the power of God's Spirit. The sacrament is also a demonstration of acceptance of the new Christian by the community.

3. *Holy Eucharist:* This sacrament relates to our need for nourishment. The heart of the sacrament of Holy Eucharist is the consecrated bread and wine at Mass that, we believe, becomes the Body and Blood of Jesus, the Christ. By consuming the Body and Blood of Jesus, the Christian commits to take on the person of Jesus in his or her actions and to live by the teachings of Jesus. In a sense, we like to think that we become what we eat, or what we consume nourishes our spiritual life and is food for our journey into God.

4. *Reconciliation:* As Catholic Christians, we believe that our sins not only affect us personally, but affect the whole community. What we do or don't do as individuals strengthens us as well as the life of the community as a whole or serves to lessen us and break down the unity and charity that should exist among us. By acknowledging our sins, by naming our demons, we demonstrate recognition of our faults and how we have broken relationships with God, ourselves and the community. In the name of the community, the priest receives our acknowledged faults. The priest represents the person of Jesus Christ in absolving us of our sins just as Jesus did with those He cured in body and soul 2000 years ago. The sensate experience in the sacrament of Reconciliation is the naming of our faults and the blessing of absolution administered by the priest in the name of Jesus and of the church community.

5. *Anointing of the Sick:* Those who are ill and face the possibility of departing the Christian community through death, are given a special anointing with oil to strengthen them on their journey into the next life and to relieve them of the sins they

have committed in this life. A priest anoints the forehead and hands of the sick person with oil and says special prayers over the person in the name of the community. The desired intent is the healing of the person's soul. Healing of the body may also take place.

6. *Holy Orders:* In ancient times the community designated its leaders. It called forth those who were to preside over public prayer, administer the sacraments, preach and teach, and provide guidance for the community in following the teachings of Jesus, the Christ. These leaders were considered priests, and were anointed with oil to designate their calling to leadership and their power to act on the part of the community. The bishop, in the name of the community, ordains the new priest by laying his hands on the new priest's head and anointing his hands with oil. The ceremony of anointing and laying on of hands for priests is the sacrament of Holy Orders. This is considered to be a permanent calling. Once a priest is ordained, he remains in this position until death.

7. *Matrimony:* The union between man and woman is considered sacred, not only for their own relationship with each other and the enhancement they can bring to each other's spiritual development, but also for the procreation and raising of children. The family is the center of the Christian community. In the sacrament of Matrimony, the couple makes a public statement of their commitment to each other, their promise of fidelity. The couple confers this sacrament on each other. The community receives their commitment in the person of the priest and agrees to uphold the couple's commitment to each other. The sensate experiences of the sacrament are the couple's spoken promises to each other and the consummation of the marriage. Like Holy Orders, Matrimony is a "vocation sacrament"; it is expected that

the married couple would uphold their promises of commitment and fidelity to each other until the marriage is ended by the death of one of the parties.

OUR SAINTS In our society it is common to look to movie stars, rock stars, sports heroes and even political leaders as our models and mentors. In our Roman Catholic Church, we look at the lives of very holy people who have gone before us to be our models. These are our saints. They do not take the place of God, but by their exemplary, Gospel-centered lives they point to God. We look at how they lived and we may attempt to imitate them.

First among our saints is Mary, the mother of Jesus. We believe in the virgin birth, that is, that Mary became pregnant without the help of a man. However, a young Jewish girl pregnant out of wedlock in pre-Christian society was subject to severe punishment, even death. When Mary was asked by the Angel Gabriel if she would be willing to carry this child, her response was one of total submission to the will of God. She risked her reputation and her life to carry and birth the God of the universe. We are grateful to Mary for her immense courage. Because of her "Yes," our God became fully one of us. For this we hold Mary in great esteem.

Throughout the first 10 centuries of the Church, holy people were frequently given the title of "saint" after their death by their local communities, by the people who lived with them and knew them. These were people who lived the Gospel teachings in an heroic way and who may have influenced many others to live good and holy lives. In the 12TH and 13TH centuries, the Church leaders established a process for naming people saints, a process of canonization. This consists of an examination of the person's life by means of objective inquiries and a certain number of miracles attributed to the holy person. Popular saints are St. Paul, St. Francis, St. Catherine of Siena, St. Anthony, St. Augustine, St. Dominic, St. Ignatius, St. Teresa of Avila, St. Jude, and many others.

We Catholics understand death as a separation of our soul from our material body. We believe that we are more than our bodies. We believe that our soul, our spirit, our individuality lives on in eternity. We believe that we can be in union with those who have gone before us. So it is quite common that we have our favorite saints and that we talk to them. We ask them to help us because we understand that they are in a better position than we are. Personally, I have asked the help of particular saints from time to time and I am always amazed at the little (and big) miracles and responses to prayer that come my way. The saints are our friends. I call them the "Heavenly Folk."

PRIVATE PRAYER AND MYSTICISM Although the Catholic Church has a very long tradition of public prayer and all of us are expected to participate in public prayer with our Christian community, we also have an equally long tradition of private prayer and mysticism. In the Gospel stories, we read frequently that Jesus went to quiet places to pray. We are encouraged to do the same. The material used in our public prayer should contribute to the content for our private prayer, meditation and contemplation. We might contemplate events in the life of Jesus, reflect on passages from the New Testament; or we might center ourselves quietly on the presence of God in creation; or we might select elements of the Old Testament such as the Psalms to lead us into quiet meditation. Many of our saints were mystics, losing themselves in true contemplative prayer.

Other private prayers may be the reading of prayers and spiritual thoughts found in the writings of our saints and mystics. Or we might be comfortable with a mantra type of prayer like the Rosary in which a single prayer is recited over and over. Some form of private prayer is highly encouraged.

PERSONAL CONSECRATION Within the Catholic Church there have always been men and women who have made the decision to dedicate themselves solely to God and thereby to forego the vocation of marriage and a natural born family. They have chosen either a life of solitude and contemplative prayer, or a dedicated life marked by the three vows of poverty, chastity and obedience. They live within a group of people with similar goals and shared vows, their community family. We call these groups "religious communities." Some are monks who live together in one monastery generally for life and dedicate themselves to prayer and good works. St. Benedict, in the 6TH century, established a complete monastic system that greatly influenced the stabilization of Western Europe and promoted the spread of Christianity. Other religious groups may live together and share a common rule of life, but the members move about among the people preaching, teaching, and caring for the needs of the sick and the poor. They might staff schools, hospitals, charitable organizations, missions, and universities. Franciscans (founded by Saints Francis and Clare), Dominicans (founded by St. Dominic), Jesuits (founded by St. Ignatius of Loyola), Carmelites, Daughters of Charity (founded by St. Vincent de Paul) are but a few of the religious communities who have served the peoples of the world for centuries.

CHURCH GOVERNANCE The Roman Catholic Church is really more democratic than it may appear. As a collective body, we believe that the Church is guided, and has been guided through the ages, by the Spirit of God (the Holy Spirit). We have had many fine leaders as well as others who have not been blessed with good administrative skills and have made tragic decisions. At times Gospel values have prevailed; at other times human egos and greed have surfaced. However, we believe that the Wisdom of God has been present to guide us, raising up holy people whose actions have contributed to counteracting poor administrative decisions. For us, our true leader is the Spirit of God.

Although the principal administrator of the Roman Catholic Church is the Pope, the Bishop of Rome, each geographical area has a leader, the local bishop. These smaller areas are called "dioceses" and each is divided again into smaller areas called "parishes." Each parish has a priest assigned to it to serve the spiritual needs of the people living in that parish. Each bishop has several advisory councils within his diocese made up of priests and lay (non-ordained) people who provide him with information needed to administer the diocese and meet the needs of the people therein. Not only is this a practical way of bringing the Gospel message of Jesus to the local people, but it is also a way of maintaining uniformity in the practices of Roman Catholicism. For example, one may attend Mass in a parish outside of one's residential area, such as when on vacation, and find that, other than architecture and possibly the style of music, the public prayer (Liturgy) of the Mass is no different than what goes on in one's home parish. This is consistent the world over, not only in our public prayer practices, but in what we believe and, other than specific ethnic customs, generally in the way we try to live.

Major decisions for Roman Catholics are made on a representational basis. Bishops from a particular country or a council of bishops drawn from all parts of the world may be called together to form councils and synods to answer problems that arise, make decisions that affect all members of the Church or of a particular area, or to update practices within the Catholic Church. There have been 21 ecumenical or worldwide councils over the last 2000 years, the first one taking place in year 49 CE. The most significant of these in the 20TH century was the calling of bishops worldwide to attend the Second Vatican Council. The purpose of this council was to look at how the Church serves the people in the modern world, our present attitudes toward our lives as Catholic Christians, and a call to revisit our roots of Christianity in order to focus on Gospel values and the teachings of Jesus. Here in the United States we have the U.S. Conference of Catholic Bishops that meets periodically to address issues pertinent to American Catholics. The bishops are expected to represent the needs of the people in their diocese. All workings and decisions of the conferences, synods and councils are public information and made available to all of us through published documents.

ORIGINS OF OTHER CHRISTIAN GROUPS   Until the 16TH century, Roman Catholicism represented Christianity throughout Western Europe and the Americas as well as in some parts of Asia. In 1517, Martin Luther, a Roman Catholic monk living in Germany, expressed his dissatisfaction with some of the practices of the Roman Catholic Church. For political and economic reasons, German princes saw this as an opportunity to express their own dissatisfaction with the pope and some Church practices. The result was the severance of ties between the German princes and the Pope in Rome. This was the beginning of the Protestant Reformation. Soon to follow was King Henry VIII in England, severing his ties with Rome over a disagreement he had with the Pope regarding his marriage. Henry set himself up as head

of the Church in England. From both of these incidents came
the formation of Lutherans and Anglicans, new forms of Christianity. Both groups retained much or only some of what they
had experienced in Roman Catholicism. Lutherans and those
inspired by the Lutheran movement began to focus their religious efforts on the use of the *Bible* as central to their Christian
beliefs and practices. Many groups mitigated or eliminated the
public prayers of the Roman Catholic Church as well as several
of the sacraments. Most Christian groups today, e.g. Baptists,
Presbyterians, Methodists, Episcopalians, can trace their roots
directly or indirectly to a connection with Roman Catholicism
in Western Europe.

My Journey through Christianity
My own personal journey through Christianity is not as clear-
cut as the preceding explanation. Rather, my journey has been
an evolution from an immature acceptance of being placed in
Christianity, through painful anger and bitterness, to a mature
conviction that where I am in my faith life is where I belong – a
sense of comfort like an old shoe.

Being a Christian was not originally my idea; it was a choice
my parents made for me shortly after I was born. My mother was
Roman Catholic and my father converted to Catholicism prior
to marrying my mother. Therefore, I was baptized as a Roman
Catholic Christian within a few weeks of my birth.

When it was time for me to attend school, I was enrolled in
our local Catholic school. In the 1940s, Catholic families were
strongly encouraged to send their children to Catholic schools
attached to nearly all Catholic churches in the United States.
Outside of a few friends in our neighborhood, we seldom associated with non-Catholics or non-Christians. As we entered

our late teens, dating and marriage with members of our own religion and our own form of Christianity was highly encouraged. I even attended a Catholic college for my undergraduate studies in Spanish and education. I believe that this attitude prevailed in most Catholic families as the Catholic Church was still, after 400+ years, reacting to the Protestant Reformation of the early 1500s.

During my college years I became seriously confused and disillusioned with my Catholic faith. As I explained, we Christians hold the teachings of Jesus Christ as found in the New Testament to be a basic guide for personal and communal holiness and for salvation. What I read in the New Testament and what I saw in practice among many followers of the Catholic/Christian faith did not coincide. I saw too many destructive and abusive behaviors performed in the name of Jesus that, to me, were the furthest thing from what Jesus taught: "You shall love the Lord your God with all your heart ...You shall love your neighbor as yourself" (Mark 12:30-31). I caught myself falling into cynicism and the same hypocrisy that I criticized in others. Greatly disturbed and disillusioned, I chose to step away from my Catholic faith for several years. Although I felt like a "fish out of water," I had to step away and find out if I had an identity, a person, outside of Catholic Christianity. And if I did, I knew that I would have to make a choice about how I would seek out faith in God – through a Christian or a non-Christian community.

One person who greatly influenced me during my college years was a French Jesuit priest and world-renowned paleontologist, Père Pierre Teilhard de Chardin. He was of French origin and died in 1955. The Catholic bishops had discouraged the reading of his theological writings as these were perceived to deviate from orthodoxy. I, on the other hand, read everything of Père

Teilhard's that I could find, many times over, and even some of his scientific monographs. He dared to suggest that the God of the universe might extend beyond the bounds of the Catholic Church. He saw all creation and every creature as holy because all were infused with the life of their Creator. This, to me, was new and mind-boggling. In Père Teilhard's theology I saw the potential for world justice, dialogue and peace. I saw a world made out of Love and for Love. Although Père Teilhard was deeply rooted in the teachings of Jesus Christ and dedicated to Catholic Christianity, he understood God as all creating, all embracing Love who transcended any institutional structure. For me, Père Teilhard de Chardin represented a personal freedom of conscience within the structure of Christianity. I began to understand that I could have a personal identity that included my own ideas and spirituality and still be a Catholic Christian.

The year 1962 marked a turning point for Catholic Christians worldwide and for me in particular. This was the year of the opening of the Second Vatican Council. In 1958, Angelo Roncalli was elected to replace Pope Pius XII as leader of the Roman Catholic Church. He took the name John XXIII. One of the first things he did was to call an ecumenical (universal) Church council at the Vatican in Rome. The 2540 delegates to the Second Vatican Council were asked to review all aspects of Roman Catholicism and to clarify our practices in light of our 20TH century context.

As much as the Catholic Church may be perceived to be authoritarian and monarchical, a Church council is a rather democratic process. Bishops from all over the world, voicing the concerns of the people who they represent, come together to deal with major issues facing the Church. In 1962 the majority of bishops did not perceive that the Church had many major issues and that the status quo was appropriate for Catholics world wide. At that time our official communal prayers were in Latin, a language few of us understood. The laity (those who were not ordained ministers) held few if any positions of leadership or responsibility in the Church. Rules were followed for their own sake. Study of our sacred writings by the laity, especially the *Bible*, was not really encouraged by the Church leaders. Ecumenical dialogue with other Christian groups and with non-Christians was practically nonexistent. But the general perception by Church leaders was that these were not serious issues. However, Pope John xxiii felt differently.

The council met for three years. As the delegates began to work on various aspects of Church life, their understanding changed and they saw where changes needed to be made. Their task was to bring the Roman Catholic Church into the modern world. Several documents were written that shed new light on how we worship as a community, how we understand the role of all people in the Church, and how we relate to our brothers and sisters of other faiths. Pope John xxiii said that the council needed to do some "spring cleaning." It was a time of fresh air for us. The result of the council was, briefly, that Catholic Christianity became much more "user-friendly."

User-friendly was what I needed in order to resume my life as a Catholic Christian. Looking back, I see this conscious stepping back into Catholic Christianity as my personal commitment to a life of Christian faith. I became an active participant in my Church again. The public prayer life of the Church changed to English and I could adapt that public prayer to my private life. I felt free to move in different circles. I read the documents promulgated by the council and felt empowered to take charge of my spiritual life. I know that I, like many of my friends, would have left Catholic Christianity if it had not been for the Second Vatican Council

So where am I now in my Christian faith journey? Since the mid 90s, I have taken the study of Christianity seriously. I have spent much more time with the New Testament getting to know the person of Jesus Christ, re-read my friend Père Teilhard de Chardin, studied Church history in detail, and traveled to Europe where I spent time in Rome and other significant places for Catholic Christianity. Besides my Bachelor's degrees in Spanish and education and my Master's degrees in bilingual education and school administration, I have a certificate for four years of study in Catholic theology. Before my retirement I was employed by the Catholic diocese of Phoenix as a school administrator and a parish education director. I took the responsibility for providing education programs in Catholic Christian scripture, theology and liturgy (our public prayer services) for the people in my local parish.

But my personal spirituality has gone deeper than that. Among all Christian groups, Catholics are well known for their recognition of saints. These people have gone before us and provide an example of spirituality and holiness by the way they lived. In 2001, I was directed to do a series of activities to make the Catholics in Flagstaff aware of our patron saint, St. Francis of Assisi. I knew very little about this man who lived and died at the turn of the 13TH century in medieval Italy. Because the success of the activities depended on me, I thought it would be wise to find out as much about St. Francis as I could. I went directly to his writings and to the early sources of his life and spirituality. In short, I discovered that his was a spirituality that completely resonated with me.

Francis was called to follow Jesus' teachings on material poverty. He gave up a wealthy merchant life style to become a poor beggar, walking through the Umbrian countryside preaching the overflowing love of God for all people, all creation, practicing charity toward all and living a life of profound material poverty. Francis saw all humankind as his brothers and sisters (as well as all creatures) because all were created by the same loving God. Therefore, war and fighting were contrary to a life of fraternity and were seen as a rejection of a God who made each of us and holds us in existence because He loves us. Protection and maintenance of material wealth and possessions frequently necessitates war. The distinction between rich and poor is based on material wealth and possessions. Therefore, to avoid war, to transcend class distinction, and to follow Jesus Christ more perfectly, Francis chose a life of complete simplicity. He understood poverty as a means to attaining peace and justice for all as well as the practice of absolute faith in God. One may think that Francis' notions were rather impractical and impossible to live by, but within the first 10 years of his conversion, he had over five thousand followers. Today there are hundreds of thousands of Franciscans in the world, all desirous of living lives dedicated to peace, justice, service to the poor, and following the teachings of Jesus Christ. There is a whole school of Franciscan theology that stems from the time of St. Francis, a way to understand one's relationship to God in terms of peace, poverty and fraternity.

Not only am I an active practicing Roman Catholic Christian who better understands my Church and strives to follow the teachings of Jesus Christ, but my spirituality is based on that of St. Francis and how he understood Jesus Christ. My prayer life centers on the Psalms and meditation on the life of Jesus. I continue to give presentations on scripture, prayer and Church history for my local Catholic parish. I am involved with programs that support peace and justice, and those that provide opportunity for the poor. And I'm happy. I'm happier than I have ever been, I'm at peace, I'm enjoying life and all those who come into my life, and I feel capable of dealing with whatever and whomever comes my way. I have come to know that life is not about me and that my existence is a total gift. What freedom!

Where does my journey go from here? Who knows? It really doesn't matter. Martin Luther King said that he had "gone to the mountain." Well, I feel that I have entered the Divine Dance of Love, the "dance" of the Trinity, probably the same thing as going to the mountain. And once one enters the Dance or goes to the mountain, then nothing else matters.

Saint Francis of Assisi, depicted in classical fashion giving a sermon to the birds, surrounded by nature. *

---

*Tile is from the private collection of Laurent Weichberger.

CHAPTER TEN

If Saint Francis Were Here
Mary Esther Stewart

He would tell us that Jesus said what He meant and meant what He said; that the Gospel was intended to be lived, not just to be read, ignored and forgotten.

He would tell us that to follow the poor Christ is to share with those who are in need. He would tell us that we are to simplify our lives so that those less fortunate can have basic necessities. He would remind us that this is God's justice.

He would tell us that he liked Christmas best of all because that is the day when God bent low to walk in our skin and to show us how much He really wants us for Himself, to share His love and His happiness. He would tell us to really celebrate Christmas!

He would tell us that war is not holy, that it is not good for anyone, and that war does not bring peace. He would tell us about his meeting with the Muslim Sultan of Egypt, how they both desired to have peace in spite of the Crusades, and how they became friends.

He would tell us about lepers. He would tell us that those who we think are the lowest members of society are also God's children and that we must accept them as we would accept Christ. And he would tell us that this is not easy!

He would tell us that all creatures are our brothers and sisters because we have the same Father. He would tell us to respect and care for the water, the air, the wild creatures, the land, the sea and each other.

And he would tell us to sing, sing a lot, because we are children of a Great King!

299

Guru Nanak

SEWA SINGH KHALSA

CHAPTER ELEVEN

Sikh Dharma

Haring Singh Khalsa

T HE FOLLOWING WORDS ARE A TRANSLATION of the first
teachings spoken by Guru Nanak, following his awakening. They
form the opening of his sacred song, Japji Sahib - The Song of
the Soul.[1]

One Spirit Beyond,
Moves within the Creation
Coordinating, Consolidating,
Continually Creating,
And this Spirit within,
Is (our) True Identity.

It does All,
And causes All
To be done.

It protects
Through all incidents
Of time and space.

It Fears Nothing
And knows nothing
Of Vengeance or Anger.

Deathless,
It comes into form.
In itself,
It has never been born.

Flowing through the cycles
Of birth and death,
It moves,
By its own purity and projection.

This understanding shall come to you
As a sweet blessing,
As a gift.

In every moment continue
In this continual remembrance.

From the start,
This was true.
All through time and space,
Is true.
Even now,
This truth is true.

Nanak says,
It ever shall be true.[2]

Within this song is the heart of the way of life and philosophy followed by all of Nanak's disciples, who became known as Sikhs. It is a declaration that the Creator and the Creation are One. Just as the dancer is one with the dance – and the dance itself, cannot exist without the dancer. Man is not separate from God; the Creator is not separate from the Creation. That which we call God – is immanent – within us and all around us, and is the reality of our True Nature. Our very essence is completely fearless, beyond anger, beyond birth and beyond death. Japji Sahib continues, through a series of 40 divinely poetic verses, describing the true, divine nature of the Spirit we share within us, and the path to realization of that spirit.

What is that power or energy, the awareness, that gives life to all creation? Sentient beings are composed of physical form, and also something which might be called a governing spirit. The word "animus" is sometimes used in reference to this. This spirit forms the basis of most religious beliefs. An important difference in perspective lies in the fact that in the West, it is regarded as personal to each phenomenal object, being the sentience of it. In Eastern teachings – it is called "heart" or "consciousness" and is regarded as impersonal and universal, as in terms such as "Buddha Mind," "Prajna[3]," or "Atman[4]."

Assuming personal ownership of this spirit which is completely impersonal is perhaps the original sin, or point of confusion. This difference in perspective results in so many mistranslations of the teachings of the great spiritual masters. What is available to the seeker simply misses the mark, or at the very least, falls quite short of it. The result is confusion, caused by identification with the body as "self" instead of with the consciousness that gives life to it. And this is what is known as bondage.

The true purpose of religion is to explain to us our true reality, and to help us simply Be ... That: Awareness, fully experiencing our *One*ness. Religion must offer the technique or technology to enable us to experience the light and grace within our own being. We have not been taught to experience our own spiritual soul, our real Love. Spiritual means – my spirit within me is infinite, and my spirit as infinite, shall relate, experience, express, and project infinity. Therein lies the Divine. There is nothing other than our spirit that we must realize.[5]

Guru Nanak offered one profound basic teaching: Ang Sang Wahe Guru, "Within every limb, God is in you." (Our very reality is God – dancing within each of the 30 trillion cells of our being, which change themselves every 72 hours.) There cannot be any power which comes to us from outside. There's a dormant power within us which has to be awakened. If in our ego minds, we have put God outside of us, then there is nothing in us, and that's why we are suffering.

The simple act of hearing the Truth, listening & trusting, is enough to start one on the path to awakening. As Guru Nanak put it: "By trusting what you hear when you listen, The Truth of your own inner consciousness will saturate your psyche with wisdom."[6] The process unfolds in its own time and way. It is not within our control, but once it has begun, it evolves towards fruition in spite of any imaginary efforts brought to it, not "because" of them.

Deeply Listening,
Recognize the ocean of virtues within you.
Deeply listening
Become in tune with Spirit,
Perfectly balanced
In your own humanity
And nobility.[7]

In trusting what you hear
when you listen –
Dharma,

The path of divine discipline and law,
Will guide your whole life.[8]

This very truth – about our true identity, or True Self (self
with a capital "S") is most important. In actuality it is "ours,"
rather than mine or yours – for all creation shares it together.
But, because we start from the perspective of seeing ourselves
as separate "individuals", we can fathom no other approach
than to begin by looking to find our "own" True Self. Nanak
never claimed this as an original revelation. This Truth has been
communicated to us by every spiritual Master, all down through
time. If you look for it you will find it, tucked away between the
oh-so-many words recorded by those who followed, in their
humble understanding of the teachings they had received. It is
this truth – that is perhaps the hardest for us to accept or believe
in, to "trust" that we are divine, for we face and experience so
many base desires and emotions so painfully every day. But it is
this truth which we must trust and believe in, in order to let go
of the limited self image that is so deeply conditioned within us.
And it is this truth that will allow mankind to find and know that
shared heart that we all have in common.

The key to a deep and complete understanding of this shared
heart lies in the words: Karta Purkh, which are sometimes translated as "God is the Doer." This is truly at the very core of the
teachings of Guru Nanak. That which we call God, the Source of
all that is, the mysterious power by which this Creation came into
existence, "does all, and causes all to be done." It is the conscious
presence which pervades all creation. It is in each and every one
of us. Without it there would be no creation. The experience
of this presence is a state of (True) Love. Sadly, instead of that
Love, our worldly experience is more one of painful duality. We

find ourselves feeling separate, not only from God, but from each other. We become lost – seeking what is sadly only a poor substitute for love, and in all the wrong places. Our challenge is to learn to love and relate to our own soul with reverence. Until that happens, truly loving or even just relating to each other will always be a struggle.

"God is the Doer" is another way of saying that everything happens according to God's Will, or Cosmic Law; including the consequences – everything. We find ourselves instantly wanting to argue this idea, and therefore never really open ourselves up to this most important spiritual teaching. We see around us so many events that we label as ruthless, cruel, or tragic and unfair; happenings that our ego selves cannot reconcile with any images we have of God. In our anger, we immediately look for someone to blame (and punish). We get sidetracked – fiercely debating good and evil and justice and injustice – when what we are really being asked to do is to let go of all of our endless judgements.[9]

The basis of Western thought and aspirations is to get rid of "evil" altogether and try and make this world a paradise to live in. In 2000 years we have not managed to do so. All of our efforts to make the world a better place than it is, begin with the presumption that we know what's best, and that the power which created the world has somehow been left in a position of utter helplessness. Since God has failed, it is up to "me" to take over and fix it and to make it as "I" think "it should be." We have even dared to imagine that without our intervention the world will deteriorate into complete chaos. In our passion, we seem to have forgotten how futile all of our good intentions and efforts have been – and worse, that mankind as a whole, seems to be the very problem we are trying to address.

This perspective of seeking to purge the earth of all evil, ignores the basic fact that this entire creation is an ongoing dance of polarities. The phenomenal world we live in is a relative world of interrelated conceptual opposites. There is a perception of "evil" because there is a perception of "good." As the Taoist sages have said, "It is the interplay of Yin and Yang." The same impersonal, light of consciousness which gives life to the saint, exists within the sinner too. Each of us has the qualities of both within us. A deep apperception[10] of this leads to an awareness that Guru Nanak simply phrased: "No one is high and no one is low." The labels of good and evil (or light and dark), are references to opposite sides of the same coin – life. And each side of life, both the bright and the murky, must (and will) have the upper hand at some time or another.

The powerful invocation, "Thy Will be Done," is at the heart of the Lord's Prayer, shared by Christ Jesus. Sadly, the level of surrender it asks for, only seems possible after one has exhausted all efforts to impose their own will on every situation in life. The eventual realization is that it is not within our power to do so. "Thy will be done" is really an acknowledgment of our own helplessness. But if we steadfastly insist that God meet the terms and conditions that we have established, we will always remain separate from the One we say we love and the One we seek to reunite with.

Actions happen, deeds are done, but the causes are infinite and incomprehensible. Everything that happens, happens because everything in the universe is exactly how it is, at this moment. Whatever we (or "another") may seemingly be doing, it is always based on two factors: [1] genetic predisposition and, [2] the complex conditioning received by the circumstances of life itself. Neither of these were ever within our control. We have

to live life in the circumstances in which we have been placed.
Sometimes we play the star, sometimes we play the fool. This
teaching appears over and over again, throughout the scriptures
of the Sikh Gurus.

> *All treasures, O Lord, come by Your Kind Mercy.*
> *No one obtains anything by himself.*
> *As You have delegated, so do we apply ourselves,*
> *O Lord and Master.*
> *O Nanak, nothing is in our hands.*[11]

> *As long as someone thinks that he is the one who*
> *acts, he shall have no peace.*
> *As long as this mortal thinks that he is the one*
> *who does things, he shall wander in reincarnation*
> *through the womb.*

> *He causes whomever He pleases to play in His play.*
> *He is beyond calculation, beyond measure, uncount-*
> *able and unfathomable.*
> *As You inspire him to speak, O Lord, so does servant*
> *Nanak speak.*[12]

Harmony between "me" and the other ("you") comes about
only when there is a total understanding and acceptance that
whatever happens, is not in the control of anyone, it depends
entirely on the Will of God or the Cosmic Law. Then, who is there
to blame or condemn anyone for anything? And all of our judg-
ments and anger dissolve into a profound sense of compassion.
"This living can be so hard. How can we not be loving?"[13]

When one has truly been able to accept that the apparent separation between "me" and the "other," does not include personal "doership," the sense of separation no longer dominates our perspective, and only then, the experience of universal brotherhood between all mankind begins to blossom. An astonishing change takes place, without any specific action on our part, apart from "the understanding" itself. There is an intuitive apprehension of this world as a net of jewels, every jewel containing the reflection of all the others – a fantastic interrelated harmony.

The Search for Truth
Everyone's journey is unique, and one never knows how many steps their own will take. The path to Truth is never linear. It covers as much ground as each one's destiny or karma requires. The sense of being utterly lost may happen many times along the way. Still, there is a longing deep within calling us ever inward. After much seemingly futile searching, it gradually dawns on us that Truth is everywhere: within us and all around us – always. But the ears to hear it and the eyes to see it have been too busy serving the ego, instead of the soul.

The great sage and poet, Kabir, known to many spiritual seekers world-wide, was a contemporary of Guru Nanak. The songs of Kabir appear many times in the Sikh Scriptures. Kabir was born to Muslim parents and yet believed to be a disciple of the famous Hindu guru, Ramananda. Kabir is associated with a period of religious reformation known as the Bhakti[14] movement. The ecstatic poems that poured forth as songs from him, were often a direct challenge to the entrenched religious viewpoints of his time. He was denounced by Hindus and Muslims alike. It was only after his death that his light and wisdom came to be revered, and then, by followers of all faiths.

This problem, regarding our openness or ability to let go of

our preconceived notions and to hear the Truth, seems to be
our greatest challenge.

I Just Laugh
by Kabir[15]

If I told you the truth about God,
you might think I was an idiot.

If I lied to you about the Beautiful One
you might parade me through the streets shouting,
"This guy is a genius!"

This world has its pants on backwards.
Most carry their values and knowledge in a jug
that has a big hole in it.

Thus having a clear grasp of the situation
if I am asked anything these days

I just laugh!

"Mankind has practiced religion for thousands of years. The
true message of the great world teachers and spiritual masters
has always been the same. We are spirit. We are always spirit.
We are all One in spirit. When spirit departs, this physical body
is called dead, but spirit is eternal. And when we are alive and
we do not recognize our own spirit, and the spirit within each
other, we are worse than dead."[16]

These teachings are not exclusive to Sikhism. All of the great
Masters have offered them to us, in one form or another. But they

have been extremely difficult for mankind to actually accept. They have been misinterpreted, overlooked, or ignored. Too often, what has been emphasized were simply methodologies which further conditioned followers into a conceptual framework of bondage, rather than freedom or liberation. Instead of love – fear and guilt have been promoted, with a heavy emphasis placed on judgment, punishment and vengeance. "Life presents a problem only because the individual thinks of himself as a fixed, separate entity and tries to make sense out of life from the point of view of this separate entity. What is more, organized religion has supported him in this misconceived notion of the separation of the individual from the rest of the universe."[17] All of the fighting between religions over whom or what God is, or what name God should be called, and what is the proper way to worship God, is all a conceptual fantasy – a tragic insanity. In Truth, there's nothing to fight about.

Two thousand years before the birth of Nanak, Lord Buddha told his followers: "All things arise because of their interdependence. Nothing has a separate, independent identity. All dharmas[18] arise out of each other and co-exist interdependently." Every new religious movement is born out of, and shaped by existing faiths, and therefore bears at least some resemblance to them. Historically, India has been a living testament to this truth. Over the 2500 year period following Buddha's words, Hinduism, Jainism, Islam, Sufism, Sikhism, and Christianity, all had significant impacts upon each other as well as having their own practices, impacted by the entire cultural heritage of India, and its peoples. Sikh Dharma, or Sikhism was very much a response to the clash between Islam and Hinduism. Nanak's entire lifework was dedicated to bringing peace between the followers of all faiths.

Guru Nanak taught that all religions share certain timeless, universal truths. It is these truths that the seeker must give their greatest attention to, not superficial differences in style, language or modes of worship. The teachings of every great teacher (Krishna, Buddha, Christ, Mohammed, etc.) were necessarily framed within the context of certain times and circumstances, certain cultures and languages. But all shared the same, one and only, source of all creation; the cause of all causes – that which many of us call God or the Absolute Reality.

These great teachings came to be honored as "jewels," by those who received them. They were offered to mankind, as a conduit through which the experience of the loving presence of God, could be transmitted. They were an offering by which we might awaken to the truth of our spirits within us and live in the Love that flows forth from the very source of our beings, instead of the fear and pain of the limited ego.

Beads on One String

Meher Baba's reference to the religions of the world as all beads on one string is a wonderful metaphor, which would have been close to the heart of Guru Nanak. The mistaken belief that each religion has a different origin and a separateness in intent is the great illusion, sold to us by those seeking to profit from divisiveness. Guru Nanak simply stated: "The Creator of All, is One." Surely, the words of the Apostle John were conveying the same truth: John 1:3 "All things were created through Him, and apart from Him not one thing was created that has been created."[19]

This entire book is an offering, a meditation on what it is we all have in common. Each contributor has offered a chapter on the spiritual tradition that they have identified with during their own life journey. As I meditate on the idea of "beads on one string," not only every religion can be thought of as a bead or jewel on this string – but more importantly, each (and every) person is a bead on that string. All races and peoples on this earth including those called "saints" and those called "sinners," all languages and cultures, all that is – all come from one Creator. The One true self, which shines in all of us, connects us infinitely more deeply than the religious tradition we follow. And the one "string" is the light of God that flows through all creation. Those who look deeply enough, lose all sense of a separate identity as a jewel, or a bead, or a person, and dissolve into the light that is the thread running through all life. Therein lies the Peace of God.

The Life of Nanak

Nanak was raised from childhood, to follow the religious practices of the Hindu Faith, but he found his world filled with prejudice and bigotry. He believed in the fatherhood of God and the brotherhood of mankind and he practiced this in his day-to-day life. All were equal in his eyes. No one was great and no one was small. He believed that it is our actions, not our birth, that determines our status. The caste system was incoherent to him. Those of the so-called 'lower castes,' were most dear to him, simply because of their humility and their helplessness. He felt an overwhelming connectedness to all around him – regardless of their caste, race or creed. He denounced the caste system and viewed the whole world as his family and all human beings as his brothers and sisters. He spoke out against injustice wherever he found it, and truly felt the sufferings of the people.

He was increasingly drawn to spiritual devotion and often spent long hours in the company of wandering yogis and joined them in singing devotional hymns to the Creator. As he grew older, it became his daily practice to rise each morning, more than an hour before dawn. He would wade out into the river near his home to bathe, and then he would sit and meditate before beginning the rest of his day. His closest and most devoted companion, happened to be a Muslim, a minstrel named Mardana, who always accompanied him in this, and throughout the rest of his life.

This devotional practice became the basic Sadhana[20] for all who later followed Guru Nanak. It is beautifully described in the following scripture:

> *One who considers himself to be a disciple of*
> *the True Guru*
> *Should rise before the coming of the light,*
> *And contemplate the Name (of God).*
> *During the early hours of the morning*
> *He should rise and bathe*
> *Cleansing his soul in a tank of nectar,*
> *While he repeats the Name the Guru has*
> *spoken to him.*
> *By this procedure he truly washes away the*
> *confusion of the mind.*
> *Then with the arrival of dawn*
> *He should sing the hymns of praise*
> *Taught to him by the Guru.*
> *He should hold the Name in his heart*
> *All through the busy hours of the day.*
> *The one who repeats the Name with his every breath*
> *Is a most dear disciple of the Guru.*
> *The disciple who has received the gift of the*
> *Lord's Name*
> *Truly wins the favor of the Supreme Lord.*

I seek to kiss the very dust
Under the feet of such a one,
Who recites the Name and inspires others to do so.[21]

One morning, in the middle of Nanak's 30TH year of age, he dove deep into the river and did not resurface. He disappeared for three days and was feared dead. It was at this time that his true awakening occurred. What exactly happened is difficult to know, but this story symbolizes the process we all must go through.

The full experience of selflessness is the gateway to knowing our own true nature. Whether we lose our self in a river, or on a mountaintop practicing spiritual disciplines, or living the life of a householder, is not the point. Either way, that part of us that is referred to as "I", "Me" or "My" – must drown, dissolving into union with the very source of all being.

There is no end to God's Praises.
To those who sing His praises, there is no end.

The longing experienced by the young Nanak manifested itself through songs of devotion. He encouraged the singing of God's praises day and night. By so doing, one can find the Love of their very soul.

Nanak sang with all of his heart, so much so, that his singing became the purest meditation. Like the Sufis and Hindu Bhaktis, Nanak taught that singing can bring about a state of divine exaltation – where identification with the limited self is dissolved, the restless wandering mind is stilled, and one surrenders in absolute entirety to God. "Chanting the Naam, the mind becomes peaceful. Anxiety departs, and ego is eliminated."[22]

If you can't see God in All, You can't see God at All [23]

How can one tell if the Teacher they are listening to is truly a man of God? Only those who love their own soul, can truly love others. And only those who love their fellow-man can truly be said to love God. Wherever there is a spirit or a soul, there is God, and those who do not see God in all, they do not see God at all. The Sikh teachings view Hinduism and Islam, (and all religions), as reflections of the one same reality. The true enemies are not people of 'other' beliefs or faiths – but ideologies of fear, hatred and ignorance.

> *In the Company of the Holy,*
> *all one's enemies become friends.*
> *In the Company of the Holy, there is great purity.*
> *In the Company of the Holy, no one is hated.*
> *In the Company of the Holy,*
> *one's feet do not wander.*
> *In the Company of the Holy, no one seems evil.*
> *In the Company of the Holy, supreme bliss is known.*
> *In the Company of the Holy, the fever of ego departs.*
> *In the Company of the Holy,*
> *one renounces all selfishness.*
> *He Himself knows the greatness of the Holy.*
> *O Nanak, the Holy are at one with God.* [24]

Dharma
The word Dharma is often defined as a body of religious or spiritual teachings. There is however a more specific term used in reference to an individual's duty, fulfilled by integrity and observance of custom or law: Svadharma. It has also been described as

the essential quality or character, as of the cosmos or one's own nature. It can also be seen as the unique part that each one plays in the grand scheme of the entire Creation. But perhaps more simply it can be described as our true purpose in life.

Knowing one's Svadharma involves, first and foremost, letting go of the ego's agenda and thereby connecting with one's spirit, or True Nature. Nanak taught that we can achieve this connection, by being completely present within each moment. "Remember God's Name with Every Breath." In every breath we seek that connection to spirit, and then our exact duty, the precise true action that life requires, becomes known to us, as it spontaneously unfolds. It is something that we rediscover in every moment. And in that moment, Peace resides.

Eleven Sikh Gurus

Guru Nanak initiated a legacy of the experience of the highest consciousness that continued unbroken for over 200 years. There were nine successive Gurus following the death of Guru Nanak. Each one carried the light onward, holding that space with grace and humility. Guru Ram Das became the fourth to receive the light. Among his many contributions to humanity – he is credited with beginning the construction of the Golden Temple. *

This temple was designed and built to be open on all four sides, symbolizing that its doors are ever open to all who wish to enter. There's only one Golden Temple in the world. While it is indeed the heart and crown of the Sikh Faith, world-wide, it is not viewed as belonging just to the Sikhs. It's not anybody's property. It is revered as the temple of the Imperial Divine Self that resides within all mankind. To this day, thousands of people pray there every day, and all who come are served and fed through a "free kitchen" manned by volunteers.

---

*Located at Amritsar, in Northern India.

Throughout history there have been many saints and sages who have declared the divine nature of the human spirit, and have truly known that Reality within. The ten Sikh Gurus were all representatives of this universal truth.

Sikh Scripture – Siri Guru Granth Sahib

The teachings, poetry and songs of all the Sikh Gurus, along with the writings of many other saints and sages, were compiled into a large volume known as the Siri Guru Granth Sahib. This scripture is honored by the Sikhs as their Guru, to this day.

The Siri Guru Granth Sahib has been called the first interfaith scripture of the world. "(It) provides to the whole of mankind a universal spiritual code. It shines with pristine purity in its originality, authenticity and the love of all true lovers of God, irrespective of their religion, caste, color, creed or status. (It) embraces within it, not only the writings of its own founder, but the spiritual poetry of saints of different religions, castes, places, ages, and different times.

The selections in the Siri Guru Granth Sahib cover a span of six centuries. In addition to the poetry of the Sikh Gurus, one will also find the divine love of Muslim (Sufi) mystics, and Hindu Saints of all the four Varnas[25]: Brahmins[26], Kashatriyas[27], Vaisha[28] and Shudras[29]."[30]

The words within this scripture are the perfect devotional language, where the heart commands the mind to serve infinity. Once these songs of the infinite are in one's heart, the truth will always seem sweet and victory in life is attainable. Meditating on the Naad (sound current) of the Siri Guru Granth Sahib, lifts one beyond fear and beyond the personality conflicts within the mind. When one reads and listens to the words of the Siri Guru Granth Sahib, it is nothing but the infinite True Self shared by all, that is being expressed. The mind dwells in pure consciousness. It is beyond time and space. There is one infinite consciousness in all creation, and it is the very presence within us.[31]

With this remembrance and meditation, the mind chooses the spirit, grace, and the seemingly remote soul, as if it were more tangible than anything else. Throughout all activities, one is encouraged to continuously relate, connect, and keep the soul with God. When eating, living, waiting, driving, anytime – remember. The very purpose in life becomes the transcendence of all sense of a self separate from God, and from one another.

Which religion one follows may be important in terms of political power or cultural influences, or family ties, but to the soul, it doesn't really matter. Each will serve the seeker in direct relationship to the sincerity and the intensity of desire that they bring to the quest. The Truth always prevails eventually, but humbly remember – that even sincerity and desire, come by Grace, rather than self-will. Sikhism's ultimate goal is to forget the self and to merge with the infinite.

All Is One
by Haring Singh Khalsa

We, whose origin is the One True Reality,
Open our eyes within this dream.

There we find ourselves at play
With the illusion of separateness
and individuality.

And then from the suffering that ensues,
A search begins
For something imagined lost.

Eventually, to realize:
It's all just dreaming.

There is no separate self.

All is One.

Always and eternally.

Our heart of hearts,
Holds this entire universe,
And everything beyond it.

All manifestation shines forth
From the simple Awareness of Being,
I Am.

Humbly,
We make our way
To this remembrance:
In the Divine,
All is Love.

In that Love,
All is Divine.

✶ ❧ ▨

*Avatar Meher Baba, Old Dharamshala, Lower Meherabad,
India on June 3, 1937.*

CHAPTER TWELVE

Modern Mysticism

Laurent Weichberger

Religion has to go, and God has to come. Definitely! *
–Meher Baba

T HIS CHAPTER IS BASED PRIMARILY *on a presentation Laurent gave at the Eastern Heritage Symposium: Beads on One String at Northern Arizona University, Cline Library Auditorium (February 23, 2002), in Flagstaff, Arizona.*

This subject of modern mysticism, where the East meets the West, is extremely close to my heart. This is where the whole book, all the different faiths and traditions, all that we have learned about from these wondrous authors comes together, and it all comes to the West. So, it's one thing for people here in the West (America, England, Australia, and Europe) to get on a plane and go to India, or go to Nepal, or Tibet or make a pilgrimage to Mecca, or whatever. But it is important to realize that there were individuals who came from the East to the West, because of their deep compassion for our situation here. They shared their wisdom with all, for what it was worth. They did not try to convert people to their faith. They simply shared whatever they had found that was true, and then they left again to go back to their respective homes.

Mehera–Meher, Vol.II p.65, by D. Fenster (Ahmednagar: Meher Nazar Publications, 2003).

There are four major figures who are vital to this discussion. In this chapter we will focus on Ramakrishna of Calcutta (we read about him already in Kelly McCabe's chapter), and he figures in to what I want to share here as well. Also, we will take note of his chief disciple, Swami Vivekananda. We will then see about Hazrat Inayat Khan, one of the finest Sufis ever to grace the West. (Karl Moeller touched upon Inayat Khan in his discussion of Sufism, because he brought Sufism to the West). And finally we shall see that Inayat Khan has a connection to Avatar Meher Baba, through Murshida Rabia Martin. Let me be totally clear and honest about my perspective on all this, since I have been following Meher Baba since 1986, and I have dedicated my life to Him.

Ramakrishna

Ramakrishna of Calcutta lived from 1836 to 1886 near Calcutta, India. He didn't actually live in the city. If you would like to read about his life, the last few years of his life are superbly chronicled in the spiritual classic, *The Gospel of Sri Ramakrishna*. Ramakrishna worshipped the goddess Mother Kali. He also engaged the Islamic and Christian faiths before his personal attainment of God-Realization. According to Meher Baba, Ramakrishna is a splendid example of a Perfect Master (Sadguru) or one who has attained the goal of all life.

Before attaining to Truth-consciousness, he had certain spiritual urges, and so he was drawn to certain different faiths, and he went with that, fearlessly. He didn't confine himself to one particular path, or way. Ramakrishna did whatever he felt he needed to do to get closer to the Truth, filled with courage on each step of his personal way. Walking this way takes courage because you can be severely ostracized by your community.

I know about this. You have to be willing to go outside of the box of your faith, of your conceptions, to remain free of everything that constrains you spiritually. That takes a lot of courage actually. He had that courage, and he achieved the goal. By the way, one of my mentors, Don Stevens, reminded me recently that the root of the word, courage, is "coeur" which is the French word meaning "heart."

Ramakrishna's chief disciple was Swami Vivekananda. As far as I know, Ramakrishna never traveled to the West, but he trained his disciples, including Swami Vivekananda, and told him to bring this Vedantic message to the West. One of the last things that Ramakrishna ever said to Vivekananda, just before he died, was this:

> *O Naren, the same Rama and the same Krishna are embodied in this body as Ramakrishna. I am speaking the truth.*[1]

Here is Vivekananda's Master saying to him directly, Have no doubts about what you've experienced with me because I am Rama and I am Krishna as one in this body. This is the absolute highest thing he could have said, because of course Vivekananda would have already full belief that Lord Rama and Lord Krishna are the Avatar, the embodiment of God in human form. So this is the state of Perfection expressing itself to the disciple, for the spiritual benefit of the disciple. It is also a form of encouragement. Mahatma Gandhi said about Ramakrishna of Calcutta:

> *The story of Ramakrishan Paramahansa's life is a story of religion in practice. His life enables us to see God face to face.*[2]

I think this is just about the highest compliment anybody can give you. Coming from Mahatma Gandhi, it means even more. In India, if you go there today, you'll see pictures of Mahatma Gandhi everywhere. I know who Mahatma Gandhi is, but I like to ask anyway: Who's that? – just to see what they might say. Sometimes they reply: He's the Avatar.

Ghandi made such an impression on the Indian people that they think he is as high as the Avatar. I don't believe he was, but that is another story. In any case, this is what Mahatma Gandhi is saying about Ramakrishna – great people saying the greatest things about other wondrous people.

Swami Vivekananda lived from 1863 to 1902, a rather short life. He was born and raised in Calcutta, and he met his Master, Ramakrishna, when he was 18 years old. So as an 18-year-old young man, named Narendra, he approached the Master, and he said to him, "Sir, have you seen God?" I guess he just wanted to get right to the point, because the answer was going to change his life. This would have been in about 1881, and Ramakrishna was prompt to respond:

> *Yes, I see him, as clearly as one sees an apple over*
> *the palm, nay, even more intently. And not only this,*
> *you also can see him.*[3]

Well, Narendra was hooked, and he decided to spend his whole life with Ramakrishna. In 1893, after Ramakrishna passed away, and Narendra had become a monk named Vivekanada, he came to America. The occasion was the Parliament of Religions in Chicago, a colossal spiritual gathering with representatives from all faiths. Vivekananda spoke to that Parliament during the period from September 11 to 27, 1893. So, in Chicago he shared about Vedanta and Hinduism. What did he share with that group of august personages? He said:

> *I thank you in the name of the most ancient order of monks in the world. I thank you in the name of mother of religions. I thank you in the name of millions and millions of Hindu people of all classes and sects. The lord says in Gita,*
>
>> *Whosoever comes to Me, through whatever form, I reach him. All men are struggling through paths which in the end lead to Me.*
>
>> *I fervently hope that the bell that tolled this morning in honor of this convention may be the death-knell of all fanaticism, of all persecution with the sword or with the pen.*[4]
>
> –Swami Vivekananda · September 11, 1893

This *Bhagavad-Gita* quote from Lord Krishna, which Vivekananda shares at the Parliament of Religions, is a perfect example of the Avataric tone we described earlier in the chapter Ancient Mysticism. It is simply incredible that any being can speak that way; it's beautiful and it is a deep challenge to the limited ego of whomever hears such a declaration. Vivekananda is credited with introducing Vedanta and Hinduism to the West. He wasn't the first to translate the Vedic wisdom into English, but he brought the wisdom to the people in a personal way, and that made an enormous impression on the Americans in particular.

Sufism Comes West

Hazrat Inayat Khan was an Indian Sufi who also came to the West. He was born July 5, 1882, and he died in 1927. He also did not live a very long life, but he sure packed in a major amount of spiritual work before he left. Inayat Khan was born and raised in Baroda, India. The title Hazrat is a muslim way of saying that a person is a great one, saintly. The symbol of the Sufis is a heart with wings, and sometimes you see the Muslim crescent moon and star inside the heart, or it may be empty, or it may have some other symbol in the heart. The Chishti order, to which Inayat Khan belonged, used this symbol extensively. He was trained as a classical Indian musician, and he became a mureed (close disciple) of the Sufi Murshid (Master) Hazrat Abu Hashim Madari. Just before Master Madari died, he said to Inayat Khan:

> *Fare forth into the world, my child, and harmonize the East and the West with the harmony of thy music. Spread the wisdom of Sufism abroad, for to this end art thou gifted by Allah, the most merciful and compassionate.*[5]

When Inayat Khan received a direct order of this nature from his beloved Murshid, what do you think he decided to do? He came West.

According to Avatar Meher Baba, Hazrat Inayat Khan was actually a high level saint of the 5TH plane, which means mastery of one's thoughts in the mental world.* Here are Hazrat Inayat Khan's words regarding his own beliefs and process:

> *The Sufi Message does not call a person away from a belief or church; it calls one to live it.*[6]

---

*For more information on planes of consciousness, see the book, *God Speaks,* by Meher Baba.

And then sharing about his sojourns to the West, he said:

> *Following my decision and the call of God, I left
> India in 1910 to sojourn in the Western world, strong
> in the courage of the most blissful command I had re-
> ceived from my Murshid and in the glory of the noble
> object he had awakened in my soul.*[7]

I can say from personal experience that anybody who has a
profound relationship with their Murshid or Spiritual Master,
feels that a direct order given to them by the Master is more valuable than all the treasures of this world. Many disciples wait for
an entire lifetime for just one direct order from their Master.

So, from 1910 for the next 17 years, Inayat Khan traveled
around America, Europe, even as far as Russia, sharing about
Sufism with those he came into contact. In America, he founded
a Sufi order, and worked extensively with one of his first Mureeds,
Rabia Martin who lived in San Francisco, to help this Sufi order
flourish.

There are many letters from Hazrat Inayat Khan to Rabia
Martin, and to others, in which he shares his tremendous belief
in her spiritual advancement and her role.* Yet, she still felt in-
adequate. It is easy to understand this, when after all she was a
Jewish female leader of a predominately male, seriously Muslim,
mystical order shortly after the turn of the century. At a time
when almost no women were being given leadership roles. Murshid Khan bestowed upon Rabia Martin the title, Murshida.

Shortly before suddenly passing away from critical illness in
India, Murshid Khan gave the spiritual charge of his Sufi order
to Murshida Rabia Martin. Now, Rabia Martin did not feel fully
qualified to discharge the huge role of being the Murshida of this

---

*We are currently working on the biography of Don E. Stevens, which will include
some of the correspondence between Hazrat Inayat Khan and Murshida Martin.
–LW

Sufi Order, despite the faith and trust placed in her by Hazrat Inayat Khan.

Murshida Martin felt that Inayat Khan's Sufi Order in the West should be handed over to a living Qutub, somebody who is consciously one with God, or the Avatar. She didn't feel that she should continue without greater guidance, and set out to find a Pefect Master (Qutub) or the Avatar (Saheb-e-Zaman*) to offer this spiritual order back to the master for guidance. According to the biography of Inayat Khan, Rabia Martin became his direct successor in America. Ultimately he appointed her Murshida over his Western Order, which extended all the way from America to Australia and into Europe. Again, Inayat Khan died rather suddenly from illness, and immediately after his death there was a split in allegiance of the Western mureeds. Why? Rabia Martin was doing her work per her orders from Inayat Khan, however, Inayat Khan also had children. And his son said, "No, no, not her. It's me. I'm the one who is succeeding my father." That became a serious split. I'm not going to talk about that split any further here, but it is important to recognize this situation, and future generations will make what they want to out of this issue. Even in the life of Mohammed (peace be upon him) there was a split immediately after his death. This was the start of the Shia (the party of Ali) as opposed to the Sunni (those who followed Caliph Abu Bakr) and that rivalry continues to this day.

Avatar Meher Baba

Baba was born February 25, 1894, and he passed away on January 31, 1969. So before Meher Baba was born, Swami Vivekananda was already standing in Chicago addressing the Americans about Vedanta and Hinduism. The spiritual fields of the West were being prepared by this ground breaking sharing of, not

---

*Another translation of Saheb-e-Zaman is Messiah, Anointed One, or "Man of the Age."

just Vedanta, but Sufism as well. Then, as we know, many people came from the East to share their spiritual values, such as the Dali Lama of Tibet. It is easy to take it for granted now, because people come from the East all the time. Buddhist monks come, Sufis come, Hindu Swamis, all these people come here. But at that time, in turn-of-the-century America, it would have been quite exotic for anyone to come from the East and share about all this mysticism, here in America. The ones who do such spiritual work are the modern mystics.

I have also been asked to share more personally, about my journey into God. I really had no direct interest in God as a child, I was more interested in playing basketball, and then *Dungeons and Dragons**. Then my father committed suicide when I was sixteen. Needless to say, that experience left me disoriented, and it wasn't until about six months had passed that I regained enough equilibrium to realize that I was deeply stuck. The abandonment by my father left me holding many unresolved issues, and I realized clearly that I needed a spiritual teacher or master. Being a teenager living in Manhattan, I at once set out in search of my master, for as any real New Yorker knows, you can find anything in New York. On the first day, I was not successful, but my intention was clear and strong and I felt intuitively it was just a matter of time (and patience), both of which I seemed to have a lot of at that point. After a couple of weeks, I went to visit Patrick (a close friend of my family) at his apartment in Westbeth. On this occasion, he already had visitors (which was rare), and I was introduced to Michael, a middle-aged University Professor of English and an accomplished Julliard musician.

To make a long story shorter, it was through Michael that I came into contact with the spiritually progressive "Unity" group of Christians, who helped to prepare me for what was ahead spiri-

---

*We used to play AD&D in Westbeth late at night with Marco and Gabriel Abularach, Mark Vincent (Vin Diesel) and Taiyoung Ahn.

tually in my life. Within a few months I again met with Michael and also the Stalker family (who he explained were followers of Meher Baba), at a midtown Manhattan coffee shop. We had just come from singing, "We are the World" at a special event that broadcast our live singing around the world, and that day I had my first direct contact with Meher Baba. It was during the conversation at the coffee shop, when Michael asked Doug Stalker if he had a picture of, "The Ancient One." This piqued my interest, as I was an avid reader of *Dr. Strange* comic books as a kid, and so this name, The Ancient One, had deep personal relevance to me.* There is no way that Michael could have known about this childhood connection. So, when Doug produced a folded piece of paper from his wallet, and handed it to me, I opened it to see a black and white photo of Meher Baba looking right into my eyes. As soon as our eyes connected, I recognized Meher Baba as the Spiritual Master I was seeking. I knew him and felt his presence. I felt the intensity of his love, grace, and peace right then and there in the coffee shop. Doug told me to keep the paper (which was Meher Baba's Universal Message). Even though it was worn, and folded (from being in Doug's wallet), I felt I had just been given an extremely holy relic.†

By that summer, I was making my plans to visit the Meher Spiritual Center, in Myrtle Beach, and at Michael's suggestion, I started corresponding with some of the Baba followers down there. In response to one letter which I wrote to David Silverman, he sent me a little card with Baba's photograph on it, and this quote at the bottom: "If you make me your real Father, all differences and contentions between you, and all personal problems in connection with your lives, will become dissolved in the Ocean of my love."‡ For some reason, as soon as I read that quote on the bottom of that little card, I said to Baba, "I am making you

---

*The Ancient One is the name of Dr. Strange's spiritual master.
†See Chapter Images section (photo #26) for an image of this relic.
‡Quote from Baba is from his message, *My Dear Workers*.

my Real Father, Baba," and I meant it. Since that time, over 20 years ago now, Baba has been my Spiritual Master, Real Father, and Beloved God who has never let me down, ever. If there are times when I do not feel his presence in my life, I know it is I who have been absent, not he. Meher Baba is the most important person (or being) in my life simply because he is the most real, and responsive, and reciprocal relationship I have ever had. His love is pervasive, and he communicates to me through multifarious mediums of communication, which would take a-whole-nother book to elucidate. Suffice it to say that through dreams, spiritual experiences, intuitions, the communication, love and care of those who are in my life, and countless other ways, Meher Baba has made himself present in my life, and continues to support and sustain me in my spiritual walk with him. Through Baba, I met my beloved wife Lilly. And it is because of Baba that I have the courage and inspiration to work with these glorious *beads* * to fashion a book that in some small way celebrates the light of His Divine Presence with the world. May it be so.

Meher Baba's given name was Merwan Sheriar Irani. He was born and raised in Pune, India, to a Persian family. His father, Sheriar, came out of Persia as a Zoroastrian in the dervish tradition, ardently seeking for God, longing for God. Meher Baba indicated that it was because of his father's intense longing for God that he was born to this Irani family.

He had a normal, if not excellent, childhood until as a young man in college he met a Perfect Master named Hazrat Babajan. She had come from Afghanistan, and now was what we would call a homeless woman living in Pune, India. She did not care for her own welfare, in the true "fakir" tradition. She slept outside under a large tree, eating only what food people brought to her, and she loved tea. If she would walk around town, shopkeep-

---

*This term, beads, is in reference to the contributing authors of this book, which was tentatively titled, *Beads on One String.*

ers would come out and say, "Please, have tea. Have a pakora,
here, have a samosa." She would eat it, of course, but she was
rather indifferent to her own comfort. She sat under her tree
surrounded by people who wanted to meet her, and talk to her.
If it would rain, she would sit there under the tree in the rain. If
it was sunny, under a scorching sun, she'd continue to sit there,
no problems. She was a most remarkable woman, and Meher
Baba called her the "Emperor," and revealed that she was in fact
a Perfect Master – consciously one with God. One day in 1914,
when Merwan was 19 years old, she kissed him on the forehead
underneath that tree. Later he said that when she kissed him on
the forehead, he also experienced being one with God. Here is
exactly what he said about that experience:

> *Babajan kissed me on my forehead in January 1914,*
> *and that very instant I experienced my infinite*
> *Ancient One state. This experience will ever remain*
> *beyond words. However, to give you some idea, first*
> *I entered the infinite vacuum. Nothing was there,*
> *no one, no Akash (primordial matter). The Gross,*
> *Subtle and Mental worlds ceased to exist, even as*
> *illusion. This was followed by the infinite bliss of*
> *Self-realisation. But soon after, for nine months, I*
> *had to go through indescribable spiritual agonies,*
> *and something urged me to come down to normal*
> *human consciousness.**

In order to return to his "normal human consciousness," he
instinctively sought out contact with the four other living Perfect
Masters in India: Narayan Maharaj of Kedgaon; Tajuddin Baba of
Nagpur; Sai Baba of Shirdi; and lastly Upasni Maharaj of Sakori.

---

* See also *Listen, Humanity*, by Meher Baba (Edited by D.E. Stevens), Appendix II,
Reminiscences pp. 245-247.

Upasni Maharaj was the direct disciple of Sai Baba of Shirdi, and it was this Sai Baba who gave God-Realization to Upasni Maharaj, who then in turn performed a tremendous amount of spiritual work with the young Merwan Irani (before he was renamed as Meher Baba). About his first meeting with Sadguru Upasni Maharaj, Meher Baba said:

> *As I approached Maharaj, he flung a stone at me. It hit me on the forehead and drew blood. That spot was the same place on my forehead where Babajan had kissed me. That hit was the first stroke of Dnyan (divine knowledge) that initiated my apparent coming down from the infinite ancient state. After several meetings and contacts with Maharaj, over a period of seven years, I established myself in the full normal human consciousness of man as the God-Man. Then I had both the infinite divine and the ordinary human simultaneously harmonised in me ...*

What an incredible story. This is the new perfect drama for the modern age. The main point here is that his experience from Hazrat Babajan was so far out that he literally needed the help of another living master to fully integrate it and to be able to work in the world himself as a living spiritual master, and as his master, Upasni Maharaj later explained, as the Avatar of the Age.

In 1922, Merwan gathered his first disciples, which he called "Mandali," which means "of the circle" (a circle of disciples) and can also mean "close family." By June of 1922, he had established his first ashram, which he named "Manzil-e-Meem," which literally means the "House of M" in Persian. Merwan spoke in Persian, his native language, as well as Gujarati, Hindi, and was fluent in English. In fact, he was a poet as well. He later founded his headquarters near Ahmednagar (in Maharashtra state India) at what is now known as Meherabad. Today there is a large spiritual center at Meherabad, and his tomb is there, which continues to be a pilgrimage destination for tens of thousands worldwide.*

As Meher Baba, he opened a free hospital, and free schools, one for girls and one for boys of every religion, sect, caste, creed. Zoroastrians and Muslims learned alongside Hindu "untouchables." Baba himself was totally against the "caste system" and worked to undo its grip on the Indian mind-set. He allowed everybody to come and he worked with all their individual temperaments, which proved to be quite difficult. Even early on in his work, Baba was living the message of "beads on one string."

In July of 1925, Baba told his disciples that he planned to keep silence for a period of one year. Upon hearing Baba's plan to remain silent, one of his disciples said that if Baba remained silent that the world would be deprived of his spiritual teaching. Baba was quick to reply, "I have come not to teach, but to awaken." This conversation was on July 9, and the next day July 10, 1925, he started observing complete silence. That "one year" stretched to 44 years of complete silence. And because he said, "I have come not to teach, but to awaken," which were some of the last words he ever physically spoke, this phrase became the catch phrase for his entire life. It is literally carved on his tombstone.

Even with this self-imposed silence, it did not hamper his activities at all. In fact, he became even more active. In order to communicate, he first started writing with chalk on a small blank slate. Eventually, a disciple suggested that he use a small board with the letters of the English alphabet painted on it, and he could point to each letter to spell out what he wanted to say.

---

*See Appendix, Sacred Places, p.364 (photo of tomb) and p. 368.

Baba settled on this method, and it was known as his alphabet board. Instead of having a normal conversation, he would listen and then spell out his response by pointing to the letters on the alphabet board. For decades, this is how he managed to talk to somebody in silence. It is a fascinating fact that many who were in conversation with Baba, while he used his alphabet board, experienced hearing him speak to them internally, and that this external aspect was somewhat redundant.

Eventually, Meher Baba's life in India settled back down to the point where he could begin a series of world travels. His first visit to Europe and the West had Baba taking a boat from India and arriving in Marseilles, France, on September 11, 1931. There's that date again, so strange. Vivekananda spoke in Chicago on September 11, and here Meher Baba is coming on his first European visit on September 11 – amazing. I believe there is some sort of giant global spiritual balancing act taking place with these dates, so much light and then so much darkness. From France, he goes to America, and then continues on this world tour.

Later, he would travel to Persia*, and then in 1938 he bought a small blue school bus in India, the kind we see driving around, only quite small. He then proceeded to load it full of his women disciples, from East and West, and they drove all around India, doing special work. He had one or two men with him, to help with the bus, the luggage, and all that, but he drove all around doing this with the women.†

Meher Baba's work and spiritual influence continued to spread and his reputation as a Perfect Master grew, bringing him disciples and followers from all over the world for the next 10 years. Then, in 1949, on October 16, he literally walked away from that life, and began what was to be known from that point onward as Meher Baba's New Life. He declared in forceful terms

*The country of Persia was renamed as Iran in 1935. Meher Baba self-identified as Persian.

†Kitty Davy was one of the disciples, from England, and she writes about this period in her book, *Love Alone Prevails,* (Myrtle Beach: Sheriar Press, 1981).

that he was leaving Meherabad, and would take up a New Life of wandering where he and those who remained with him would rely "wholly and solely on God," and those who were not with him would be sent back home. Only one or two remained at Meherabad, where he had already built his tomb and which was one of the only possessions he kept in his name. He said something like: Sell everything. Sell the hospital. Sell the school. Sell all the pots and pans. Sell everything that's in my name – except one thing, the little piece of land where we built my tomb, just keep that tomb and that land, so that if I should die you can put my body there. Everything else, get rid of it. Everything else that belonged to him was either sold or given away.

Most everybody in his circle was shocked by this, especially since it occurred at the height of Baba's popularity as a master. They must have thought: What do you mean, you're leaving? Where are we supposed to go? What are we supposed to do?

He told them to either join him in this New Life, or go home. The disciples initially said they wanted to join him, but then it got complicated, when Baba showed them a long list of conditions under which they would be allowed to remain with him during the New Life, which had no termination date.

So, he gave all these conditions, you can read about it in the books about Baba, and he was clear that this is what the New Life would be about. One of the points was that the New Life companions must always be cheerful. Baba's disciple Eruch clarified this for us in Mandali Hall* one day, saying, "It doesn't mean always be smiling, or giddy, or laughing." But those disciples who did join Baba, if they were found to be in a bad mood, or crying over this or that, Baba just sent them right home. Boom – gone. Another condition was that no one should relate to him outwardly as if he was a spiritual master. He was to be known as their elder

*Mandali Hall is where Baba sat with his Mandali (close disciples) at Meherazad, India.

brother, and spiritual companion, not a perfect master, nothing like that. All that, he said, belonged to his old life.

Baba was really quite sincere about his New Life. They ended up sleeping anywhere, in orchards, on train platforms, in abandoned buildings, anywhere. What did they eat? They begged for food, and Baba distributed whatever food they managed to acquire. He took this New Life extraordinarily seriously, and the companions who accompanied him have given a brilliant account of that period of Baba's life in a book, *Tales from the New Life* *.

It is important to realize that at this point, Baba had thousands of followers in India, hundreds who lived with him personally, and there were followers all over the world who were in regular contact with him. But he was adamant that if anyone did not like his conditions for remaining with him, they should simply go home.

Some asked, "If we do go home, and then you return, can we join with you again?" But he refused to answer that question, and other questions about the meaning of the New Life. What we do know is that some went home, and twenty† set out following him while at the very end of the New Life, there were only four left who didn't get sent home. Four survived the conditions. He gave up that phase of the wandering in India in 1952, so he was on the road for quite awhile. Sometimes they were walking, sometimes they would get a ride on a bullock-cart, or whatever. But once he ended that phase, he entered another phase which he named the "Fiery Free Life." He said this meant he had become completely free of all attachments and bindings. This is all very mystical talk, you know? But he was serious about these different phases of his life.

Baba eventually said the disciples could buy the land of Mehe-

---

*For a story about the creation of this book, see *Sexuality on the Spiritual Path*, pp. 48-49 (London: Companion Books, 2007).
†From *Lord Meher* p.3435: four women and 16 men accompanied Meher Baba on the New Life, so 20 people plus Baba.

rabad back, get the pots and pans back, and life returned to what would be externally normal, however the atmosphere around Baba had shifted. He started things up again at Meherabad, but it was with a different flavor, a different tone. Certain special work had been done on a mystical level. After this turning point, two things stand out as notable differences: one is that his work with the West took on a greater external importance, and a universal spiritual center was founded by him, and for him, in Myrtle Beach, South Carolina. Another aspect that became predominant was that he held "Sahavas" gatherings, and other large spiritual events in India, which served to bring hundreds of people together in the close company of the Master.

A "sahavas" is a group of chosen people living day in and day out in the intimate company of the Master, and they are invited by the Master to participate in his life this way. Such a sahavas is extraordinarily rare. In the occasion described by Don Stevens*, there was a "four language group" sahavas. One week was devoted to each of the four main language groups of India, where people would come from all over India, and Baba also allowed two from the West.[8] For example, there was one week of just Hindi-speaking followers of Baba, another week was just for Telegu-speakers, etc. For that sahavas at Meherabad, Baba dictated seven special messages, which were posted for all to read. Here are two of them:[9]

1. "Real happiness lies in making others happy. The real desire is that which leads you to become perfect in order to make others perfect. The real aim is that which aims to make others become God by first attaining Godhood yourself."

2. "Desire for nothing except desirelessness. Hope for nothing except to rise above all hopes. Want nothing and you will have everything."

---

*For a detailed description of sahavas with Meher Baba one should read the book *Listen, Humanity* by Meher Baba and Don Stevens, a wondrous volume. -LW

This notion of sahavas is somewhat foreign to most in the West. Simply the idea that anyone would travel ten thousand miles at great expense, just to be in the physical presence of Meher Baba for a few days, whether he said anything or did anything at all, is not easily understood. What if he would just be sitting? Then they would come and just sit with him. Or what if he was pacing back and forth? They might ask a question; he may answer, he may not. This is known as sahavas, or "darshan," (depending on what the situation is), but in any case he would want those who came to be totally natural, and worry free. He would say something like: If you have something to ask, tell me. If you want to go do something else, then go home, just go. But if you are here, be with me, don't think about what is going on elsewhere, just live with me while you are here.

It was all very natural. What a tremendous blessing to those who took such an opportunity! And because he was in silence, he dictated those seven messages and had them put up around Meherabad, so that while people were milling around each day, after a meal, or on their way to bed, they could read what he had said. Of course he also gave spontaneous discourses on spiritual subjects, or had discussions with the group, or whatever was most natural for the situation.

Let's continue to look at Baba's life and work during 1952, since it is a pivotal year for him and his Western followers in particular. First of all, this year marked his first visit to the Meher Spiritual Center in Myrtle Beach. This center was created by some of his American followers who acquired 500 acres of land in South Carolina, and gave it to Baba as a gift*. The story of the creation of this center is long and involved, however an important point is that he also had certain guidelines that he wished followed, and this center met all of them 100 percent. This

*The land itself was actually a gift directly from Elizabeth Patterson to Meher Baba, and she worked with many others to establish the Meher Center.

center is still there today, and they preserve it in an immaculate way, working to maintain the atmosphere that he brought there and it is kept in perfect shape just as it was when he personally stayed there. I encourage many to go there for personal spiritual retreat, and I go as often as possible.

Now, on May 24, 1952, while traveling from Myrtle Beach towards Ojai, California, Baba and his women disciples had a very violent car accident, a collision with another car, near Oklahoma City, in a little suburb called Prague. He was thrown out of the car, with half of his body crushed – his face, his nose, his mouth, and his leg was broken. Baba was bleeding profusely from his head onto the rich soil of heartland America.* He had previously stated that America wanted his blood.

Later he explained that the car accident in America served a spiritual purpose – to break the back of the Kali Yuga: the machine age. Those disciples traveling with Baba got help and two ambulances arrived. Baba himself had ordered the medics to take his beloved, Mehera, in the first ambulance, and then him to a little medical clinic in Prague. The doctor working there, Dr. Ned Burleson, was totally astounded. He later shared that while treating Meher Baba, who was obviously lacerated and suffering with a broken leg, he noticed Baba was so happy and cheerful. Dr. Burleson reported that Baba had a glow and a real happiness which seemed incomprehensible under the circumstances. Baba later indicated that a tremendous spiritual work had been accomplished through this particular accident, and that is why he was so very happy. That doctor who treated him became one of his followers. Now if you go to that little clinic today, they have put up Baba's picture on the wall, and they have a little bookshelf below his photo with Baba's books. They like him a lot. All of this is in a little town in Oklahoma; it's quite bizarre.

---

*There is now a blossoming Heartland Meher Baba Center at this location.

Something else happened in 1952 that is also important. As we had mentioned previously, in 1945, Murshida Rabia Martin wanted to find the Qutub, or the Saheb-e-Zaman, to get continual guidance for her Order of Sufism. If I were in such a position I would probably do the same thing. She had heard about Meher Baba from some of his Western disciples, and so she sent for one of her mureeds (a disciple), Francis Brabazon in Australia, and told him to come to America, so that he could bring her to India and finally meet Meher Baba. She was inwardly convinced of Baba's divinity. So, dutifully, Francis Brabazon came from Australia to America as requested, and then before they could make the journey, Rabia Martin died of cancer. Just before she died, she appointed as her successor Ivy O. Duce. A Murshid (or a Master) initiates another Master, it doesn't just happen on its own. In almost every spiritual tradition there is a process. So when Rabia Martin chose Ivy Duce she entrusted her with the instruction to find Meher Baba, and to give him her Sufi Order.

In fact, Rabia Martin had already entrusted her own spiritual welfare and those of her Mureeds to Meher Baba's guidance, through correspondence with Baba, but this would take the matter to another level of officially laying the order at Baba's blessed feet. These are radical decisions. We are discussing the fate of Inayat Khan's Sufism in America, and it was not considered lightly by anyone. The reality of this process would come to offend a tremendous number of Sufis in America, Australia, and Europe. People like things to be the way they want them to be. Why so few trusted the wisdom of Murshida Rabia Martin, who was hand picked by Hazrat Inayat Khan as his own successor in the West, is a mystery. Perhaps it was because she was Jewish, or perhaps because she was a woman. In any case, many did not want Hazrat Inayat Khan's Sufism given away to anybody. Nonetheless,

this is exactly what Murshida Rabia Martin, and then Murshida
Ivy Duce, went on to do. Murshida Duce found Meher Baba at
Meherabad, and gave him her Sufi Order. She was convinced of
his spiritual status, and she said, "Please take it." Baba replied
that he would accept the Sufi Order, but that she would have to
remain as the functioning Murshida. He made it clear to her
that he would guide the order, but that it was her destiny to be
the Murshida of this Sufi Order. Essentially he said, You guide it
and I'll guide you. He warned her to remain 100 percent honest
and not to pretend to have a level of spiritual advancement that
she did not experience.

Naturally, she wanted to just give the whole affair over to him,
but he would not allow that. He said something like: Yes, I accept
it – here, take it back now and do as I instruct you. Go back to
America. Be honest. Tell people that you're not one with God.
Tell them that you're still longing for God. Be honest about it,
and through your honesty I'll guide you and I'll guide the rest
of Sufism.

So she did as instructed, and she went back to America serving
as the Murshida of Sufism Reoriented under Baba's direction
until her death. All this was totally under Meher Baba's direct
guidance. For a detailed account of how the order went from
Murshida Rabia Martin to Meher Baba before even Ivy Duce got
involved, Don Stevens wrote a wondrous article titled, "Who
Brought the Sufis?"* I think that's as close to the actual history
as we will ever get, because he was a mureed of Murshida Martin
at that time in 1945, and was directly involved with Meher Baba
in the creation of the new Sufism Reoriented under Murshida
Duce.[10]

Okay, lets move on to February 10, 1954, a special day for
Meher Baba, as it is the day he decided to publicly declare his

*This article is available at: www.jaibaba.com/mandali/ds/broughtsufis.html

Avatarhood in India. He waited until he was just about 60 years old to publicly share with the world his experience of his own divinity. So at the age of 60, he finally starts openly telling people: All right, so I didn't tell you before, but now I can tell you – I am the Avatar. Wow! To his close disciples, some of whom already knew this, it was not a great stretch. They had already accepted him as a God-realized Perfect Master. Upping it one notch like that, sure, no problem, so he's the Avatar, great. To some other disciples, and a lot of other people, this was real news. After he publicly declared himself to be the Avatar, he said to his disciples they could tell other people as well. One of Baba's closest Mandali, Eruch, confided in us that he was not sure whether Baba really was the Avatar, even though it was his job to read out Baba's messages, and whatever Baba dictated from his alphabet board, to thousands of people who would come for Baba's darshan programs. So, it was not a requirement than anyone believe this or not, it was just the time to make it known. Baba himself later declared:

> *Now is the time for all to understand that I am God in human form.*[11]

Remember we discussed Jesus earlier, and he spoke directly to his disciples, saying something like: Hey, so you know that I'm the Christ but do me a favor and let's not tell anybody else. Here we have Baba at age 60 saying basically: You know I'm the Avatar, and go ahead, it's okay, now you can tell the whole world.

So they did, and the word started to spread father and wider about Meher Baba, the Avatar. There can be no doubt that by the late 1960s Baba was one of the most popular, if not the single most popular, Spiritual Master in the world. How else could I have heard about him, in a coffee shop in New York in early 1986?

Getting back to Meher Baba's life, we find that on October 7, 1954, he completely stopped using his alphabet board in favor of unique hand gestures. His gesture for a woman was to place his thumb and finger around his wrist, like a bracelet. His gesture for forgiveness was reaching both hands in toward his heart and then giving and releasing. He gave forgiveness. Baba's sister, Mani, once told us that she noticed his gesture for love was the same as the gesture for forgiveness.

In July of 1956, Baba made a 2ND visit to the Meher Spiritual Center. Now just think about this: the 1950s in South Carolina, and this guy comes over from India saying: I'm the Avatar.

This story may help give the context of how unreal this all was for the American psyche at this time. Baba came down from New York with some disciples, got off the train in South Carolina and naturally he had to use the toilet. At the train station he sees not one but three bathrooms: Men, Women, and Colored. So he used the bathroom for colored people. Segregation was everywhere, and he did not ignore it, instead he just gave his love to the people in South Carolina, and all over America. He traveled all over America, and shared freely of his wisdom, and his love. He just gave love, and then he went back again to his home in India. This is East meets West. It is important to note here that those who traveled with him reported that whenever an African-American person came to see him, Baba would stand up and greet them with even more respect than the average visitor.

After this, he went to Ojai, California, still in 1956. There is a center there called Meher Mount, an incredible place founded by Jean Adriel, Alexander Markey and Agnes Baron. If you've never been to Ojai, make the visit; it is so beautiful. Baba also went to Australia a number of times, 1956 being his first visit down-under. And then, in September of 1956, he published his long-awaited seminal book, *God Speaks*. If you only ever read one Meher Baba book, that is the one to read.[12] He stated many things about the relevance of this particular book, and that it was the dissemination of His Divine Knowledge in the world. He said that since technology is rising to its height, so spirituality also should rise to its height. These forces should be kept in balance.

In December of 1956, just as Baba had fully recovered his health from the 1952 car accident in America, he has a second accident, this time in India. The intriguing thing about these two car accidents is that in Oklahoma, there were only women in the car with Baba, whereas in this car accident in India, there were only men in the car with Baba. I think this is worth mentioning, because America is often criticized as being too masculine in energy, too warlike and aggressive in its foreign policy tendencies, too much testosterone. And the East is frequently referred to as being supremely feminine, expressing the qualities of compassion, nurturing and other deeply spiritual qualities. So isn't it amazing that with America there are only women in the car, and in India there are only men in the car? Another thing to note is this: in the accident in Oklahoma, one side of Baba's blessed body was badly crushed, whereas in the India accident, it was the opposite side of his body that was severely injured. As a result of the 1956 India accident, Baba's hip joint – literally called the universal joint – was almost completely demolished.

The doctor said he would never walk again. But he did. Here is a saying from Baba (as told to Filis Frederick):[13]

> *Inscribe these words in your heart: Nothing is real but God. Nothing matters but love for God.*

Still not finished with his work in America, we find that Baba makes a third visit to the Meher Spiritual Center, this time in 1958. Again, people from South Carolina, North Carolina, Georgia, New York, California, and all over would come just to see him for an hour, or less. What an unlikely place to build a Universal Spiritual Center, you might think. He could have created a more accessible center in Chicago, San Francisco, New York or even Albuquerque. He did visit San Francisco and New York and many other places in America, but he made his center in Myrtle Beach. Also in 1958, Baba made his first visit to the center created for him in Australia, now known as Avatar's Abode.

This marks the end of his world traveling period. The next 10 years of Baba's life are enjoyed in a residential compound where he lived and worked with his "resident Mandali" in greater periods of total seclusion. Then, in July, 1968 he declared, "My work is done 100 percent to my satisfaction." At this time also, Baba would make cryptic remarks that his life would soon be ending.

By January 30 of 1969, as a result of the two automobile accidents, and other work that he had done for decades in India that created a wearing out of his spine.[14] Baba was suffering tremendously physically. He would have chronic violent muscle spasms move throughout his body, so much so, that his body would rise up off his bed in convulsions. His disciples would literally hold him down to keep him from falling off his bed.

The last night, January 30, 1969 – and I heard this directly from the Mandali who was his night watchman in this story – Meher Baba was resting in the company of his night watchman, Bhau Kalchuri. It was just the two of them, and Baba was trying to rest, and Bhau says it was amazing that after so many months of intense physical suffering, suddenly Baba had a really totally restful day. He told us he was so happy that Baba could just rest. Then Baba turned to him, at 10 P.M. that night, and he communicated with hand gestures,* saying, "Remember this: I am not this body." And Bhau received that. At 11 P.M., something very unusual happened according to Bhau, Baba looked at him and instead of gesturing said out loud, in Hindi, "Yad rakh ..." which means, "Remember this..." But he spoke out loud for the first time in 44 years, and then continued with the rest using hand gestures: "I am not this body." Bhau was stunned. He had never heard Meher Baba speak, because he joined Baba after the silence had commenced. And then at midnight, Baba just gestured the whole thing again, "Remember this: I am not this body." The next day, Meher Baba passed away, and was buried in his tomb at Meherabad.

Bhau said to us in India, "I never told anybody that Baba spoke out loud." For 32 years he kept quiet about this experience of Baba speaking out loud. We were all stunned and shocked at this report, as we listened to Bhau in India during July 2001. Did this really happen, is Bhau telling us the truth, or was this some spiritual experience meant only for Bhau? Or was it something else entirely? Many are doubtful of this story, but that is what I was told. God only knows.

Conclusion

I have some special words from Baba that were given out to the press in a filmed interview made by Paramount Studios, for a newsreel, back when you saw the news before they played the feature film in the movie theater. There was no television. This is what Meher Baba says in 1932 in London during the film[15] using his alphabet board. Of course, in the film he remains silent. The Paramount film has a static text introduction in black and white, very old school:

---

*Meher Baba had given up the use of his alphabet board in 1954 relying upon hand gesturing instead.

India's Mute Messiah
London – He hasn't spoken for 7 years!
Shri Meher Baba pointedly proclaims his message to the world
– by interpreter.

Then Baba starts to dictate:

> *My object in coming to the West is not with the inten-*
> *tion of establishing new creeds or spiritual societies,*
> *and organizations. I see the structure of all the great*
> *religions of the world tottering. The West is more*
> *inclined towards the material side of things.*
> *I intend to bring together all religions and cults like*
> *beads on one string, and revitalize them for individ-*
> *ual and collective needs. This is my mission to*
> *the West.*

Questions & Answers:
The next section of this chapter is dedicated to questions that I
received at the Beads on One String Symposium (NAU, February 2002), and then finishes with Meher Baba's explanation
regarding the "Ten Principal States of God," originally published in *God Speaks*, as I describe them for this publication,
and a prayer.

DENISE: What does the name "Baba" mean?

LW: A number of years ago I actually wrote an article about
what the name "Meher Baba," means, so I feel very happy that
you asked that question. In India, you know there's a word for
"father," right? That's not the word "Baba." That's a different
word. But, if you have somebody in your life who's like a father-
figure, a mentor, a guide, somebody who you feel you can go

to for spiritual guidance, they call that person, "Baba." Maybe Ameeta can add something to that, but that's my experience of the word "Baba."

AMEETA VORA: A lighter note on the word "Baba," you see a lot of sadhus[16] walking around, and usually they're just referred to as "Baba ... Ah, there goes a Baba." You know? A couple of months ago there was a guru who had come from India. He was referring to himself, and he goes, "You know how you see those Babas walking around the streets of India?" And he was referring to himself that way. Yeah, so it does mean "mentor," or whatever. But sometimes just the wanderers are also referred to as "Babas."

JIM COURSON: What is your intention, or goal, with following Baba, what is it about for you?

LW: That's a very good question, Jim. I think you asked me about that before, but I'm going to have a different answer this time. It's not what it used to be, I can tell you that. After 15 years[17] with Baba, I can sort of boil it down to something extremely simple. I'm aiming for simplicity. Like the sticker on my day-runner says, "Simplify." On the spiritual path I think it's very important to have simplicity, and not complications.

So what does that mean to me? It means "Am I pleasing Meher Baba?" Which does not mean, "Am I pleasing Jim, and am I pleasing my wife Lilly, am I pleasing Ameeta?" That's not what it means. It means, "Am I being true to Baba within me?" Meher Baba as a spiritual master to me is an external reflection of who I really am. Because of my ignorance of who I really am, he's very helpful as a reflection. But when I become who I really am, there won't be any separation. I will know that Meher Baba is the same as the Real me. Until I achieve that union, that Oneness with Meher Baba, I rely upon the reflection to help me realize that inner self, that Real me. And the best way in my current process to do that is to continually ask, in every situation, in every moment, as often as I can remember: Am I pleasing you? Then listening for his voice within me that may say, Please do this. Would you do that? Would you rest? Would you listen to Lilly – just this one time? You don't like to listen, but listen to Lilly this time. {audience laughter}.

So pleasing Baba may mean pleasing Lilly. It may mean pleasing Jim. But Baba may say something to me internally, that inner voice of Baba, and I may say to Baba, "Sure, I'll do it." And Jim may say, "What?" And Lilly may go, "Jim, what's he doing?" And Thom may say, "I don't know." {audience laughter}. But that doesn't matter, because pleasing Baba is more important than pleasing anyone else. That's what it means to me right now.

JONI HAUG: Rather than a question, what I have is something to relate. The story that Karl Moeller brought up, about the Sufi student who asked a question whose answer he wasn't ready for.[18] Something less than a year ago, I got to sit with a group of people, with a Hopi-initiated priest, who was asked by one of the other ladies, "Had we entered the point of no return, in terms of the change in the world, or was there still time or things that we could do to avert that?" And he answered her, and she didn't like the answer, so she paraphrased her question and asked it again. And his answer the second time was, "You didn't listen the first time. I already answered your question." And let it go at that.

LW: Yes, thank you. I think we had one other? Yes, don't be bashful. It's okay.

RUBY: When you try to listen to Baba, and follow Baba, is that separate from following God to you?

LW: It's identical to me. The only difference would be that I totally respect and honor if somebody else has another aspect of God

that they connect to. I don't require that everybody say, "Baba."
I say, "Baba." You may say something else. Somebody else may
say, "Moses." Somebody may say, "Mahavir." For me, the way
I look through my eyes, they're all just manifestations of the
same Truth. That "beads on one string" analogy is very potent,
because the string is the Truth that runs through each bead. The
bead itself is the manifestation. One bead looks like Buddha. One
bead looks like Mohammed. One bead looks like Meher Baba. It
keeps going like that. If you look at the bead, somebody may say,
"No, no, this bead is orange, that one's red, this one's square,
that one's round." But the string that goes through the core of
the bead is the Truth. So if you look beyond the surface, you find
the same Truth inside the bead. I experience that Truth as Meher
Baba. Anybody else? {audience clapping}.
ASPEN WEICHBERGER (age six): What does Jesus mean?
LW: Ooooh, big question: "What does Jesus mean?"
KM: Jesus means, "Suffer the children to come unto me."
LW: Yes, absolutely. I think Jesus means, "Find some way, any
way, to love God." And then you'll make Jesus happy.
{Aspen and India Knoles go on the stage and start dancing. Tirza
Newman joins them, and also starts dancing ... }

*The Ten Principal States of God according to Avatar Meher
Baba*[19]

   1. "God in the Beyond-Beyond." Baba says this is the original
state of God, and that it is unknowable, indefinable. It's the original state of God before Creation existed and before consciousness
arose. He said that if you try to describe this original state of God
with words, you can't do it, and what you end up doing instead is
describing the second state of God.
   2. When you try to define the indefinable you end up with

the second state of God which he says is "God in the Beyond." This is a state of God where there is latent consciousness, and it's the formless infinite God that is not manifest in Creation. It is beyond Creation. This is the formless infinite state that the Muslims call "Allah," the Hindus refer to as "Paramatma," and Christians refer to as "God the Father."

3. Then we have God as the "Emanator, Sustainer, and Dissolver" of Creation. The Hindus call these states respectively, "Brahma, the Creator; Vishnu, the Preserver; and Mahesh, or Shiva the Destroyer (or dissolver)."

4. Then we have God as an embodied soul. That state of God enters the Creation. God says, "This Creation is here for Me to experience ..." God enters the Creation, and according to Baba, the first forms that God inhabits in Creation are gaseous forms. The first seven gaseous forms are the beginning of evolution,* and that state of God associates with these states of matter to experience Creation.

5. After this, we have God as a soul in the state of evolution. God literally moves through the Creation, using different forms to gain greater and greater experience, greater awareness, greater consciousness. It's a little bit different than the evolution of Darwin, because it's tied to a spiritual journey, and a spiritual purpose. The purpose is to realize Divinity consciously.

6. Then we have God (soul) as a human in the state of reincarnation. Remember this is not a different God from the earlier states, it is just a different experience that same God is having. As the philosopher said, "We are not human beings having a spiritual experience, we are spiritual beings having a human experience." So here God has become a human being, but the journey isn't over. There are things to unlearn, there is a lot of baggage to unburden oneself of, and that baggage was obtained

---

* "Actually the consciousness of the soul utilizes the stone-form only after innumerable cycles and ages of diverse experiences through diverse species of forms, of which there are seven major different kinds of most, most-finite and most, most-gross gaseous forms, which cannot even be concretely grasped nor imagined by ordinary human beings." -God Speaks, by Meher Baba, p.13 (New York: Dodd, Mead & Co., 1973).

in the subhuman forms. There are feelings and thoughts that just are not true such as lust, greed and anger. This all has to be purified. This occurs naturally in the spiritual process of reincarnation. During this process individuals can move closer and closer to the Truth of who they really are. Who are they? They're all God, but a human being in the state of reincarnation normally does not experience being God.

7. As this reincarnation process is a purification process, it brings us to the state of a spiritually advanced soul, who is more pure than the average human being. Such a soul experiences being closer to the Divine Presence within themselves. The God within is now clearer to them than it is to the ordinary human being, and this experience has them behaving in a more saintly manner. Simply put, they're more spiritually advanced than most of us.

8. This is the state of one who arrives at purification of consciousness, where there is no feeling of separation from God, there is no "I" and "thou," no lover and Beloved, there is only One. Total complete Oneness with God is experienced, by the soul – *perfection*. God IS but Creation is not, and the I am God state is experienced – that one is called, "God as Divinely Absorbed." That experience of being one with God, according to Meher Baba, means that you experience that you are God, and that the Creation is really non-existent. In other words, it means that the Creation existed to bring you to the point where you say: Oh, I'm God.

When you have that experience, the Creation no longer has substance, it no longer has meaning or value for you. Because you become everything, the Creation vanishes as nothing. With a divinely absorbed person – "God as Divinely Absorbed" – they do not experience the Creation, and according to Baba, that person usually drops their physical body (dies) after three days. The body falls away. Why? Because the human form no longer serves any purpose. The purpose for the human form has been served when the consciousness becomes one with God. Some people don't like this idea at all. They say: I don't want that.

I know a lot of people who don't want that. They have no idea what that state means, they just don't like the sound of merging with the infinite, and they think it means loss of individuality. Baba is clear that it is an individual attainment of infinite bliss, infinite consciousness enjoying the limitless.

9. So the one who experiences being one with God, and their Creation consciousness vanishes; they just exist in the bliss of being one with God, which is the experience of infinite knowledge, infinite power, and infinite bliss, for that one individual. With no consciousness of Creation, the infinite Power has no scope, so it is really the Infinite Knowledge of "I am God" and the Infinite Bliss of being that consciously. Now, there are certain individuals whose destiny it is to come back into Creation consciousness and help others to become one with God. They do come back, a journey of return to Creation consciousness, with their transcendent God consciousness – of being one with God, fully intact. They return into the Creation, and then they start saying things similar to a prophet or Avatar, but they may not gather a following or lots of disciples. Still they say things that most people don't usually say, and to a select few that they are destined to help they disclose: Oh yeah, by the way, I am now one with God. You wanted that? Well come over here, I'll help you. I'll make you one with God, but you have to do exactly what I say, because I just did it. So if you want that, I will give it to you directly.

What happens is, somebody becomes God consciously, and

when they come back, if their destiny is to help one, or maybe two people to achieve that, they're known as a, "Liberated Incarnate Soul." They have what Hindus call "Moksha," or liberation, because they are literally liberated from the bondage of reincarnation and karma. They can help one or two people attain that state, and they don't normally attain to public prominence. The Hindu Saint, Muktabai, the sister of the Perfect Master Jyaneshwar, is a great example of a liberated soul.

10. Then we have the 10TH primary state of God, which is the show-stopper. That's the one who comes back into Creation consciousness and they are honored as a Spiritual Master, a Prophet. They have a circle of disciples. They make a big impact on the world. That's a "God-Man," or a "Man-God." The difference is this: a Man-God goes through the evolutionary process, arriving at Oneness and then comes back – so the Man-God has taken this huge journey and then comes back. The God-Man is the Avatar, and this is the most unusual case where the living Perfect Masters of the time bring the formless infinite God directly into a male human form. The living masters around Buddha brought Siddhartha down into form. The living masters around Jesus brought him down into form. The living masters around Mohammed, around Krishna, all were brought into form to live as the world Prophet, the Avatar, the Christ. When I say brought into form, I mean that while the mother carried the fetus to term and all that naturally happens still happens, the soul that incarnates in that form is brought there by the Perfect Masters of that Age. The God-Man is an individual whom all of humanity comes to know and respect on some level. He becomes a household name. A God-Man stops the show, and everybody eventually looks and says: What, whoa, who is this?

A Man-God, a Perfect Master, may do their work, and may

be somewhat obscure or they may gain a large following. They help their circle of disciples realize the Truth. People who are on the spiritual path may say, Yeah, there's a Perfect Master. But the whole world may or may not ever come to know who they are. They're one with God, and they make others one with God as a Man-God, but the whole world may never know them. However, with the God-Man, the Avatar, people the world over invariably come to say: Holy cow, that life was totally incredible! And the whole world comes to know that God came again in human form.

What I have shared above is directly from Meher Baba, it is not my experience. I re-articulate it only because of the tremendous help it has been to me, since I started reading *God Speaks* in 1986, while attending college. Even with all these explanations from Meher Baba, and the intricacies of the spiritual path, I am reminded to keep the focus on what is important, as Baba says: "God is not to be learned or studied or discussed or argued about. He is to be contemplated, felt, loved and lived."[20]

Lastly, I cannot close this chapter without sharing a profound interfaith prayer that Meher Baba dictated using his alphabet board. This is the Master's Prayer[21] that he gave in conjunction with the Prayer of Repentance (not shown). Just as they asked Jesus, "How should we pray," so they asked Baba, as they have asked all great spiritual beings. This was his response from silence:

The Master's Prayer

O Parvardigar,
The preserver
and protector
of all:

You are
without beginning
and without end

Non-dual
beyond comparison
and none
can measure you.

You are without color
without expression
without form
and without attributes.

You are unlimited
and unfathomable
Beyond imagination
and conception

Eternal and imperishable.

You are indivisible
and none can see you
but with eyes divine.

You always were
You always are
and you always will be.

You are everywhere
You are in everything

and you are also
beyond everywhere
and beyond everything.

You are in the firmament
and in the depths,
You are manifest
and unmanifest,
on all planes
and beyond all planes.

You are in the three worlds
and also beyond
the three worlds.
You are imperceptible
and independent.

You are the Creator,
The Lord of lords,
the knower of
all minds and hearts.

You are omnipotent
and omnipresent.

You are knowledge infinite
power infinite
and bliss infinite.

You are the ocean
of knowledge,

all-knowing,
infinitely knowing,
the knower of the past,
the present,
and the future,
and you are
knowledge itself.

You are all-merciful
and eternally benevolent.

You are the Soul of souls,
the one with infinite attributes.

You are the trinity
of truth, knowledge, and bliss.

You are the source of truth
the ocean of love.

You are the Ancient One
the Highest of the High.

You are Prabhu
and Parameshwar.

You are the Beyond God
and the Beyond-Beyond God also.

You are Parabrahma,
Allah,
Elahi,

Yezdan,
Ahuramazda,
and God the Beloved.

You are named Ezad,
The only one worthy of worship.

✳   ❖   ▣

Epilogue
Laurent Weichberger

TODAY IS SEPTEMBER 11, 2008 and I want to tell a story. Jim Courson encouraged me to state (outside of the framework of chapters and themes), what is important. So, I came up with what is most important, but never wrote it down. Then, yesterday, on the way to school with my daughter, Aspen (now in 8th grade), we were being delayed because of road construction. This got us into a conversation about the state of the roads, and that Romans built better roads than Americans, and she said the Roman roads lasted, "like a thousand years." That lead to a conversation about when the Romans lived, and from there to when Jesus lived, and then to the fact that the Western calendar revolves around the birth of Jesus (which somehow escaped her memory, don't ask). She sipped her hot blackberry tea with milk from a travel mug, trying to wake up. Then we got to the fact of multiple faiths, and multiple calendars, and then we talked about violent conflicts between faiths, and faith prejudice (literally pre-judging someone based on faith). Aspen did not like that at all, and we tried to figure out a solution to these problems. We talked about how everyone on the planet just needs to move towards peace, and healthy loving relationship, and spiritual understanding. She then said exactly (word for word) what I wanted to write at the end of this book, but never told anyone. I will quote her instead, since I can't say it any better: "Why don't they just sit down and have tea together and see who the other person really is?" So, the next time you meet someone who seems to be from a different culture, and perhaps have a different faith, why not ask them, "Want to join me for a cuppa?" *Om.*

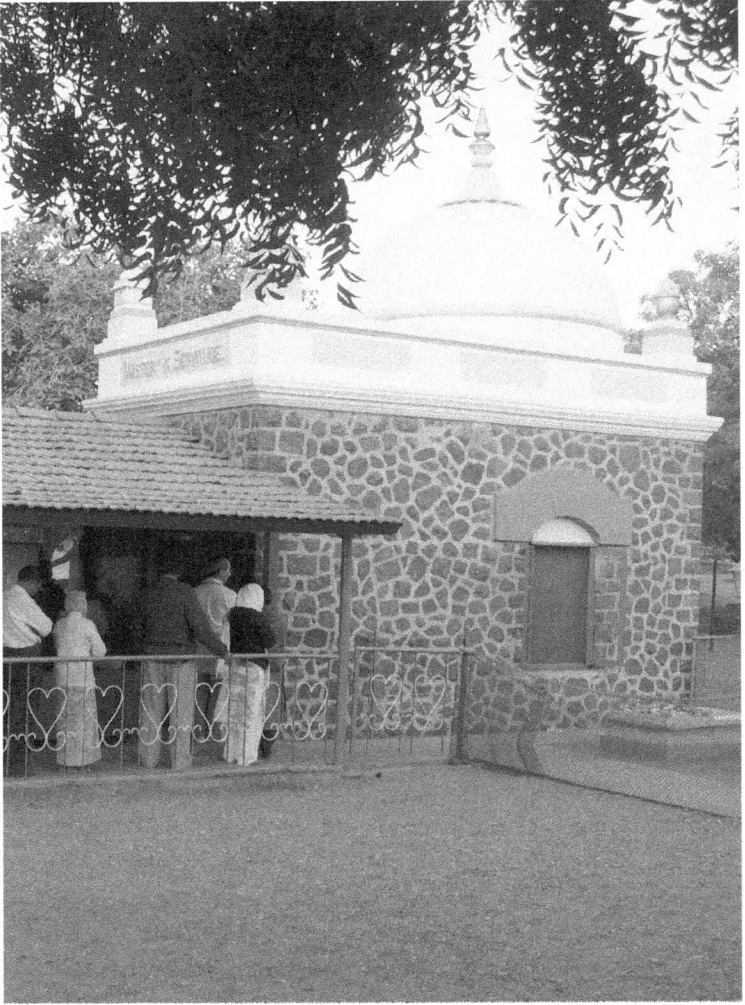

The Tomb * *(Samadhi) of Avatar Meher Baba, at Meherabad, India, November 27, 2007.*

---

*Meher Baba's motto, "Mastery in Servitude" can be seen above the door. Also at the top of each corner of the tomb roof, around the dome, can be seen detailed models symbolizing four of the great spiritual traditions: A Christian cross, a Hindu temple, a Muslim mosque, and the Zoroastrian fire brazier, with flames rising.

Sacred Places

Laurent Weichberger

MEHER BABA PERSONALLY VISITED, AND in some cases also explained the spiritual significance of, many of the most sacred places of the world.[1] While an exhaustive study of all the sacred spots that Baba spent time visiting is beyond the scope of this chapter, it is abundantly clear from what I have been able to easily research of how he honored and loved these places, that he saw all faiths as expressions of the One Truth. In addition, he seemed to delight in being able do his spiritual work at a location where the atmosphere contained holy spots belonging to multiple faiths, as if this was helpful to him for some reason.

Zoroastrian

- Baba visited the Zoroastrian Fire Temple in Udwada, Gujarat, India with some of his men Mandali around November, 1914.[2]

Hindu

- Baba visited Kailash Temple, and Indra Sabha, as well as other caves at the Ellora Caves, India.[3]
- Baba with his close Mandali went to the center and tomb of Sadguru Ramakrishna of Calcutta in India. This was during the New Life phase of Baba's work. About Ramakrishna, Baba remarked, "Ramakrishna was Rama & Krishna personified!"[4]
- In April 1949, Baba visited the town of Ayodhya, India which is well known as the birthplace and home of Lord Ram. At that time, according to Bhau Kalchuri, "In Ayodhya, Baba

contacted a subtle conscious yogi known as Aisruddin, who was much revered. Afterwards, Baba indicated that he wished to contact sadhus. The mandali gathered a hundred and four sadhus in one place. Baba did his work of bowing down to them and giving the sadhus a few rupees each before leaving by train for Gonda."[5]

• Meher Baba visited Shivaji's Forts (near Satara, India).[6]

Buddhist

• Baba visited Sarnath, India on January 19, 1939 with some of his women mandali.[7] He returned to Sarnath again during his New Life phase with his companions in December, 1949.[8] Sarnath is where Buddha preached his first "sermon" (or taught the Dharma) and initiated his first disciples, shortly after receiving Enlightenment. It is one of the four holiest places of pilgrimage for Buddhists the world over.

Jain

• Jain temples at Mount Abu, India.[9] According to Eruch Jessawala (as related to me by Don Stevens), when Baba would stay overnight at the temple complex, he would roll himself in a blanket and sleep on the steps to the main Jain temple. Eruch was Baba's companion on these visits.

Christian

• When Baba was in Muree, India with a group of close Western disciples (including Kitty, Norina and Elizabeth) on Easter, Sunday, April 16, 1933, he visited a church. According to Bhau Kalchuri:

> *It was Easter Sunday and Baba visited a Christian chapel with the group, remarking, "All worship*

*returns to me. The sigh within the prayer is the same
in the heart of the Christian, the Mohammedan, or
the Jew. They are all indivisibly longing for the same
God."*[10]

- Meher Baba visited St. Theresa of Avila's place.[11] He gave it high spiritual honor, explaining to those with him about holy places and calling it one of, "the four centers of Europe."
- While in Assisi, Italy, on August 7, 1932, Baba visited a cave that had been used by St. Francis of Assisi.[12]
- When visiting Venice, Italy on August 18, 1932, Baba saw St. Mark's Cathedral and he indicated, "This church is one of the four great spiritual centers of Europe. The whole structure corresponds to the Avatar's twelve disciples of the inner circle and one hundred and eight disciples of the outer circles."[13]
- While in Cairo, Egypt on August 25, 1932, Baba visited a cave used by Mary, Joseph and the baby Jesus during their flight from Herod, and while living in exile in that land.[14]

Islamic - Sufi
- Meher Baba went to the Qutub Minar (and climbed up the inside staircase), in Delhi, India.[15]
- In Delhi, Baba visited the Tomb of Qutub Nizamuddin.[16]
- On more than one occasion, Meher Baba bowed down at the tomb of Qutub-e-Irshad Khwaja Saheb Mu'inuddin Chishti in Ajmer, India.[17]
- On November 11, 1951 Meher Baba sat in seclusion in the cave of the Sufi Qutub Zarzari Bakhsh, who was Shirdi Sai Baba's Master, near Khuldabad, India. He also visited the tomb of this Sufi Master, and various Muslim shrines in Khuldabad.[18]
- Baba visited a mosque (and tomb) of the eighth Imam of Shiite Muslims, in Meshed, Iran (Persia).[19]

Sikh
- Meher Baba visited the Golden Temple of the Sikhs, in Amritsar, India.[20]

Meher Baba

WORLD WIDE:
- Meher Baba's tomb at Meherabad, India.
- Meher Baba enigmatically remarked that "a place on the Ligurian coast of Italy," was one of the spiritual centers of Europe.[21]
- While in California, on August 2, 1956, Baba visited "Meher Mount" a spiritual center created for him by Jean Adriel, Alexander Markey, and Agnes Baron near Ojai, California at the summit of Sulphur Mountain.[22]
- The Meher Spiritual Center in Myrtle Beach, South Carolina is the universal spiritual center in America, founded by Meher Baba himself, in conjunction primarily with Elizabeth Patterson.
- Baba did special spiritual work at the "Manonash Cave" at Hyderabad, India.
- Meher Baba's first automobile accident site, near Prague, Oklahoma (USA).
- Meher Baba's second automobile accident site at Satara, India.
- Meher Baba has a special fondness for the "Agha Khan's bungalow" (where Baba cared for some masts), in India.
- Meher Baba did special seclusion work at the Panchangani cave, India.

PUNE, INDIA:
- David Sassoon hospital where Baba was born.
- Meher Baba's childhood home, and Pumpkin house.
- St. Vincent's High School where Baba studied as a boy.

- Qutub Hazrat Babajan's tomb, Pune, India.

PLACES OF MEHER BABA'S OTHER MASTERS:

- Qutub e Irshad Sai Baba, Shiridi, India.
- Sadguru Upasni Maharaj's tomb, Sakori (near Shirdi), India.
- Qutub Tajuddin Baba's tomb and the asylum where he was incarcerated, in Nagpur, India.
- Sadguru Narayan Maharaj's tomb, Kedgaon, India.

Other Places

- On September 13, 1931, Baba visited Glastonbury, England (home of the "Chalice Well" associated with the Holy Grail).[23] It is not clear from the literature whether or not he went down to the well.
- Baba visited various spots in China, including Hong Kong.[24]

While this is just an opening attempt at such a study, I have no doubt that future generations will make an exhaustive account of all the places that Meher Baba visited and what he said about those locations. I hope the above overview helps amplify the message that all faiths are expressions of One God, who loves us dearly and wants our love in return.

About the Contributors

☼

MARY ESTHER STEWART lives in Flagstaff, Arizona. She is a retired educator, a widow, grandmother and artist. She spends her time drawing, painting, writing, gardening, and enjoying her grandchildren. Esther works with Franciscan groups in promoting the spirituality described in her chapter. She has published several articles in Franciscan periodicals, both in America and in the United Kingdom. She works with two Franciscans in promoting the writings of St. Bonaventure, a 13TH century Franciscan theologian, and she gives days of reflection on Franciscan Spirituality. She is an active member of San Francisco de Asis Roman Catholic Parish where she teaches Church history and gives presentations on the Psalms, the New Testament, and Franciscan themes.

HARING SINGH KHALSA is a graduate of the University of Washington, and works for the U.S. Postal Service. He and his wife have a son and a beloved granddaughter. Haring was born and raised a Christian, and his father was a Presbyterian minister. Somewhere towards the end of his high school years, he decided that the Truth could not possibly be the exclusive property of any one faith and began a quest to learn what wisdom might be found in other spiritual traditions. In 1972 he began studying both Kundalini Yoga and Sikh Dharma with Yogi Bhajan, taking vows as a Sikh the same year. He began teaching Kundalini Yoga in 1974 and became a minister of Sikh Dharma. He has been practicing and teaching yoga and meditation and living a vegetarian, primarily ayurvedic lifestyle ever since. Haring delights in the experience of human kindness – whenever and wherever it may be found, and is especially grateful for the gift of sometimes being allowed to play a part in it.

THOM KNOLES was born into an American military family in post-war Europe. Thom was reared in international settings that exposed him to diverse cultures. As a boy living in Asia, he developed an early interest in Eastern philosophy and alternative approaches to psychology. While still a teenager, Thom qualified as a yoga instructor; by his early twenties, he had become a renowned teacher of Vedic meditation. Thom's scholarship in the Sanskrit classics and knowledge of the Vedic sciences has gained him worldwide recognition. In India, he is widely revered and is described as another "maharishi" (great seer). By the late 1970s, Thom's research was focused in cognitive neuroscience and its relationship to revelations then emerging in quantum mechanics and Vedic psychology. In Europe, Thom participated at the highest level in now-legendary think tanks and in groundbreaking research into consciousness. His synthesis of modern scientific theory with proven techniques of Eastern philosophy and spiritual practice give him a unique perspective from which to teach, and the ability to present the attainment of expanded consciousness as man's birthright, rather than as something miraculous and all but unattainable. Today, Thom is one of the world's most sought-after consultants, mentoring people at all levels of society in sustainable approaches to personal and corporate development. His client base is global and includes some 12,000 students. An exponent in the direct lineage of the Shankaracharya tradition, Thom has become the world's foremost instructor of Vedic meditation outside of India, and is a leading authority on the Vedic worldview. Anyone interested in learning more about Thom and about Vedic Meditation may visit his website: www.introtomeditation.com.

KELLY W. MCCABE lives in Flagstaff, Arizona with his wife Tessie and stepsons, Jayme Barbosa and Alex Padilla. He was a monk in the order of Sri Ramakrishna and Swami Vivekananda for 15 years. In 1992 he started his shop, Sacred Rites, in downtown Flagstaff where he sells sacred art and musical instruments from around the world. In 1999 he founded The Temple of the Divine Mother where he performs Puja Sunday mornings, offering prayers for the well-being of our planet and worship of the Sacred in all of its beautiful manifestations. He can usually be found in his shop playing his shakuhachi flute or singing with his sansula kalimba. His first music CD was *Sacred Rites Sacred Flute*. He is currently working on a CD of Sanskrit healing prayers and experimenting with sound healing. Music, sacred art and the Divine Mother is what makes his heart sing. Please visit him, when in Flagstaff, at Sacred Rites, 8 N. San Francisco St., Flagstaff, AZ 86001. He can be reached via email: kellymccabe@mac.com.

LAURENT WEICHBERGER has traveled to India where he stays primarily at Meherabad, a spiritual center founded by Avatar Meher Baba near Pune. In 1997, he moved with his wife & daughter to Flagstaff, Arizona. After settling in "Flag," he co-founded a small spiritual center to freely share the light of divine presence with one and all. Participation at gatherings included people of all faiths. Laurent's first book, *A Mirage Will Never Quench Your Thirst: A Source of Wisdom about Drugs* (Myrtle Beach: Sheriar Foundation, 2003) brought Meher Baba's drug message to a modern audience. He has since contributed to a number of books by Don E. Stevens on practical spirituality, including *Meher Baba's Gift of Intuition* (2006), and most recently *Sexuality on the Spiritual Path* (2007), both from Companion Books. Laurent works as a IT Program Manager at an international investment bank.

KARL MOELLER has been affiliated with the Chishti and Qadiri Sufi Orders of Pakistan and India for almost 30 years. He is a computer industry professional. He is a pianist, keyboardist and composer with multiple album credits and video soundtracks. He is married to a psychotherapist. His novel-in-progress received Honorable Mention in a recent writers' symposium. He has crashed badly on a motorcycle. He has worked as a 3-D animator, as a sound designer on a feature film and has an EMMY Award for Outstanding Achievement in Sound. He believes, as sci-fi author Robert Heinlein does, that "specialization is for insects."

AMEETA VORA takes pride in bringing the Eastern and Western culture together. Ameeta has lived in Flagstaff since 1995 and is very involved in the community in many ways (philanthropic, cultural and volunteering with Hospice). She is a dedicated mother and wants to make sure that her American-born daughter understands and enjoys her heritage. She works at the American Cancer Society as a Quality of Life and Relationship Manager which involves working directly with cancer patients. She aims to minimize the suffering and improve the quality of life of her clients.

GEETA VORA's Jainism started when she was a child. Although born in an ancient Hindu tradition, she found herself attracted to Jainism, their discipline and their very beautiful, simple life. At a very young age, she accompanied a girlfriend to a Sthanak, and started learning this faith, and practicing its disciplines. Her love for Jainism drew her to a man who grew up in a Jain faith, and they had three beautiful children, the eldest and the most beautiful of all is Ameeta!

LOPON TSULTIM WANGMO is a Tibetan Buddhist, and her title "Lopon" means she is qualified to teach. She lives in Kentucky with her little cat Punki and her two kittens (now about four or five years old). Her current study has her preparing to practice counseling using principles of Buddhist psychology for mental health.

YAAKOV WEINTRAUB has traveled many roads on his spiritual path, but always returned to his roots and love for Judaism. He shares, "The seeds of this love were planted by my beloved father, Henry (Chaim) Eliyahu, and mother Dora, who emerged from the ashes of the holocaust with their hearts and spirits still intact, to raise us in a home filled with love and caring. I am deeply indebted to them, and the rest of my family, who have always been there when I needed them." Yaakov has performed as a dancer with the Erick Hawkins Dance company and the Parparim Ensemble, and is a long time student of Aikido, Tai Chi, and music. He has a degree in Electrical and Computer Engineering, and has been involved in starting two successful businesses. He shares, "I am deeply grateful to Meher Baba, my ballet teacher Maestro Zsedenyi, Erick Hawins, and Rabbi David Ingber – from all of whom I have learned so much. My endless gratitude and love to my beloved life partner Jessica, for her understanding, support, and deep love."

WAYNE SMITH is a high school teacher of personal, social, and religious education and helps to edit "Neti Neti," an international Meher Baba newsletter. He is married to Naomi and has two children, Joe and Lucy.

DON E. STEVENS assisted in editing Meher Baba's seminal books, *God Speaks* and *Discourses*, and narrated and edited *Listen, Humanity*. He is the author of *Meher Baba, the Awakener of the Age* (Myrtle Beach: Sheriar Foundation, 1999) as well as several

small books concerning Baba groups and activities. Avatar Meher
Baba pointed out (more than once) that Don was in fact one of
his own Mandali. Don was a Vice President at Chevron Research
(formerly Standard Oil of California) and is now retired, living
in Paris. Despite retirement, he manages to travel around Europe to attend to his numerous Baba groups, and frequently to
America and India, to continue work for Meher Baba which he
knows is necessary.

JANE CHIN was born in Taiwan, spent her childhood in Saudi Arabia, and came of age in the United States. Although Jane's native
tongue was Mandarin Chinese, she learned Queen's English at
the British Section of the Saudi Arabia International Schools
in Riyadh. Jane now dreams in American English. Jane first
trained as a scientist, earning a doctorate degree in biochemistry and launching her healthcare career in cancer research. She
subsequently crossed over healthcare's business divide where
she worked as a medical science liaison. She quit the corporate
life in 2004 and became an entrepreneur to follow through on
a mission to change pharmaceutical industry practices. Jane
sees herself as a member of the "Bridge Generation," where her
multi-continental, multi-cultural, and multi-career adventures
have helped her form bridges between different worlds. In 2008,
she embarked on an experiment to spend 366 days doing what
she loves, to see what success, if any, may follow. What emerged
is Jane's personal journey to reconnect with the Heart Mind and
Inner World Peace. She chronicles her lessons learned in the
website: WhatILoveToDo.com.

End Notes

✧

1.   It is somewhat ironic that as I edit this chapter (September 11, 2008), in Flagstaff, I have received not one but two invitations from my friend Adele Wolkin and the Los Angeles Meher Baba group to be a guest speaker at their Meherabode Meher Baba meeting. I accepted and we shared two lovely circular gatherings with them on June 8, 2008 (topic: The New Humanity), and October 19, 2008 (topic: Meher Baba's Gift of Intuition). So, apparently this old pattern really is shifting. Thank you Baba, and Adele.

2.   In a discussion of this chapter over dinner November 11, 2007.

3.   For the story of Abraham and the sacrifice of his son, see Genesis 22:1-14, and see also the *Qur'an*, Surah "The Arrangers" (Al-Saffat) 37:83-111.

4.   Bharata was also exceptionally humble in that while he assumed the role of King during his beloved brother Rama's exile, he refused to sit on the throne, instead placing Rama's sandals on the throne, and he sat next to the throne.

5.   St. Catherine of Siena, who was a "real saint" according to Meher Baba. I prayed in her bedroom, at her family home in Siena, and it was wondrous. See *Lord Meher*, p. 3818. For the life of St. Catherine, read: *Saint Catherine of Siena*, by Alice Curtayne (Tan books and Publishers, 1980).

6.   During a conversation about a draft version of this chapter on March 20, 2008 in State College, PA.

Throughout the endnotes, "Lord Meher" means: *Lord Meher*, by V.S. Bhau Kalchuri, (Myrtle Beach, SC: MANifestation Inc). Quotes from Meher Baba © 2008 Avatar Meher Baba Perpetual Public Trust, Kings Road, Ahmednagar, MS India 414 001, unless noted otherwise.

1.   From *Lord Meher*, Volume 19, p. 6347.

2.   From Ma Jaya Sati Bhagavati at Kashi Ashram in Sebastian, Florida.

3.   Karl Moeller wrote to me on September 10, 2007: "Sufism is not a faith separate from Islam."

4.   This is a 2007 estimate from Nation Master.com Statistics on the United States, at www. nationmaster.com/country/us-united-states (visited September 22, 2007)

5.   This is a 2007 estimate from the CIA, printed in The World Factbook at www.cia.gov/library/publications/the-world-factbook/print/xx.html (visited September 22, 2007).

6.   See the encyclopedia Britanica online at: www.britannica.com/eb/article-9034123/Fertile-Crescent.

7.   Regarding Moses, his is somewhat of a special case, as Meher Baba indicated: "Moses was on the 6TH plane. His seeing the land of Israel but not being able to enter it is symbolic of his experience on the 6TH plane of seeing God, but not yet merging in Him. Though when he dropped his body Moses realized God." (From *Lord Meher*, p. 5264). On the

world stage, Moses is definitely considered a prophet, which is why I included him in the prophetic tradition.

8.   Ba'ha ullah (also Bahaullah) is the founding figure of the Baha'i faith. According to *Lord Meher*, Volume 4, p. 1240, footnote 1: "Bahai is a mystical religion founded in Persia during 1863, by Bahaullah (Hussein Ali, 1817-1892), who emphasized the spiritual unity of all mankind. Bahaullah translated is the 'Glory of God.' Bahaullah was a follower of Bab, the title of Ali Mohammed of Shiraz (1819-1850), who was a Qutub." For more information see: info.bahai.org/bahaullah.html.

9.   For the genealogy of Abraham, see Genesis 11:10-26. For the life of Abraham, see Genesis 11:27-25:9.

10.   For the genealogy of Lord Jesus, see the New Testament, Gospel according to Matthew 1:1-17.

11.   For Jacob marrying Leah and Rachel, see Genesis 29:21-28.

12.   For God changing Jacob's name to Israel, see Genesis 32:24-32.

13.   For the life of Joseph, a son of Jacob and Rachel, start at Genesis 30:22.

14.   For David being from Bethlehem, see The Old Testament book, 1 Samuel 16:1-13.

15.   For the earliest complete New Testament, see the "Codex Sinaiticus" at www.sinaiticus.com/ and for scans of the actual Greek writing go to: www.textexcavation.com/codexsinaiticusscans.html

16.   For a great example of the honoring of a Prophet from God, see the story of Jonah starting in the Old Testament book of Jonah 1:1.

17.   For Jesus mentioning himself as God's Son, see the New Testament John 10:22-39.

18.   For Jesus as the way, truth and life see John 14:6.

19.   See the New Testament book of Matthew, Chapter 16:13-20.

20.   Quote from Meher Baba on Jesus from *Lord Meher* (Volume 3, p. 1034-1035).

21.   Islamic calligraphy from, Sufi, Expressions of the Mystic Quest (Avon Books).

22.   *Ibid.*

23.   For the annunciation, see Luke 1:26-38.

24.   For the similarities of Arabic and Hebrew names, words, and common usage, compare the Arabic greeting "Salaam aleikum," to which the response is "Alaikum assalam," and the Jewish greeting "Shalom aleichem," and the response being, "Aleichem shalom." The words mean, "Peace be upon you." The Arabs and Jews remain close siblings, even thousands of years after the original split between Abraham's sons, Ishmael and Isaac. Thank you to Shelley Silbert for her sharing of the Hebrew version via email (September 18, 2007). As she commented regarding the above similarities, " ... unfortunately, the most painful conflicts sometimes arise between siblings ..."

25.   For the idol worship problem in the Old Testament (Pentateuch) see the *Bible*, book of Exodus 20:22-23.

26.   Quote from *Qur'an*, www.hti.umich.edu/k/koran//browse.html (viewed in 2002).

27.   Quote from *Hadith* from www.geocities.com/~abdulwahid/hadith/qudsi.html (viewed in 2002).

28.   Karl Moeller noted this was also true of the written *Qur'an*.

29.   Basra is still a city in what is now Iraq. Hazrat Rabia lived from 714-801 CE. She was a poet mystic of the highest order. Good references for her life and work include: *Muslim*

Women Mystics: The Life and Work of Rabi'a and Other Women Mystics in Islam, by M. Smith, and *Doorkeeper of the Heart: Versions of Rabi'a*, by Rabi'a al-Adawiyya and C. Upton (Pir Press, 2004). The poems rendered into English by Upton are inspired translations, and he has a good overview of Rabia's life in the introduction.

30. Don Stevens related, "One time when he was in India to visit Meher Baba, Baba had specifically arranged that Don (who was with Baba's Mandali, Meherjee Karkaria) stop [the car] as they ascended the ghats to see a spot where Shivaji fought one of his major battles against the Moguls ... When Don was with Baba on their arrival at Meherazad afterwards, Baba asked Don about his thoughts on this and at that time confirmed that Shivaji was indeed one of three minor incarnations of the Avatar, all in India." Excerpted from an email clarification by DES to LCW on October 12, 2007, Subject Re: Shivaji.

31. Quote is from: *Meher Baba is Love, Sayings from the 1958 Sahavas* (Myrtle Beach, South Carolina, © 2007 Avatar Meher Baba Trust).

32. Quote about Rama by Sadguru Ramakrisha is from *The Gospel of Sri Ramakrishna*, p. 189, ©1942 Swami Nikhilananda, Ramakrishna - Vivekananda Center. The phrase "Brahman Absolute" means the Supreme Reality of the Vedic path.

33. Whether Hanuman was literally an animal of the type monkey is doubtful, but that's how Hanuman is portrayed culturally.

34. The best version of *Ramayana* that I have seen in English is the deeply inspired *Ramayana*, by William Buck (University of California Press: 2000).

35. The best version of *Mahabharata* that I have seen in English is also by William Buck, *Mahabharata*, (University of California Press: 2000).

36. Quote about Krishna by Meher Baba from: *Discourses*, "The Place of Occultism in the Spiritual Life," pp. 197 (Myrtle Beach: Sheriar Press, 1987).

37. Hafiz quote and story of Baba's gesture is from *Lord Meher*, Vol. 20, pp. 6712-6713.

SUFI
BIBLIOGRAPHY/REFERENCES
BOOKS:

- The Holy *Qur'an*, translated by Marmaduke Pickthall, Sh. M. Ashraf, Lahore, Pakistan.
- *Unseen Rain, Quatrains of Rumi*, by J. Moyne and C. Barks (Threshold Books, 1986).
- *In the Tavern of Ruin, Seven Essays on Sufism*, by Dr. Javad Nurbaksh (pub. 1978. Italics in the original), p.107.
- *Sufi Symbolism*, by Dr. Javad Nurbakhsh (Vol. 1) (Khaniqahi Nimatullahi Publications).
- *Suhrawardi's 'Kitab Adab al-Muridin'* ('A Sufi Rule For Novices') translated by Menahem Milson (Harvard University Press, 1975).
- *Ihya Ulum-id-Din*, by Muhammad el-Ghazzali (Vol.4), p.238.
- *The Tale of the Reed Pipe*, by Massud Farzan (Dutton, 1974).
- *Sufi Essays*, by Seyyed Hossein Nasr (Schocken Books, 1977).
- *Hadiths* found in Sahih al-Bukhari, (one of the trusted *Hadith* sources).
- *The Sufi Orders in Islam*, J. Spencer Trimingham (Oxford University Press, 1973).
- *The Walled Garden of the Truth: The Hadiqa of Hakim Sanai*, by Hakim Sanai translated by Major J. Stephenson (1908), published: (Samuel Weiser, 1972).

WEBSITES:

Internet websites are ephemeral in nature. Not all of the following pages will be available in perpetuity. However, there is a wonderful website which maintains earlier versions of thousands of websites: www.archive.org.

- www.uga.edu/islam/sufismwest.html – listing of Western Islamic and non-Islamic Sufi organizations.
- www.uga.edu/islam/Sufism.html (listing of Eastern Orders and famous Sufis).
- www.sufiajmer.org/html/khwaja_moinuddin.html (Chishti Order site in Ajmer India).
- www.wahiduddin.net/sufi_poetry.htm (excellent site with examples of classic poets).
- www.sufistudies.net/world-community/shabistari.html (analysis of Shabistari and Rumi).
- www.themodernreligion.com/basic/madhab/madhab-nec.htm (the Islamic madhabs, or schools of Islamic law).
- www.books.guardian.co.uk/print/0,3858,5326079-99931,00.html (Turkish Sufism).
- www.sabiree.com/sufism/sama_book/role_of_sama.htm (Chishti Sama),
- www.almusaffir.com/modules/myalbum (Qawwali music).

VEDANTA

1. Study was published in the "International Journal of Neuroscience" in 1986.

2. For stories about the life of St. Francis, including his levitation (flying) see: *The Little Flowers of St. Francis*, by Raphael Brown (Image, 1971).

3. Platt Cline was a founding publisher of *The Arizona Daily Sun* newspaper.

HINDU

- This chapter is excerpted from the yet to be released book, *From the Mississippi to the Ganges (and Beyond)*, Kelly W. McCabe. This material is copyright © 2008 and all rights to this work belong to Kelly W. McCabe. Kelly gives full and free permission to Laurent Weichberger to use this chapter in his book.

JAIN

1. Tirthankara is a Sanskrit word, which means literally "ford-finder," or one that marks the destination. This means the Master is one who helps you cross the river of suffering and ignorance, to find the other shore of God-consciousness.

2. Mahavir means "the great victor," in Sanskrit.

3. Past and present represents yesterday and today, as well as this lifetime and previous lifetimes. Obviously, Jains believe in the reincarnation of the soul.

4. Jiv Daya is love and mercy for all souls. If you have love then you can have Daya (Mercy)... Love for all living beings, from bacteria, to the insects, and up to human. Jiv means any soul, Daya means mercy, but mercy comes with love. – GV. You don't have to love it, but you still have to be merciful. I just think Compassion should be afforded to all souls, and that universal love is important, Jiv Daya stems from universal love. – AV. 5. Geeta says, "Every act of Jainism is based in science. Take for example the way we treat water before its ready for consumption. First thing each morning,, we take fresh clean water, wherever it comes from, then this water is boiled. But if the water has a different color

than pure water, you put Alum, and let the dirt or impurities settle to the bottom and then the water is filtered and then boiled again. Then the water is allowed to cool. Since this is part of every Jain household's ritual every morning, Jain kitchens are equipped with large vessels to purify water. The cooled water is filtered again; finally it's put in a small earthen pot. And then we put the pot in placed is a clean safe spot int eh kitchen where it is ready to be used for everything. One is always mindful of placing the pot carefully sothat it can't hurt anything or anybody. That is the law of science, that you drink clean, pure water. The religion has taught us how to live a healthy life." (Dictated to Laurent in Flagstaff, September 8, 2008).

6. Ameeta says, by "eat all of it" a Jain means, all. In India, it is a traditional Indians eat without utensils. So, before a meal, you thoroughly wash your hands and then sit to take your meal. After the meal is complete, as Jains, we wash our fingertips with the water we are drinking with dinner, into the plate, then swirl that water around in your plate, so that every last grain (and leftover whatever in your plate) is cleaned and mixed together, so that when you drink that, nothing is left. And that is a Jain kid's bane, and their exercise in humility. Jains do not waste food. It is a very scientific religion. Geeta says, "The scientific reason for this practice is that we don't create an environment of cleanliness. Once the plate is ready for final cleaning and if there are no food particles to go into the garbage, none goes onto the earth, there is no rotting food, no pests due to collecting garbage and a clean environment – a green environment."

7. See http://www.lifepositive.com/Spirit/world-religions/jainism/jain.asp.

BUDDHIST

1. Lao Tzu *Tao Te Ching*, (Penguin Books, 1963) p. 57.

2. See: *The Great Disciples of the Buddha: Their Lives, Their Works, Their Legacy*, by N. Thera & H. Hecker, p.7. The word "Tathgata" is Sanskrit meaning, "one who has thus gone (Tath-gata) and, one who has thus come (Tath-gata) as well as, some have argued, one who has gone to That (Tat-gata). Still others assert that the name means, "one who has found the Truth. It is the name the historical Buddha Gautama uses when referring to himself." From en.wikipedia.org/wiki/Tathagata, accessed September 2008; sourced from Nyanatiloka, Buddhist Dictionary, 4TH ED. (Buddhist Publication Society, 1980).

3. What the Buddha Taught, by W. Rahula, P.xv (New York: Grove Weidenfeld, 1974) [hereafter "Rahula"].

4. See http://en.wikipedia.org/wiki/Kapilavastu

5. See http://en.wikipedia.org/wiki/Bodh_Gaya

6. Rahula, p.xvi.

7. Rahula, p. xv.

8. See Sutta, NO. 16 found in *The Middle Length Discourses of the Buddha, A New Translation of the Majjhima Nikaya*, by Bhikkhu Nanamoli and Bhikkhu Bodhi, (Wisdom Publications, 1995), [Hereafter "Buddha Discourses"].

9. Dhamma = "Dharma," and Nibbana = "Nirvana."

10. See Sutta, NO. 26, the Ariyapariyesana Sutta or *The Noble Search, from Buddha Discourses*.

11. Saint Francis of Assisi is historically the first Stigmatic.

CHRISTIANITY

1. See *The New Testament*, Acts of the Apostles.
2. Letter to the Smyrnaeans.
3. It is not the purpose of this chapter or this author to explain the history of Christianity. There are many fine books on the subject that I suggest those interested in the subject should consider.

SIKH

1. This translation of Japji Sahib is available through the bookstore at www.xlibris.com.
2. *Japji Sahib – Song of the Soul* – translation by Ek Ong Kaar Kaur Khalsa.
3. Prajna: Universal Intelligence; Perfect Wisdom; All-inclusive Truth which is Love.
4. Atman: Self (with a capitol "S") which is the spiritual guidance working through the intuitive part of man; the Divine Self within mankind; God within; Pure indivisible Being; Its existence is Light.
5. Yogi Bhajan (Siri Singh Sahib Bhai Sahib Harbhajan Singh Khalsa Yogiji, 1929 -2004)
6. From the 13TH Pauri of Japji Sahib.
7. From the 11TH Pauri of Japji Sahib.
8. From the 14TH Pauri of Japji Sahib.
9. The phrase, "Judge not, and you will not be judged," from *Holy Bible*: Luke 6:37.
10. The process of understanding something perceived in terms of actual experience. A profound recognition of the truth of it.
11. Sukhmani Sahib | |8| |6| |.
12. Sukhmani Sahib | |8| |21| |.
13. Sujata.
14. Devotion. Guru Nanak is associated with this same movement.
15. *Love Poems From God*, by Daniel Ladinsky.
16. Yogi Bhajan.
17. *The Final Truth*, Ramesh S. Balsekar.
18. "Dharma" is used here to reference a body of religious or spiritual teachings.
19. *Holman Christian Standard Bible*.
20. Spiritual Practice.
21. Guru Ram Das was the 4TH in a legacy of ten Sikh Gurus.
22. *Sukhmani Sahib*: Ashtapadi 22.
23. Yogi Bhajan – the very motto by which Yogiji lived his life.
24. *Sukhmani Sahib*: Ashtapadi 8II3II.
25. Hinduism categorizes human society into four "Varnas", and these categories define the group's social standing in marital and occupational matters. Therefore, Varna means "arrangement" in the context of social hierarchies.
26. Brahmin – "scholarly community," including teachers, doctors, and other scholars.
27. Kshatriya – "warriors and rulers or politicians community."
28. Vaishya – "mercantile and artisan community."
29. Shudra - "service-providing community."
30. "Sri Guru Granth Sahib Darshan" – Bibiji Inderjit Kaur Khalsa, Ph.D.
31. Yogi Bhajan.

MODERN MYSTICISM

My research about Ramakrishna and Vivekananda done at www.geocities.com/neovedanta, and the publication which is the cornerstone of their wisdom tradition, *The Gospel of Sri Ramakrishna*, by Swami Nikhilanda (Ramakrishna-Vivekananda Center, 1985). My Research about Hazrat Inayat Khan done at www.sufiorder.org/murs.html, and *Biography of Pir-o-Murshid Inayat Khan*, 271 pages (downloaded as *Biography*.pdf as the original book is out of print), unless otherwise noted.

1. Vivekananda's given name was Narendra, in the Ramakrishna Order he was named Swami Vivekananda. See Life and Teachings of Swami Vivekananda: Part 6, The Teachings of Vedanta at www.geocities.com/neovedanta/sv7.html (visited Sept. 2008).

2. www.geocities.com/saradavidyamandir/guide.html (visited Sept. 2008).

3. www.geocities.com/neovedanta/sv3.html.

4. www.geocities.com/neovedanta/a32.html.

5. www.ruhaniat.org/lineage/HIKBio.php.

6. www.sufimessage.com/introduction.html.

7. *Ibid.*

8. The two men invited from the West were Don Stevens from America, and Francis Brabazon from Australia.

9. The two sahavas sayings by Meher Baba are from *Lord Meher* (Vol. 15, p. 5262).

10. www.jaibaba.com/mandali/ds/broughtsufis.html (accessed September 10, 2008).

11. From *82 Family Letters to the Western Family of Lovers and Followers of Meher Baba*, by Mani S. Irani (Myrtle Beach: Sheriar Press, 1976), p. 267, letter is dated, "Meherazad, December 14, 1966" (p. 3 of 7).

12. For more about the importance of God Speaks and other words from Meher Baba see the book, *Meher Baba's Word and His Three Bridges*, by Don E. Stevens with Norah Moore and Laurent Weichberger (London: Companion Books, 2003).

13. www.meherabode.org/library-speaker/Filis_Frederick.php.

14. The special spiritual work that wore out his spine was that of literally bowing down to many thousands of people over his lifetime, especially the poor, lepers, and holy people of all faiths.

15. From Paramount Newsreel, April 8, 1932. YouTube has it on-line: www.youtube.com/watch?v=rt4xVI2odKw (accessed September 11, 2008).

16. From *Mehera*, by Mehera J. Irani with Janet Judson & Shelley Marrich (New Jersey: Beloved Books, 1989). See also, en.wikipedia.org/wiki/Mehera_Irani.

17. Ameeta was born and raised in Mumbai, India in a Jain family, speaks and writes fluent Hindi and Gujarati. A "sadhu" is a Hindu holy man, or renunciate, often homeless and frequently wearing orange.

18. Fifteen years is counting from 1986 to 2001 as this Q&A session was held February 23, 2002 in the Cline Library Auditorium at Northern Arizona University.

19. During his presentation on Sufism earlier that day, Karl Moeller had told us this story.

20. The explanation I give is based on the section "The Ten States of God," by Eruch Jessawala, from *God Speaks*, by Meher Baba, (Walnut Creek: Sufism Reoriented, 1973), 2ND Edition Revised and Enlarged (3RD Printing, 1997), pp. 157 – 189. ISBN 0-915828-02-2.

21. From *Lord Meher*, Volume 11 & 12, p. 3783.

22.   As given by Meher Baba, August 1953 at Dehra Dun, India (original in Gujerati). Source: *The Life Circulars of Avatar Meher Baba*, Ed. Swami S. P. Udaseen, p. 33-34. See also *Lord Meher*, p. 4209.

APPENDIX: SACRED PLACES

1.   We know that Meher Baba did not visit Israel or Palestine, so the holy locations were naturally in countries that he did visit.
2.   See Lord Meher p.p. 205-207.
3.   *Ibid*, p. 3737. According to Bhau, Meher Baba visited "Cave #32, called Indra Sabha - meaning the Assembly of Indra" at the Ellora Caves, in Ellora, India on November 12, 1951.
4.   *Ibid*, p. 817.
5.   *Ibid*, p. 3329.
6.   *Ibid*, p.p. 3171 - 3172, see also p. 883.
7.   *Ibid*, p. 2372.
8.   *Ibid*, p. 3508. See also: en.wikipedia.org/wiki/Sarnath
9.   *Ibid*, p. 1963. See also: en.wikipedia.org/wiki/Dilwara_Temples
10.   *Ibid*, p.1767.
11.   *Ibid*, p. 1834, see also p. 5433, and p. 3818.
12.   *Ibid*, p. 1690-1691, see also p. 1834, and p. 3818.
13.   *Ibid*, p. 1699, see also p. 1834.
14.   *Ibid*, p. 1705.
15.   *Ibid*, p. 1184, see also p. 2377, also p. 2673 and p. 2929.
16.   *Ibid*, p. 2377.
17.   *Ibid*, p. 406, see also p. 2393.
18.   *Ibid*, p. 3737.
19.   *Ibid*, p. 1370.
20.   *Ibid*, p. 2929 & p. 1184. Also, see the photo of the Golden Temple in the "Chapter Images" section of this book (Image #31).
21.   *Ibid*, p. 1834.
22.   *Ibid*, pp. 3138 - 3139, and 5061. See also: www.mehermount.com
23.   *Ibid*, pp. 1412 - 1413. Thanks to Joni Haug for searching whether Baba went to Glastonbury the first time I showed her the site www.lordmeher.org. I had no idea!
24.   *Ibid*, pp.1672 - 1675. While they were not "sacred places" for the most part, it is difficult to know what Baba was doing in China exactly.

Photo and Image Credits

✿

- Photographs of Buddha statues are from the book, *Where Every Breath is a Prayer*, by Jon Ortner (New York: Stewart, Tabori & Chang, 1996). For more photos by Jon Ortner please obtain his book, *Sacred Places of Asia, Where Every Breath is a Prayer* (Abbeville Press: 2001). Also see *Buddha*, by Jon Ortner (Welcome Books, 2003), and another on American slot canyons, *Canyon Wilderness of the Southwest* (Welcome Books, Deluxe Edition, 2008). All photos of Lord Buddha from, *Buddha*, by Jon Ortner (Welcome Books, 2003). Photographs, and captions for those photos, copyright © 2008 by Jon Ortner. Used by Permission. All rights reserved.
- All photos of Avatar Meher Baba are courtesy MSI Collection India, and are used by permission. Opening photo for chapter, Modern Mysticism, Avatar Meher Baba, Date: 3RD June 1937, Location: Old Dharamshala, Lower Meherabad, Photographer: Padri © 2008 by MSI Collection Inida. All rights reserved. Opening photo for chapter, Listening, Mehera J. Irani with Avatar Meher Baba, Date: 1936, Location: Meherabad, Photographer: Mani © 2008 by MSI Collection Inida. All rights reserved. Photo in Chapter Images section (Image #25), Avatar Meher Baba, Date: 1965, Location: Poona Darshan, Photographer: Beheram © 2008 by MSI Collection Inida. All rights reserved.
- Cover image is a sculpture: "Luminous Return" by Haidee O. Cooke (4' x 5' - White Marble Bas Relief) copyright © 2008 by Haidee Cooke. Used by permission. All rights reserved.
- Photos of contributors, in the Chapter Images section (images #4, 5, 18, 19, 21, and 24) taken on November 4, 2007 in Flagstaff are by Betsey Bruner, copyright © 2008 by Laurent Weichberger. All rights reserved.
- Photo in Chapter Images section (image #20) of the ironwork window, copyright © 2008 by Ameeta Vora. Used by permission. All rights reserved.
- Chapter Images photo #31 of the Golden Temple, courtesy of Haring Singh Khalsa.
- Original artwork for the opening of chapter Sikh Dharma: "Guru Nanank Dev Ji" - oil, by Sewa Singh Khalsa, and in the Chapter Images section (image #23), "Ek Ong Kar" - gouache, by Sewa Singh Khalsa. Both are copyright © 2008 by Sewa Singh Khalsa. All rights reserved. Used by permission. Reprints available from sikhphotos.com
- Photo in Chapter Images section (image #15) of Jessica and Yaakov Weintraub is by Michael Priest. Photo: © Michael Priest. Used by permission. All rights reserved.
- Original artwork, opening drawing in Christianity chapter, "Trinity," and The Cross in Chapter Images section (image #22) are both copyright ©2008 by Mary Esther Stewart. Used by permission. All rights reserved.
- Photo in Chapter Images section (image #17) of Thom Knoles is by Jeff Kober and copyright © 2008 by Jeff Kober. Used by permission. All rights reserved.
- Photo in Hindu chapter of Mother Durga is copyright © 2008 by Kelly William McCabe. Used by permission. All rights reserved.

.

Acknowledgments

*

It may seem silly, but first and foremost I need to acknowledge the "beads" for all they have shared in their chapters. Thom, Kelly, Ani, Ameeta, Esther, Karl, Haring Singh, and Yaakov. Each of you has opened your heart wide, and given of your hard earned wisdom to the general reader. I am so happy to know each of you, blessed really, and there are not words to properly express my love for you. You are so precious, and this publication will share your light with the world. Being with you for these seven years has been a huge part of my spiritual unfoldment. Thank you.

I give my wholehearted gratitude to Avatar Meher Baba. I know you are here now with me and for all that we have been through together, are going through, and whatever I will experience with you, I celebrate your Divine Presence in my life.

Giant "thank yous" to Ed Legum for doing the initial book layout and design work, thereby setting the stage for the whole print project, and for your glorious cover design. To have your involvement on this project means the world to me, even if we went back and forth about titles.

My deep appreciation for Alison Govi, as she offered to help me bring the Ed design work in for a landing at a time when she has many other (and more profound) issues in her life. Your dedication makes me so happy my friend. You gave countless hours of your life when you had many more joyful possibilities. May God bless you continually and may Baba give you brownie points.

Grateful acknowledgments are due to Deborah Sanchez, Wayne Smith and Sevn McAuley at Companion Enterprises for their support of this publication, and especially Don Stevens for going the extra mile in writing a Foreword to this volume. All my love to my Big Bear.

Thank you to Jane Chin, Ph.D. for her luminous Introduction. I knew you had it in you, and it is great work.

Peace to Daniel J. Sanders for being the best transcript creator in the universe. If there were a superhero who had the power to turn audio into text, that would be you. Also, your editing suggestions helped me a lot. Great work, man.

My deep gratitude to Jon Ortner for his tremendous support in supplying me with my favorite of his Buddha photos: Laurent's chapter, Ancient Mysticism opening image, "Buddha from Ayutthaya," as well as Lopon Tsultim Wangmo's chapter, Journey into Tibetan Buddhism, opening image, "Buddha in Sarnath, India," and lastly, the Chapter Images (Image #6) of "Maitreya Buddha." Jon, you are a real spiritual brother, and we have to meet soon! Thank you for sharing with us so gracefully. Om.

Thank you Pat Sumner, and Christine and Martin Cook, for your fine work with Baba's precious photos from Mani, always a pleasure to work with you.

Thank you to Haidee O. Cooke and Michael Cooke for sharing Haidee's fantastic artwork with me, just as I needed art for this book cover. She is available for commissions, contact: haideecooke@yahoo.com.

I so appreciate the editing, honest feedback, and support of the following people who helped me fashion this book into something worthy of placing into Meher Baba's in-box: Lilly and Aspen and Cyprus, Joni Haug, Jim Courson, Betsey Bruner, Jane Chin, Esther Stewart, Karl Moeller, Wayne Smith, Deborah Sanchez, Anne Weichberger, Sarah Weichberger, and Dieter Jacobs.

Thanks to Ralph Schmid for his THIRDiDESIGN rendering of the three figures for the chapter, Ancient Mysticism.

Special thanks to Thom Knoles for being so supportive of

the 2002 Eastern Heritage Symposium, Beads on One String, that we got to this point seven years later. How do you like 'dem apples? Your support of my spiritual work, and life, mean more to me than you know, even if I can't ever seem to reach you on the phone any longer.

Much love to Betsey Bruner for your friendship, and for constantly encouraging me (since 2002) to share this interfaith message with the world. Your spectacular photos and press coverage have helped us tremendously. –LW

This book was designed by Edmond Legum
and set into type by Alison Govi.

The text face is ITC Bodoni, a faithful interpretation
of Giambattista Bodoni's original 18th Century
type by Janice Fishman, Holly Goldsmith,
Jim Parkinson, & Sumner Stone.

www.ingramcontent.com/pod-product-compliance
Lightning Source LLC
Chambersburg PA
CBHW031231090426

42742CB00007B/153

9780952509790